Japanese Literature

Japanese Literature

A HISTORICAL OUTLINE

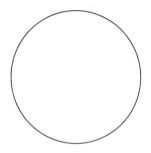

EDWARD PUTZAR

Adapted from
Nihon bungaku, Prof. Hisamatsu Sen'ichi, gen. ed.

THE UNIVERSITY OF ARIZONA PRESS
TUCSON, ARIZONA

1973

About the Editor

EDWARD PUTZAR'S interest in Japanese literature began when he was stationed in Kyoto with the U.S. Army from 1953 to 1955. Subsequently he spent a year at Kyoto University, studying under Akihiro Satake, later continuing his research into Japanese literature in Berkeley at the University of California where he did his graduate work before joining the University of Arizona faculty in 1962. His chief area of research has been the popular writing of late medieval and early modern Japan, a period of special interest to Japanese literati since 1945. Putzar's translations include several works from that period.

This book is an adaptation of *Nihon bungaku* (*Japanese Literature*) published first in Japanese by the Yushindo Publishing Company, Tokyo, 1960. The work was produced under the general editorship of Professor Hisamatsu Sen'ichi, with the various sections composed by the following scholars:

Inukai Takashi
Abe Akio
Nishio Koichi
Tesaki Masao
Nakamura Yukihiko
Hasegawa Izumi
Saegusa Yasutaka

THE UNIVERSITY OF ARIZONA PRESS

I. S. B. N. 0–8165–0357–5
L. C. No. 70–189229

Dedicated to Dana and Beth

from both of us

Foreword

THIS IS THE FIRST balanced, comprehensive history of Japanese literature to appear in English since 1889, and it is of course a translation of the work of Japanese scholars. Both of these circumstances should be of interest to students of Japan. Japanese scholars do not always see their own literature in the same light as Western experts. Certain writers and works are ranked much higher in Japan than in the West; and Japanese scholars put less emphasis on individual modern writers than on the schools or cliques with which they were affiliated. In this context, it can be said, then, that Edward Putzar's translation provides not only a great deal of information previously unavailable in English, but also clues to how the Japanese perceive their literature.

Japanese literature is gradually finding an audience outside Japan, thanks to the excellent translations, critical studies, and anthologies that have appeared in English in recent years. The production of American scholars in the years since World War II has been particularly impressive, and several Japanese writers have achieved international reputations through English translations of their works. But readers in need of a comprehensive history of Japanese literature have had nowhere to turn but to W. G. Aston's pioneer work of 1889. Tastes have changed since Aston's time, far more material is available to scholars now, and one of the most fascinating eras of Japanese literature was only beginning when Aston wrote. For many years, therefore, there has been a need for a new history of Japanese literature in English. It was in response to this need that Edward Putzar undertook this translation of Professor Hisamatsu's *Nihon bungaku*.

The present work carries the history of Japanese literature down to 1945 and the end of World War II. Since then there has been a tremendous output of important and interesting literature, including works by older writers, well established before the war, such as Tanizaki and Kawabata, and by younger men, for example, Mishima Yukio. Perhaps it is too soon to write a history of post-war Japanese literature, but one will appear eventually, and can be anticipated with interest.

ANTHONY CHAMBERS
Arizona State University

Contents

Introduction

JAPANESE LITERATURE is quite old. Its written form dates from the early seventh century, and we can reasonably assume several centuries of oral tradition existed before that. But the early period of literacy in Japan, beginning with the importation of Chinese writing in the fourth century, is obscure. Who were the Japanese? Where did they come from? And did their language, with its extraordinary continuity from the earliest records to the present, even exist before their conquest of the islands?

It seems likely that the Japanese are a relatively new people on their land, perhaps even as young as the legendary date of 660 B.C. for the Creation. That was a time of migration by various peoples of eastern Asia toward the northern rim of the Pacific Ocean. Perhaps the Japanese were part of that movement. We may ask, too, although no answer seems to be at hand, whether their conquest of the islands during the first centuries of the Common Era may not have been a decisive cause in the formation of the people themselves.

The historical outline presented in this book, as the authors are well aware, is merely a graph, a few lines describing complicated and vital events with almost complete abstraction. Such outlines are useful as maps are useful guides to a land, but their limitations are much the same. Time, the earth's textures, sky, and the heartbeat of all life—these things are not recorded and yet they are as much a part of literature as they are of the world. The moment of man on earth, as viewed by the traditional histories, is now undergoing re-examination in the light offered by various sciences—linguistics, cultural anthropology, transactional psychology, to name a few. Our view of man surely needs much broadening, much revision. We should anticipate a future of revision not only of our knowledge but also of our feelings about literature based on a wide range of experience, of study, and imaginative speculation. Our experiences at times seem to be outdistancing the development of structured aesthetics, of perception schemes that give those experiences meaning. Novelty is thrust upon us by way of the speed and eclecticism of the modern world, past our defenses, such that the art of the twentieth century typically stands too far ahead of its audience (perhaps even ahead of its creators). Aesthetics, the study of perception, acquires new dimensions without really abandoning the old, and so at times the richness of our choices in the matter of viewing ourselves and the world becomes unbearably confusing. Time perspective, for example, has entered the vocabulary of aesthetics in this century and has changed every art. In ways that seem to be different from any explored in the past, we are aware of the total field of man-universe and of the inadequacy of schemes that would set man apart. This disposition to see man as a creature of the universe is famous in Japanese literature and perhaps it should be regarded as central to Japanese aesthetics. Given this quality in the Japanese outlook it is hardly surprising that at times we find quite modern sensitivities in writing from the distant past. *The Tale of Genji* is filled with such discoveries. Still, the equations can be drawn too roughly and without regard for the sure changes that time has created in us all. Japan of today is not the Japan of the eleventh century.

Our modern aesthetic seems to be exploring a scheme which might be called time/mind, in which multi-level and multi-patterned interpretations are as necessary to its functioning as wave/particle interpretations are in considering physical phenomena. Consider the process of translation, in which we attempt to change the messages of one language into the messages of another. Questions of taste and felicity aside, translation involves such a complexity of cultural problems on both sides of the equation that we may feel that translation is impossible, that it is too damaging to all concerned. We may even come to agree with John Ruskin who condemned repairmen, "translators of old boots," as being bad for the economy as well as for the feet—and advocate formal prohibition of the whole business of translation. At any rate, attempting translation from the Japanese is surely one way to become aware of the total patterning of cultural life that is language. We cannot help but wonder and have doubts about the relationship between two languages represented by the translation. Perhaps we should regard all translations, whether they appeal to us or not, with great caution and admit that in basic dimensions we can only interpret or, to put it another way, we can only construct equivalents. Think of what was surely left out of the original writing as being too obvious to require statement for the reader and you will understand that the culture, not simply the text, is the major focus in the process of translation. Like the two sides of an equation, the original and the equivalent may appear to be unlike one another while offering reasonable descriptions of their respective elements.

The Japanese language seems to be related to languages of the Asian mainland, such as Korean and Mongol, although conclusive evidence about its filiations is still lacking. Japanese has been greatly influenced by Chinese, particularly through vocabulary loans, but structurally the two languages are quite different. Because of the extensive use Japanese has made of the Chinese writing system, and because of extensive cultural borrowings in art, architecture, dress, religion, and other areas, there sometimes grows in the minds of foreigners, people who are not Japanese, an illusion of identity between the two cultures. Indeed it is true that strong cultural influences have reached from China to Japan for two thousand years, touching nearly every aspect of Japanese life. However, it is a measure of the strength of Japanese self identity, as well as a clear statement of where this self identity does *not* lie, that Japan is still pursuing its own dynamic way in its own unique style.

The way in which the Chinese script, the figures called characters or graphs, is used in Japanese is quite complicated and varies with styles of writing as well as historical periods. Only several thousand graphs (of the nearly fifty-thousand available) are used in writing modern Japanese, but the whole range of styles presents us with by far the most complicated writing system in the world. Still, and paradoxically, a good deal of Japanese belles lettres, much of the best in fact, was written primarily in the simple syllabary called *kana,* a script of about fifty letters that is generally adequate to express all of the spoken language. The usual way of writing Japanese mixes Chinese graphs and the *kana* syllabary. In form the two styles of the syllabary (*hiragana* and *katakana*) developed through simplifications of complicated Chinese graphs. Readers who wish to study about Japanese writing and language should consult Roy Miller's book *The Japanese Language* cited in the Selected Reading List.

In adapting this book for English readers I have tried to follow current American practices in romanization of Japanese names (family name first), translation of office titles, use of *"no"* between family and given names before 1600, and established translations of book titles. This last matter has presented problems of tracing down translations or renditions, of accepting translated titles, and of seeking equivalents where more literal renditions seemed hopeless. Doubtless I have failed here more often than in other areas, but alternate titles are common in the early periods, and Japanese scholars are far more permissive than their Western colleagues about the proper reading of Chinese graphs. Finally, I wish to acknowledge with thanks a grant from Faculty Research Support in the Humanities and Social Sciences at the University of Arizona which enabled me to begin work on this book.

EDWARD PUTZAR

Early Ancient Period

A.D. 400 TO 794

by

INUKAI TAKASHI

Historical Background

THE SPAN OF TIME which we shall call the early ancient period begins about A.D. 400 with the establishment of the ancient Japanese state and continues to 794 when the capital of Japan was moved from Nara to Heian, the present city of Kyōto. Before that time, during the Jōmon period from about 4000 to 1000 B.C., the population lived in a gathering economy, supporting themselves through hunting and fishing. Female shamans occupied a high place in Jōmon society, and by means of their magic revealed the workings of superior spiritual powers. The deities, spirits of the natural world, were the center of religious worship, and the communal life of the kinship group was imbued with a religious and magical atmosphere in which the community or group acted in accordance with the will of the gods.

Beginning with the Yayoi period, about the second century B.C., we find the earliest traces of agricultural life, based on wet-field rice cultivation, and thereafter Japan shifted to an economy based on permanent agricultural villages. Also at the beginning of the Yayoi period appeared bronze and iron implements introduced from the continent. Gradually the productive power of the people was enlarged as the islands responded to man's efforts to tame and control nature. Within a relatively brief period of time a surplus in agriculture allowed for the emergence of distinct social classes and eventually the chief of what had been a primitive society grew in social and political importance until, as leader of a tribal state, he gained control of the whole group. Doubtless also another strand in this development was that the more powerful clans were able to dominate the lesser ones as much through control of magic and ritual as by their military strength. Thus when we reach the time of the ancient mound tombs in the later Yayoi period, the process of concentration of power into the hands of one of the great clans was completed and formed what is known as the Yamato Court.

During the several decades after 450 the Yamato Court seems to

3

have completed a general unification of much of the country. Within the structure they developed, each tribal state made use of ceremonies based on magic in the administration of its own people. Therefore we are probably safe in assuming the existence at that time of magical prose and poetry along with a variety of traditions which were the seeds of literature. It is evident, however, that because of the unification imposed by the dominant Yamato Court, the traditions of the various other clans were either absorbed by the Yamato people or else effectively obliterated. Some of the variety of this early material is still visible in the literature composed centuries later, but in studying it we need to keep in mind the distortions introduced by the Yamato Court for their own political motives. We believe that there existed a considerable body of oral literature or epic poetry which contained historical reflections of a kind of Heroic Age (to give a name to the period from the second to the fifth centuries during which the hero image probably expressed the feelings and thoughts of a non-individual and homogeneous society), but politically motivated alterations in the later recording of this material raise great difficulties in the way of our attempts to understand its original form.

Communication between Japan and the continent seems to have existed from Yayoi times and over the centuries the advanced culture of China greatly stimulated and contributed to the ancient Japanese world. Indeed it is likely that the dominance of the Yamato Court over tribal coalitions owed much to its having been best able to make use of knowledge from the mainland. The importation of Chinese writing in the fourth century, the transmission of Buddhism in the sixth century, and the swift introduction of many other elements of Chinese learning increasingly strengthened the Yamato Court. From the end of the sixth century to the beginning of the seventh, as the government established by Prince Shōtoku (573–621) completed its adaptation of the administrative system developed in China during the Sui and T'ang dynasties, Japan reached the point of setting up a centralized national government with absolute power vested in the emperor. Prince Naka no Ōe (who became Emperor Tenchi, r. 662–71) with Nakatomi no Kamako and others succeeded in destroying the powerful Soga clan which was the primary opposition to the imperial house and thenceforth from 645, the year of the Taika Reform, through the Jinshin Rebellion of 672 the process of centralization of national power accelerated. The authority of the emperor and the power of the national government reached a high point during the courts of Emperor Temmu (r. 673–86) and Empress Jitō (r. 690–97). The Taihō Code was completed in 701 during the reign of Emperor Mommu and thereafter a system of government based on administrative and penal codes (*ritsuryō*) was the standard of the Yamato

Court. With the moving of the capital from the Asuka lands of the Fujiwara to the new city of Nara in 710, a new era began in Japanese history and led to a reformation of the *ritsuryō* system in 718. The span of years from 729 to 749, known as the Tempyo Era, saw the greatest flourishing of Chinese culture in the Nara capital. Nonetheless, from the point of view of political realities, there was a gradual breakdown of the balance between imperial authority and the privileges of the aristocracy—an equilibrium established in theory by the *ritsuryō* system—beginning in the last years of the Asuka capital. The new direction which emerged was quite opposite the ideal of the Taika Reform. Among the general population there was acute poverty and suffering, and within a short period of time the *ritsuryō* system along with other areas of the social structure had effectively collapsed.

Such was the general situation of Japan at the end of the early ancient period during which the Yamato Court was by far the major source of movement in Japanese cultural life. Of special interest to us is the fact that nearly all of the literature surviving from this early period was part and product of the *ritsuryō* state. The literature was recorded by the privileged class that supported the *ritsuryō* system, and thus it is only through the writings of that aristocratic group that we are allowed a glimpse into the time of orally transmitted literature. Further, even the more remote provinces were under the cultural influence of the central Yamato region from which they acquired political and cultural attitudes that greatly colored their literary arts. We need then to be aware of the continuing presence of Chinese culture in Japan at that time and of the fact that literature too was emerging in intimate relation with the social evolution of the Yamato Court. There are two general tendencies in the literature of the *ritsuryō* period: one toward epic poetry, which was a reflection of the experience of the people, and the other toward personal, lyric verse. In both areas, however, there remains a distinctive quality of the voice of the ancient Japanese people which continues out of the period of oral literature into the time of recorded, written literature and which somehow escaped complete transformation and extinction within the written medium commanded by the aristocracy.

Before the introduction of Chinese, no writing system existed in Japan. And even though Chinese graphs or characters were known in Japan during the late fourth century, a general knowledge of Chinese writing among the aristocracy does not seem to have prevailed until after the end of the reign of Empress Suiko (r. 592–628). The literature of Japan before that time was orally transmitted.

We know nothing at all about the first growth of oral literature in the distant past and we can only suppose that it is nearly as old as the beginnings of the Japanese language. What we can know of the oral tradition derives from the materials of Shinto prayers (*saishi*), songs in praise of deities, dancing songs, some verses from the song and dance festivals of youth (*utagaki no uta*), stories telling of ancestors' achievements, and other compositions intimate to the religious life of the people. Such materials, recorded in the earliest documents, are the literary remains of a communal life extending from the primitive societies of the Jōmon and Yayoi periods down to the establishment of the ancient state centered on the worship of *kami*. This literature reflects a development paralleling changes in the social role of language, moving away from the homogeneous and non-individual social pattern. Perhaps it should even be regarded as a kind of epic or heroic poetry, drawing a silhouette of the ancient people. And yet, because it lacked written expression, the details of this picture remain obscure. With careful examination of the various documents remaining from the *ritsuryō* period—an examination supported by knowledge from such fields as ethnology, history, and archaeology—we may be able to offer hypotheses about the substance of the oral literature, but such a broad study has yet to be completed. It is a problem of the genesis of literature itself and we can only offer tentative explanations based on religious beliefs, emotion, play and imitative impulses and so forth. Yet it remains true that in the life of the Japanese during the period of oral transmission, worship of the deities was always intimately blended with daily existence. This means that in the literature, be it poetry or prose, associated with a religious occasion there still was not the least differentiation between what may be called the aesthetic elements and the practical elements. Language was reinforced with movement of the body, with hand gestures and rhythm, such that in a general sense the religious life of the people may be regarded as the foundation of literature. Still, the sources of literature are doubtless too complicated for us to accept one theory at the expense of all others for a time when modes such as epic and lyric were all totally fused as one expression.

Generally speaking, at this time the advanced culture of the continent reached Japan by way of the Korean peninsula, which was also the path by which Chinese writing reached Japan. It is likely that in Japan of the mid-seventh century those who could read Chinese and use Chinese writing were limited to native Chinese and Koreans who had become Japanese citizens, and to a small number of Japanese serving powerful men of the court. We may well say that literacy in Japan was then limited to the Yamato Court. Materials surviving from the ancient period include an inscription on a sword from the Province of Higo in Kyūshū (ca. 430) and the inscription on a bronze mirror preserved in the Hachiman Shrine of Suda in the Province of Kii. Little writing indeed dates earlier than the time of Empress Suiko, but from the end of her reign we find considerable writing activity in and around the court. In contrast to the inscriptions in Chinese just mentioned, we have some examples from that period of Japanese language expressed by means of Chinese graphs on such relics as a stone monument in Iyo from 595, an inscription on a statue of the Yakushi Buddha in Hōryūji, the seventeen-point code issued by Prince Shōtoku in 604, and the *Sangyō gisho* (*Notes on the Three Sutras*) from about 610. During the reign of Empress Suiko there is mention of two histories, *Tennōki* (*Imperial Records*) and *Kokki* (*National Records*), which were compiled by Prince Shōtoku and Soga no Umako jointly, but both works were destroyed in 645 with the defeat of the Soga clan.

Around the beginning of the eighth century two major forces were at work in the recorded literature of the *ritsuryō* state: one affected revision of the history of national unification under the Yamato Court; the other moved to reaffirm the heroic tradition, and was stimulated by the Chinese governmental structure then being tried in Japan, a structure which was, of course, Confucian in outlook. It was a period that seems to abound with the spirit of narrative poetry. In such a milieu the old traditions, songs, deity stories, and histories which had been preserved in the oral tradition of the whole people were collected and reorganized by the Yamato Court. Such materials, in written form, constitute the two oldest extant histories of Japan, the *Kojiki* (*Record of Ancient Matters*) and the *Nihon shoki* (*Chronicles of Japan*). Those works, besides drawing on the ancient oral traditions, were written to a considerable extent as histories and genealogies of individuals then ruling Japan. Inevitably this resulted in sizable discrepancies between the oral traditions on one hand and recorded literature composed for political reasons by the Yamato Court which was emulating the Chinese model. It is certain also that many distortions arose through the use of Chinese language and script in these documents. Thus in his preface to the *Kojiki* the editor, Ō no Yasumaro (d. 723), comments on the problem of language: "To relate everything in an ideographic transcription would entail inadequate expression of the meaning of the old language; to write altogether according to the phonetic method would make the story of events unduly lengthy." The "phonetic method" indicates the technique of using one Chinese graph to represent one syllable of Japanese. Obviously the lively spirit of narrative folk poetry suffered considerable restraint when faced with the problems of representing the Japanese language by means of Chinese graphs. Though we may suppose epic verse to have existed in the oral tradition, in the process of transcription it was inevitably turned into prose literature. Only through the most careful study shall we be able to throw light on the literature of the Japanese people prior to its transformation by writing.

With the establishment of the *ritsuryō* system of government and a certain maturing of Japanese society, there appears an awareness of a new circumstance or quality of life among the officials and aristocrats who made up the court. There was a kind of emotional awakening and a new consciousness of personal individuality. In great part such changes were stimulated by the extensive contacts Japan had with the varieties of Chinese culture and especially Chinese literature. Perhaps too by that time the clear decadence in the *ritsuryō* state prompted reflections on the inner nature of man and encouraged individualism. Whatever the case, such elements clearly pointed the way toward a future blossoming of individual, lyric poetry—in contrast to the realm of non-individual prose literature—and soon gave birth to a new literary consciousness. One result of this change was the blossoming of aristocratic literature in the *Man'yōshū* (*Collection for a Myriad Ages*), the development of which parallels the cultural transformations of the years from the Asuka-Fujiwara capital to the middle of the Nara period (ca. 550–750).

Folk poetry and song continued to flourish as before, but the world of aristocratic literature gradually drew apart from the oral folk tradition and, while still finding inspiration and nourishment in the folk tradition, produced the flower of that literature in the creation of lyric poetry. Indeed it would hardly be an exaggeration to claim that as the time of Japan's most brilliant recorded literature. And not least among the achievements of the period was the free adaptation of a foreign writing system which presented great limitations when brought to the Japanese language. In overcoming difficulties connected with use of the Chinese writing system, in solving the problem of expressing the Japanese language in writing, the ancient Japanese created, with a phonetic use of Chinese graphs, the syllabary of the *Man'yōshū*, known as *man'yōgana*.

Norito and *Semmyō*

In the primitive world of early Japan man was at the mercy of uncontrollable and often dreadful forces of nature which were personified as spirits called *kami*. The *kami* brought happiness as well as grief to the world and they were thought of as the supreme powers directing the activities of men—and the people, therefore, relied on the intervention of the *kami* for their benefit and, indeed, based their life activities on the spirit world. The *kami* were things of worship and in turn the people responded to indications of the wishes of the *kami*. On special occasions certain magical words were addressed to the *kami*, or, through human intermediaries, the *kami* spoke to men, and those utterances were known as *norito*. The role of priest or shaman may be thought of as manifesting the words of the *kami*. Clearly the motive (taking *norito* in the sense of "magic words") is the idea that in language exists a mysterious spiritual power; and to the ancient Japanese that feeling became a belief in what was called the "word spirit," *kotodama.* It was thought that the will of the *kami* was expressed in language which, if auspicious, would produce good results. Faith in the *kotodama* was the motive behind the use of magical language, and the *norito* thus acquired a rhythmical quality which was appropriate to the techniques of oral literature and which also enhanced their magical force. *Norito,* then, indicates the literature of magic and prayer which developed in primitive Japanese society.

Magical words or phrases used in the primitive society were probably great in number and all part of the oral tradition, but presumably some were transmitted with less care than others and did not survive into recorded literature. Our glimpse of the primitive *norito* in fact is limited to such items as congratulatory phrases (*yogoto*) offered to the ruler in hope of a long and prosperous reign, the "fire kindling" *yogoto* chanted by Kushiyatama no Kami in the first book of the *Kojiki,* or the passage on Emperor Kenzō in the *Nihon shoki.* Of course even when the primitive *norito* were transmitted down to the historic period their development paralleled that of society and they were transformed along with changes in the form of *kami* worship. We may well suppose that *norito* were continually evolving in the primitive society, but when we reach the time of the Yamato Court the *norito* become fixed as the ritual prose and poetry of national and court worship (later known as Shintō). The later examples of *norito* are what we find in the *Engi shiki* (*Regulations of Engi*) composed in 927, and as prayers offered by men to the *kami* the *norito* underwent changes along with the ceremonies of the court. Only a few *norito* retain vestiges of their earlier forms, but through them and the long tradition of *norito* we can grasp in outline what *norito* were in their primitive form.

on p. 43 it gives 907 ?

In the *Engi shiki* there are twenty-seven examples of *norito,* all of which achieved a fixed form after the establishment of the Yamato Court. They were written down by means of Chinese graphs used phonetically, although their language is, of course, Japanese. We believe that the *norito* were composed at the time when various ceremonies were regularized by the Jingiryō (Religious Ordinances) section of the Taihō Code of 701. A number of these ceremonies provide a chance for inferences about the *norito* during the period of oral transmission, particularly in such rituals as *ōharai* (national purification), *toshigoi no matsuri* (grain festival), *ōtono hogai* (prevention of disaster), and *Izumo no kuni miyatsuko kamu yogoto* (prayers of the Miyatsuko family of Izumo). The *norito* of the *Engi shiki* are concerned with driving out personal sin or spiritual pollution, avoiding calamities of nature, and prayers for the prosperity of the people and the imperial family. In them is stated the necessity for purification, and an abundant harvest is prayed for—the *norito* being offered up to the *kami* as well as read aloud by a group of court officials. Simple presentation of the *norito*, without reading, was known as the Presentation Ceremony (*sōjōshiki*); reading the *norito* aloud was called a Rescript Ceremony (*semmyōshiki*). Those which were read aloud supposedly show traces of the primitive form of *norito* which included words spoken by *kami* to men. Thus some scholars have suggested that the word *norito* is related to *norikudasu*, "proclaiming from on high," but in fact its etymology is still unclear.

The *norito* form is more effective as oral literature than as written literature since it sought a magical effect through the word spirit, *kotodama*. The *norito*, as prayers recited in the presence of the *kami*, made considerable use of rhythmic elements and certainly generated a feeling of solemn unity between man and the remote *kami* through the liberal use of such devices as repetition of words, antithesis, and enumeration. In following ancient materials they were stereotyped, of course, and the *norito* do at last appear in rigid ceremonies, but individually they vary in style from simple to quite complex. Each *norito* has a preface followed by a text in two parts. The first part gives a statement of the origin of the ceremonial occasion, the *matsuri*, plus a legend in some detail reviewing the achievements and praising the efficacy of the *kami*. Within these legends (close to myth in some instances) we find traditions which do not appear in either the *Kojiki* or the *Nihon shoki*. The second half of the *norito* then strings together prayers and congratulatory statements, in elaborate and elevated language, and ends with a summary or conclusion. The language of the *norito*, based on a feeling for the magic power of words, may well have contributed to the epic and lyric literature of the early ancient period.

The meaning of *yogoto* is "fine words" or "fine language" and the term is linked with another of great antiquity: *kagen*, meaning "auspicious words." These were congratulatory expressions, based on the idea of word magic and developed during the period of oral transmission. Whatever the range of the earlier *yogoto*, those remaining today are exclusively congratulations offered to the emperor in celebration of his long reign. Examples of *yogoto* appear within the *norito* of the *Engi shiki*, and in such passages as *Nakatomi no yogoto* ("Yogoto of the Nakatomi Clan") recorded in the *Teiki* (*Records of the Uji Great Minister of the Left*), the diary of Fujiwara no Yorinaga (1120–56). Again, though the dates of their composition are unknown, through the *yogoto* we see the outlines of traditions omitted in the two early histories of Japan. Considering the closeness of *norito* and *yogoto* we might classify them together, but we should keep in mind that *yogoto* do not embody any suggestion of prayer.

Semmyō derived from the *norito* in form but were imperial commands from the emperor to his retainers. Like the *norito* they were written in Japanese—in contrast to the *shōchoku,* imperial proclamations written in Chinese. *Semmyō* were especially composed for important occasions—succession of an emperor, change of the era name, announcements of reward or punishment, the death of an important retainer.

The term *semmyō* generally designates some sixty-two proclamations found in the *Shoku nihongi (Continuation of the Chronicles of Japan)* of 797. Apparently the *semmyō* were read aloud in a fixed rhythmical style. Included in the collection are many *semmyō* dating from the Nara period after the accession of Emperor Mommu in 697. They resemble *norito* in part with their solemn prayers for the prosperity of the state, but otherwise their practical contents are closer to straight prose, touching in many particulars the social and political thought of the time. The influence of foreign ideas—Buddhism first of all—is important in the *semmyō* and throughout we find a heightened political awareness, in contrast to ideas centered on the power of the *kami.*

From the point of view of development of a writing system for the Japanese language, the *semmyō* style (*semmyōgaki*) is interesting, since the Chinese graph equivalent in meaning to the Japanese word being used was written in large figure, while Japanese particles and the variable endings of Japanese verbs and modifiers were written in small Chinese graphs, using one graph to stand for the sound of one Japanese syllable—the phonetic technique of the *Man'yōshū.* If we substitute letters of the Japanese syllabary (*kana*) for the small graphs in *semmyōgaki,* then the text closely resembles the modern style of writing Japanese in the mixture of Chinese graphs and *kana* known as *kanamajiri.*

A narrative, story-telling element, we may suppose, was present from the beginning in *norito* of ceremonies in the primitive society. We may suppose too that lyrical song elements were part of ceremonies that reflected subjective or emotional expression of the society. Both elements figure in the *norito* and in this form developed as their social context evolved. Gradually the narrative aspects separated from the ceremonial context and by way of stories, *monogatari,* about traditional heroes and *kami,* emerged as narrative literature. The song elements also acquired lyric forms and with repetition through their role in community life grew into poetry. We are suggesting that the "magic" and prayer of the period of oral transmission were the materials out of which lyrical and narrative literature developed. With the beginning of recorded literature we see in *norito* and *yogoto*, with their ritualistic language of court religious ceremony, qualities of oral magic and prayer literature from an earlier time which felt the power of the *kotodama*. Story and lyric remain blended in the *norito*, but through them we can still gain a suggestion of the sources in pre-literature of these two modes.

The written literature of the early period that was developing into narrative and which attempted an objective statement of events was that of legend and the brief account or story known as *setsuwa*. Narrative elements were part of religious oral literature, and on ceremonial occasions it is likely that the past deeds of the *kami* were recited to explain the origin of the ceremony. In time stories of the *kami* grew into hero stories about the ancestors of the various clans; apparently these stories gradually separated from their ceremonial contexts and became part of the lore of the various clans. Further, we may suppose that legends and *setsuwa* were transmitted as part of the broad spectrum of social life on matters pertaining to the land and the people. Possibly such stories evolved into narrative poetry, too. But as the various clans became subordinate to the Yamato Court, materials that were inconsistent with or in conflict with the traditions of the imperial house were gradually rationalized and subordinated. By the time of recorded literature, history in the form of legends and stories underwent extensive alteration due to political motives, and the ancient traditions of various groups, traditions which had considerable vigor, lost their quality of narrative poetry and reappeared as prose. It is not certain exactly when literature first attained written form in Japan, but it seems to have been about the middle of the sixth century, perhaps when the history work known as the *Kyūji* (*Ancient Words*) was completed. The *Kyūji* is now lost, but it seems to have been written and then altered a number of times. With the adoption of the *ritsuryō* model of state organization during the last half of the seventh century, conditions were ripe for a history which would serve as a model for the nation. The idea of a national history grew out of the creative spirit of the Court, political concepts which had long ago crossed over from China, ambitions toward establishing an imperial system, and, of course, the opportunity to compose a new version of the past on the basis of the *ritsuryō* system. This effort in composing national history resulted in the *Kojiki* (*Record of Ancient Matters*) and the *Nihon shoki* (*Chronicles of Japan*) completed by the Yamato Court early in the eighth century and based on records which had by then passed through many layers of development. These histories were written within a framework that established each of the various clans in a formal relationship to the imperial house, the whole designed to strengthen the imperial house's claim to authority.

In both the *Kojiki* and the *Nihon shoki* there are passages containing elements of oral literature. The *Kojiki* indeed goes to some trouble to preserve that quality, while the nature of its material reveals a complicated, stratified society. In examining those works we will need to consider both their literary spirit and their legends and stories which were essential to the development of narrative literature and which date from before the establishment of the Yamato Court.

The Histories *Kojiki* and *Nihon shoki*

In his Preface to the *Kojiki* the editor and compiler, Ō no Yasumaro, describes the circumstances of its composition. He says that Emperor Temmu, distressed by the many inaccuracies and fabrications of the *Teiki* and the *Kyūji,* which were in the hands of the various clans, wished to select and pass on to later generations those true precepts which would be the basis of national rule. The emperor then commanded one Hieda no Are to "commit to memory" the *Teiō no hi tsugi* (*Imperial Annals*) and the *Sendai no kyūji* (*Words of Previous Reigns*). The task of editing and recording those works remained unfinished until Empress Gemmei in 711 ordered Ō no Yasumaro to resume writing down the words of Hieda no Are. The completed work was offered to the throne in 712 and is the history in three scrolls, or books, known as the *Kojiki.* The imperial command mentioned in the Preface, however, raises a number of problems: what was meant by "commit to memory"; whether the person known as Hieda no Are was a man or a woman; and whether the imperial commission itself might have been identical to that given to the historian Prince Kawashima and others in 681. Our difficulties are further compounded by a case having been made that both the Preface and the text are in part apocryphal.

The first book of the *Kojiki* tells of the era of the gods: the creation of heaven and earth, the story of the Plain of High Heaven, and the generations of the descendants of the deities. Into the basic narrative are inserted such stories as that of the Storm God, Susa-no-o, and Ōkuni-nushi, thus bringing together myths of the Izumo gods and myths of the Plain of High Heaven. The result is to tie the creation of the land itself to the interpretation of the source of imperial authority. The second book covers the period from Emperor Jimmu to Emperor Ōjin—theoretically, from 660 B.C. to A.D 310, the first date being the legendary founding of the Yamato Court, the second being the unification of the country. This part of the account deals with the era of man, but there are parts of the story heavy with myth. The final book of the *Kojiki* develops the story from Emperor Nintoku, the "virtuous Confucian emperor," to 628, through the reign of Empress Suiko and the

establishment of Buddhism. That the history ends with the reign of
Empress Suiko seems to be recognition of a turning point at the beginning of the mature period of the ancient state. In its free use of
Chinese graphs the *Kojiki* attempts to record the Japanese language, at
least in so far as writing techniques of the time would allow.

The *Teiki,* one of the sources of the *Kojiki,* was a history written in
Chinese, focusing on the circumstances of imperial succession and the
genealogy of the ruling house. The work known as the *Kyūji* was apparently an account of the origin of the imperial house and the national
government; it included anecdotes about the imperial family, traditions of the various clans, plus native myths, legends, *setsuwa* and
songs. The work may have been written in Japanese. Whatever the
materials, they seem to have been selected and organized around the
imperial family. The *Kojiki,* drawing from both works, attempted to
present a single, unified history of the origin of the state and the
imperial house. The main lines of its structure are that the emperor
rules the land by command of the heavenly *kami* and that the various
clans made up a great family around the descendants of the heavenly
kami, joining together to unify and develop the nation. The legitimacy
of the imperial rule was thus demonstrated historically, and the
Kojiki developed a political scheme which would make it acceptable to
all. One consequence of this design of the *Kojiki* was that the concrete-
ness of epic poetry—as we believe it to have existed in myths and
legends of folk literature until the formation of a national state—was
lost. Inevitably there was a good deal of intellectualizing in the composition of the *Kojiki,* but despite this it retains an echo of narrative
poetry that communicates the vigorous spirit of the ancient Japanese.

The *Kojiki* also preserves a number of *setsuwa* which developed
in the context of the *matsuri,* religious ceremonies closely related to the
lives of the Japanese people. If we examine such stories as the Stone
Door of Heaven, the Luck of the Sea and the Luck of the Mountains,
Susa-no-o, Ōkuni-nushi, and Yamato-takeru, free of a restricting historical framework, then we discover pastoral and heroic images of the
ancient people. Through its sources we need to clarify the meaning of
the *Kojiki.* When the text is analyzed and the materials in it are re-
stored to their original form, we find it to be a marvelous storehouse of
narrative folk literature.

The *Nihon shoki* was completed in 720, during the reign of
Empress Genshō, eight years after the *Kojiki.* It is a history edited by
Prince Toneri (d. 735) and others, by order of the Prince's father,
Emperor Temmu (r. 673–86). Ō no Yasumaro seems to have assisted
in its compilation. The whole work consists of thirty scrolls or books
(a book of genealogies is no longer extant) with the era of the gods
taking two books. The first part of the *Nihon shoki* incorporates varying

interpretations of the mythological period with an introductory device
("One source says . . ."), while the remaining twenty-eight books
present the history of Japan from Emperor Jimmu to Empress Jitō
(r. 690–97). The arrangement approximates one imperial reign for
each book, with detailed accounts of each reign—the same pattern as
the Chinese dynastic histories. The original title of the work may have
been *Nihongi,* but the present title has been used since the early Heian
period. The *Nihon shoki* was long valued at Court as the true history
of Japan and was frequently the subject of lectures delivered at the
imperial palace and collected in a work called *Nihongi shiki* (*Private
Notes on the Nihongi*), but the Nara period work of that title has not
survived. In medieval Japan Shintō scholars began to study the
Nihon shoki.

The *Nihon shoki* is one of a collection of histories of Japan
known as the *Rikkokushi* (*Six National Histories*) which we shall list
together with the years each covers. All follow the model of the Chinese
dynastic histories, and all are written in Chinese.

Rikkokushi (*Six National Histories*)
  1. *Nihon shoki* (*Chronicles of Japan*) 30v. Completed 720. Coverage to
     697.
  2. *Shoku nihongi* (*Continuation of the Chronicles of Japan*) 40v. Com-
     pleted 797. Coverage: 697 to 791.
  3. *Nihonkōki* (*Latter Chronicles of Japan*) 40v. (only 10v. extant). Com-
     pleted 840. Coverage: 792 to 833 (extant portions 796 to 816).
  4. *Shoku nihonkōki* (*Continuation of the Latter Chronicles of Japan*)
     (*Chronicles of Japan Continued*) 20v. Completed 869. Coverage: 833
     to 850.
  5. *Nihon montoku tennō jitsuroku* (*True Record of Emperor Montoku*)
     10v. Completed 879. Coverage: 850 to 858 (one region only).
  6. *Nihon sandai jitsuroku* (*True Record of Three Reigns*) 50v. Com-
     pleted 901. Coverage: 858 to 887.

The compilation of the *Nihon shoki,* representing the historiography of the imperial house, stands directly in line with the design
begun under Emperor Temmu who was responsible for the *Kojiki.* In
the *Nihon shoki,* however, we find a growing awareness of the world
outside Japan which reflected Japan's self-consciousness as a nation
during the formation of the *ritsuryō* state. This awareness generated
a need for historical writing on the Chinese model which could compare
with the Chinese histories. Such records and documents as were preserved at court and in the various clans, along with the *Teiki, Kyūji,*
and the *fudoki* (gazetteers), were the most likely materials for the
Nihon shoki, and Chinese sources, too, were widely consulted. But in
contrast to the *Kojiki* which labored to reproduce the Japanese language on its pages, the *Nihon shoki* attempted to bring decisive authority to its writing through use of Chinese—except for some poems and

special old phrases—and Chinese rhetoric which relied on historical incident and written sources. The emphasis of the *Kojiki* is traditional and intrinsically Japanese, while the *Nihon shoki* seems externally oriented. The contrast here may well be taken as representing the dual consciousness of the Yamato Court of the Nara period. The *Nihon shoki* throughout leans strongly toward the political and the pragmatic, and it is conspicuous in its rationalizing of history. The quality of reporting in the *Nihon shoki* is clearly high, but the literary value of the work is slight and its chronological arrangement hinders the reader's grasp of its stories. In many places too rigid adherence to Chinese stylistic demands has destroyed any immediacy of expression. Nonetheless, such passages as the "Records of Emperor Temmu," and especially the description of the Jinshin Rebellion in 672, were written near in time to the events they describe and portray with unusual detail and vividness the qualities of Emperor Temmu, retaining the flavor of epic poetry. We should mention too that myths and *setsuwa* are preserved in the *Nihon shoki* which are not recorded in the *Kojiki*.

Gazetteers: *Fudoki*

The *fudoki* (the gazetteers: literally, "records of wind and earth") may have been compiled as part of the court project that resulted in the *Kojiki* and the *Nihon shoki* since they were designed to survey the actual conditions in each of the provinces. The plan of those works is mentioned in the *Shoku nihongi* under the entry for the fifth month of 713. In that year the court ordered the use of suitable Chinese graphs in writing the names of districts and villages in all provinces, a record of the products and nature of the soil of each region, old stories and noteworthy incidents, all of which was to be transmitted to the capital. The result of this order was the compilation of a *fudoki* in each province. The surveys were not all completed at the same time for the whole country, and it seems likely that some years passed between the completion of the first and the last. We believe that, despite their later loss, the *fudoki* were once complete for the entire country, but only five are surviving today from the old provinces of Izumo, Harima, Hitachi, Bizen, and Bungo. During the Heian period, in 925, compilation of gazetteers was resumed by imperial decree, but most of the *fudoki* of that period have also been lost.

The style of the older gazetteers varied considerably, some being written in Japanese, some in Chinese, some in the *semmyō* style, and so forth, and the material recorded is colored by the particular province. Among the extant *fudoki,* however, only the one from the province of Izumo (*Izumo fudoki*) is complete; it was submitted to the Court in 733. That document seems to be a working manuscript rather

than the archival version. The remainder of the five *fudoki* exist only
as partial works about which we have no details on dates or compilers.
The *Harima fudoki* seems to have been completed soon after the
imperial order of 713, but in that case the extant document is not the
official copy. The *Hitachi fudoki* may have been completed before 723
and is attributed to Fujiwara no Umakai. Its Chinese is in the elegant
style of the Six Dynasties and T'ang periods, which alternates phrases of
four and six graphs. The remaining two works, from Bizen and Bungo,
were each composed on the same plan and possibly were prepared
under the direction of the military government of Kyūshū, the Dazaifu
as it was called. In addition to the works we have mentioned, there
exist fragments of *fudoki* from the later Heian period and from medieval manuscripts now collected in a volume known as *Santei kofudoki
itsubun* (*Recension of Fragments of the Old Fudoki*) by Kurita Hiroshi
in 1898. The fragments total 179 lines and deal with forty-one provinces.

The gazetteers offer glimpses of the life and customs of the provinces, and in their place-name etymologies, anecdotes and stories there
is a good deal from the oral, folk tradition native to the provinces and
not influenced by the central Yamato region. We are given in the
setsuwa of the *fudoki* legends and stories of heroes and *kami* which
amplify regional qualities and differ substantially from similar material in the *Kojiki* and the *Nihon shoki*. From the *fudoki* come such
legends as *Kunihiki* (land-augmenting: Izumo Province), *Urashima*
(a fisherman: Tango Province), *Shiratori* (white bird: Bungo Province), *Otome no matsubara* (maiden-pine-wood: Hitachi Province)
and *Fuji no tsukuba* (Mt. Fuji of Tsukuba: Hitachi Province).

The *fudoki* are loosely structured and do not present narrative,
organized history as do the *Kojiki* and the *Nihon shoki*. Perhaps
for this very reason they are closer to the life of the provinces. Through
them at least we can more clearly study related materials in the histories, and by the same token the *fudoki* are important in the history
of Japanese literature.

Family Histories: *Ujibumi*

The term *ujibumi* means "clan documents" and works in this
category preserve traditions about the origin of a particular clan, its
genealogy, and the achievements of its ancestors. *Ujibumi* were among
the source material of the early histories and they are thought once to
have existed in considerable quantity. Today, however, only two speci-
mens remain from those early years: the *Takahashi ujibumi*
(*Takahashi Family Documents*) and the *Kogoshūi* (*Collection of Ancient Words*). The Takahashi documents were submitted to Emperor

Kammu in 792 by the Takahashi family at the outbreak of a struggle between them and the Azumi clan. For a long time both groups had participated in the management of the Naizenshi, the imperial commissary, and the *Takahashi ujibumi* was presented to the Court as evidence on behalf of the family's claims. In a similar way the *Kogoshūi* emerged from a conflict between the Nakatomi and the Imbe (also written Imibe or Imube) clans, both of which were concerned with palace ceremonies, and was presented to Emperor Heizei in 807 by Imbe no Hironari. The collections are partisan, of course, setting out the origins of their respective clans and elevating them as far as possible. We may expect distortion and fabrication, but still those parts of the *ujibumi* that seem most ancient contain legends which are at variance with some legends in the *Kojiki* and the *Nihon shoki,* and there are parts that impress us as being authentic ancient family documents as well as prototypes of ancient *setsuwa.*

Stories: *Setsuwa*

We have two ancient collections preserving some of the old *setsuwa,* the anecdote or story literature, a genre that was to become prominent in the early medieval period. The *Jōgū shōtoku hōōteisetsu* (*Anecdotes from the Life of Prince Shōtoku*) deals with Prince Shōtoku and while of uncertain date is tentatively placed earlier than the *Kojiki.* The text is primarily in Chinese and the stories are heavily colored with Buddhist teachings; however, this collection is the source for later *setsuwa* about Prince Shōtoku. The other collection is the *Sumiyoshi taisha jindaiki* (*Record of the Age of the Gods of the Great Sumiyoshi Shrine*) dating from 731 and recording legends of the Sumiyoshi Shrine. It was presented to the Office of Religious Matters, the Jingikan, by the chief priest of the Shrine. The text is in Chinese and some of its *setsuwa* repeat those of the *Nihon shoki.*

The works we have thus far mentioned represent narrative literature centering on the imperial house and concerned with supporting its authority. It is a literature directly tied to the narrative literature of the period of oral transmission. But we find another side of ancient literature represented in the *Nihon ryōiki* (*Miraculous Tales of Japan*), the usual abbreviation for the full title, *Miraculous Tales of the Immanent Consequences of Good and Evil in Japan.* This is a collection of Buddhist *setsuwa* current during the spread of Buddhism in the Nara period. It was compiled by the monk Keikai of the Yamato Yakushi Temple, probably between 810 and 823. While the text itself was produced in the Heian period, stories from the Nara period are most common. Altogether there are 116 stories, arranged chronologically from the time of Emperor Yūryaku (r. 456–79) to that of

Emperor Saga, contemporary with Keikai. Most of its stories derive from folk traditions and from Buddhist texts, including miracle stories current in the provinces outside of central Japan, plus some secular folk tales. The purpose of the collection was to encourage good conduct and to further the chance of attaining paradise after death through presenting exemplary stories of the consequences of good and evil deeds. Here and there are passages which realistically describe the life of the common people of the time. The writing is Chinese, but with a Japanese flavor, and we learn from the Preface that the *Nihon ryōiki* was modeled on two Chinese collections: *Meihōki* (*Ming pao-chi: Rewards of the Next Life*) and *Hannya genki* (*Pan-jo yen-chi: Study of Wisdom*). The *Nihon ryōiki* embodies reactions of the Japanese as they first encountered Buddhism and as literature introduces complexities into the development of *setsuwa*. It became in later generations the model for collections of Buddhist stories.

As we have mentioned, the early narrative literature of Japan dates from the early eighth century—such works as the *Kojiki, Nihon shoki,* and the *fudoki*—and while it is not yet literature in the sense of belles lettres, through it we can glimpse the outline of narratives from the period of oral transmission down to the time when the stories were committed to writing. Considering that Japan at that time did not have a writing system of its own, and that only a few of its people had reached literacy through the borrowed Chinese script, there was inevitably some obscuring of native traditions in the first attempts at writing. To write Japanese in the medium of Chinese script presented severe difficulties, and it was at first next to impossible to record the language, literature, feelings, and thoughts of the people. Most certainly in the process of becoming literate the Japanese suffered considerable loss in their traditional oral material. Inevitably too the ruling class, the group able to use the Chinese script, exercised a good deal of selective editing for political ends. Thus, while the Chinese script itself fostered a new literature in Japan, we could scarcely expect the immediate development of a new prose literature in view of the limitations of the orthography and the politically centered world of the ruling class. Despite these limitations, documents of the period convey traditions of the oral period, and when literary qualities are retained as well, such writings are valuable indeed. Some works seem so close to oral literature that they may have been recorded without any alteration, still vitally alive in oral rhetoric and expression. In breadth of imagination as well the lively spirit of epic poetry characteristic of the ancient Japanese appears. Even though transformed through writing, it was inspiration for a new world of magnificent lyric composition in later years. At the same time that oral literature was maturing into written literature, a part of the oral tradition continued in a wide and deep current in which new material nourished the creative literature of the people. At the end of the ancient period this popular literary energy again became visible in writing through the stories (*setsuwa*) on Buddhist themes.

Early Poetry

As part of the magic and prayer literature which developed in the *matsuri*—religious events of the primitive communal society—we find a narrative vein in which lyric and song elements are blended. We believe that a great number of songs were current in Japan, songs which developed within social groups and were therefore close to the life of the people and expressive of their shared feelings. This material was song-poetry, and in the course of many generations it continued to be created and reformed, new pieces were composed as the old songs were put aside or forgotten. Some of the songs, linked with myths and legends, were recorded in such documents as the *Kojiki* and the *Nihon shoki*. Fortunately they have been preserved more or less in their ancient form, directly from oral tradition, written down syllable by syllable in the cumbersome technique using one Chinese graph to stand for a single syllable of Japanese. Perhaps we should regard these lyrics as the cradle of later Japanese poetry, but since they represent a time before an awareness of formal literature, certain cautions are necessary in our interpretations. For example, this song from the *Kojiki:*

Yakumo tatsu	Multi clouds
Izumo yaegaki	Rising, multi cloud
Tsuma gomi ni	Wall making,
Yaegaki tsukuru	For their spouses
Sono yaegaki wo	Oh! Oh! That clouding wall.

Until recently this poem was regarded as the earliest example of *waka,* thirty-one syllable poem of 5–7–5–7–7 syllable pattern, supposed to have been composed on the occasion of the marriage of the deities Susa-no-o and Kushinada-hime. *Waka,* which became the dominant form in Japanese poetry, was regarded as having sacred origin, this story being told in the Preface to the *Kokinshū (Collection of Ancient and Modern Times)* about 905. But in fact the *waka* form was not resolved until quite late and this suggestion of great age cannot be accepted. We can only venture to say that the content and expression of this poem from the *Kojiki* are ancient and unsophisticated, and that it could have evolved into the *waka* pattern. Probably the song was originally a folk song associated with a house-building celebration (*nii-muro-hōgai*) that had a long popular history. There are many songs of that kind in the *Kojiki* and *Nihon shoki,* and in fact, putting legends aside, those two works are indeed treasures of ancient poetry.

In the aristocratic Court society of the seventh and eighth centuries, new conditions of community life nourished the emergence of individual consciousness, and this, as the motive of poetry, led gradually to expression in poetry of the individual's personal feelings. The process we are describing is that of a gradual movement of lyricism away from the world of a communal voice and into the realm of independent, individualistic poetry. Expressed another way, the shift was from songs that were sung to poems that were written. The ancient lyric elements became the nuclei of the new styles and contributed to the emergence of individual lyric poetry, stimulating the marvelous flowering of lyricism and distillation of the *waka* form that we have in the *Man'yōshū*. And yet along with this formalizing trend the ancient song tradition persisted outside of the Court, and we discover this lively folk genre in the *Man'yōshū* and again much later in Japanese poetry.

During the period of oral literature the *norito* provided a foundation for literary development, and the song element in those prayers may have been purely emotive utterances before growing into a language rich in musical qualities. The ancient songs seem to have acquired their forms gradually and came to be performed independently of the *norito*. Possibly they were sung in the various rituals of the communal society—words, music, and dance all together—where they would heighten the fraternal consciousness of the group. Communal production and agriculture, as well as other seasonal activities including the exchanges of romantic poetry called *utagaki,* held magical and religious significance. It is apparent that a variety of songs were often sung within the context of communal life. Those songs which survived over a long period of time seem to have done so by virtue of their close ties with beliefs and rituals of the community, and since they were an intimate part of the life of a homogeneous society, revealing the communal life and feelings of the people, a proper term for them would be "folk songs." Indeed, those songs show rich development in both form and content over a considerable length of time, and doubtless circulated widely throughout Japan. Eventually some were preserved in the *Kojiki* and other works. Part of the evolution of ancient songs included their sometime association with communal magical events or mythical and legendary narratives. To the body of folk songs also we may add songs from such groups as the professional reciters (*kataribe*). Nor should we neglect the nearly certain evolution of some songs as narrative poetry which included theatrical elements. In the *Kojiki* a group of poems seems to have the elements of epic poetry—those about the deity Yachihoko-no-kami. It seems likely that such narrative poems (*monogatari uta*) were given a model in the early histories; then after the formation of the Yamato

Court similar songs were recorded in the provinces and later incorporated into collections of Court songs. To be sure, in the hands of Court poetry scholars such provincial songs were altered, but they were preserved as major songs of the Court and probably were performed to musical accompaniment. The *Kojiki* and *Nihon shoki* record the names of various songs, for example: *kume uta* (songs of the palace guards), *sakahōgai no uta* (a wine offering song), *amagatari uta* (referring to the song of Section 60, Emperor Yūryaku—The Leaf in the Cup) and *shirage uta* (songs with quick tempo, or songs from Silla, the ancient Korean kingdom). There are also records of the names of the melodies (*buri*): *hinaburi, miyahitoburi, amataburi,* and so forth. The relationship between the old song-poems and the various melodies referred to in the histories is examined in the *Kinkafu* (*Koto Song Music*) dating from the early Heian period. We may suppose from this evidence that the old folk songs, narrative poems, songs of the Court, and so forth, were influential materials in the composition of the old histories.

In the *Kojiki* and *Nihon shoki* are collected altogether about 240 songs which, without the duplications, total some 190 individual examples. Almost all are folk songs, narrative poems, or Court songs that had a long history and were fixed in writing only at the beginning of the eighth century. Many of the Court songs were connected with myths and legends and thus had narrative elements in them, but they do not seem to have existed as independent songs before the time of recording. Some songs had been linked together and synthesized early, while others seem to have been purposefully linked together as narrative at the time the histories were composed. The histories also include songs purportedly composed by the *kami* called *waza uta;* those had, or were made to have, relevance to particular social events. From the end of the period, at a time close to the composition of the *Kojiki,* there are a few poems which may be regarded as the works of individual authors, but in general it is difficult to accept at face value the recorded legends about the poems or their attributions. Dates of composition are obscure. The poems reflect a wide span of time and social conditions and some represent the old poetry, without distortion, from before recorded literature or the addition of legend. We find in these lyrical folk songs qualities that are part of the shared feelings of the community and expressing these feelings directly, concretely, and sensuously. Poems that contain the seeds of narratives are also present and we see throughout a vivid reflection of the Japanese world before literature itself was divided into "higher" and "lower." An example of what we mean is the *Kojiki* poem above (*Yakumo tatsu . . .*). The following poem, attributed to Oto-Tachibana-Hime, wife of Yamatotateru-no-Mikoto, clearly originates in a romantic folk song associated with the spring field burning in the Sagami district.

Sanesashi	O you, my lord—
Sagamu no ono ni	Who once stood among the flames
Moyuru hi no	Of the burning fire and spoke to me
Ho naka ni tachite	On the mountain-rimmed
Tohishi kimi wa mo	Plain of Sagamu.

(*Kojiki,* Section 84)

In studying such a poem we need to consider both its significance as an independent song, and the legend or *monogatari* in which it appears in the histories. For instance, poetry in the *Kojiki* passages about Ōkuni-nushi-no-Mikoto, Yamatotateru-no-Mikoto, and about the women close to Emperor Nintoku make us aware of a literature that is lyrical and highly romantic, here and there verging on the epic. Aside from our speculations on the legends with which the poems are associated, we cannot help but recognize in the poems themselves a spirit and direction close to narrative poetry. In both histories we find poems given a certain attribution of authorship along with circumstances of their composition—despite their basis in legend. What in fact is at work in such attributions is the emerging tendency toward individual lyric poetry at the time of the *Kojiki.* Thus independent songs, which were the products of one or another group in society, were altered and subsequently assigned places in the histories as compositions of partic-ular individuals—providing further impetus for the step into the world of individual lyric poetry.

The histories present poems of many different forms, visible to us only as they emerge after a long period of development and change but in sum defining many if not most of the forms that were part of the evolution of Japanese poetry to that time. In short, we find the whole range from amorphous types that were fixed neither in length of line nor in the number of lines in a poem to well defined *chōka* (long poems) and *tanka* (thirty-one syllable poems, also called *waka*) using lines of five and seven syllables. Generally speaking, all poems in the *Kojiki* and *Nihon shoki* are based on the alternation of short and long lines, but it was the five- and seven-syllable lines that emerged as standard. We cannot be certain what the reasons were for settling on the five-seven pattern as the basic poetic lines in Japanese, but besides such reasons as might be found in characteristics of the language and people, we need to weigh carefully the possible influence of Chinese poetry.

For convenience we shall list here the major forms of the poems in the *Kojiki* and *Nihon shoki.*

Poems without fixed pattern.
Four-line poems that repeat a long-short line combination.
katauta (half poem): three lines of 5–7–7 syllables, sometimes repeated
    to produce a dialogue.

sedōka (head-repeated poem): six lines in the pattern 5–7–7/5–7–7; this
    developed from a chorus being added to the *katauta*. The final lines in
    each half are identical.

chōka (long poem): three or more of the 5–7 syllable couplets, with a
    final extra line of seven syllables.

tanka (short poem), or *waka* (Japanese poem): thirty-one syllables in
    the pattern 5–7–5–7–7.

Because most of the poems were based on oral tradition, considerable
use is made of such devices as repetition of words and lines, antithesis, and homophony which add greatly to their rhythmic beauty. It
may have been natural within the ancient communal society that a
song form embodying repetition and movement also would be part of
the technique of oral transmission, but, as Japanese society matured,
poetry broke away from the limitations of repetition, and attempted
lyricism and condensation of feeling. In general, the ancient poets seem
to have gradually settled on forms of an odd number of lines rather
than even number. The early *chōka* thus appear with an even number
of lines, but in time the final seven-syllable line was added. The five-
line *tanka* probably evolved in the same way, although various theories
have been offered that see the form deriving from six-line poems, a line
added to four-line poems, or breaking off the last five lines of the later
chōka. In fact there is still no certain answer to the problem. Neither can
we be sure about the date of the form. Even though the remarkable blossoming of individual lyricism was due to the emergence of *tanka,* the best
we can offer is that among the various poem forms it is relatively new
and does not, it seems, date from much before the Taika Reform of 645.

    In addition to the songs collected in the ancient histories many
are preserved in such works as the *fudoki* (20 poems), *Jōgū shōtoku
hōōteisetsu* (4 poems—earliest collection of anecdotes from the life of
Prince Shōtoku), *bussokuseki no uta* (21 poems—Buddha's footprint-
stone poems, the form is that of the *tanka* with an extra line of seven
syllables), *Kinkafu* (*Koto Song Music;* 22 poems) and *Shoku nihongi*
(8 poems). The total from these and other sources comes to about three
hundred poems, in addition to which there are poems in the *Man'-
yōshū,* beginning with Volume 13, that are strongly colored by
the ancient song style. The *Kinkafu* of 981 (a work only discovered
in 1923) records the words, melody titles, and musical notation of
old songs called *ōuta* (great songs—signifying those songs performed
on ceremonial occasions at court). Five of these songs are nearly
identical with poems in the *Kojiki* and *Nihon shoki.* The *bussokuseki
no uta* are twenty-one poems carved on a stone monument at the
Yakushi Temple in Nara. The following poem is an example of this
form.

Mi ato tsukuru	This gravestone I make
Ishi no hibiki	And the sound of it
Ame ni itari	Echoes to Heaven
Tsuchi sae yusure	And the earth trembles
Chichi haha ga tame ni	For my father and mother
Moro hito no tame ni	For all persons

The poem is inscribed in *man'yōgana*—one Chinese graph used phonetically to stand for one syllable of Japanese. The poem seems to be in praise of the Buddha and the form (5–7–5–7–7–7) is found only in such poems. In that style, as in all Japanese poetry, the syllabic line occasionally may vary with the addition of one or two extra syllables (*jiamari*) and remain within the limits of the form.

Lyricism

During the creation of the *ritsuryō* state the old folk songs and poetry slowly lost some of their collective or group characteristics. As techniques of writing the Japanese language developed and as individual consciousness matured within the aristocratic society, poetry moved toward the expression of individual lyricism, the feelings and emotions of the individual poet. An intimation of this mode was apparent in the *Kojiki,* with its studied attribution of many traditional songs to individual poets. As we have indicated, even after the adoption of Chinese writing in Japan, that part of society able to achieve literacy was practically limited to the ruling class associated with the Court, and subsequently this group was most important in determining the character of recorded literature. But mastery of a writing system easily led to the expression of individual emotion. From the time of the Taika Reform through the Courts of Ōmi and the Toba Fujiwara—about 645 to 710—every type of Court ceremony became the setting for individual expression, under the influence of Chinese literature, and by distillation of emotion produced individual lyricism in Japanese poems and songs. The *discipline* of poetry which was part of this Chinese influence, through prose as well as poetry, doubtless prompted the formalization of the 5–7 syllable pattern, the *chōka,* and the *hanka* (or *kaeshiuta*—the *tanka* envoy to a long poem) which were the most prominent expressive modes in poetry. One turning point in the emergence of individual lyric poetry was, therefore, the expression of emotion *in writing* which was accomplished in the refined world of the *ritsuryō* aristocracy. And the new direction taken thereafter was to poetry and literature that was *fabricated,* rather than an art unconscious of itself and its past.

The beginning of lyric poetry implies, of course, an awakening in the poet of a sense of his own individuality. In the communal society, without writing or formalized political organization, there were shared feelings and concerns, but there would hardly have been a place or form for the awareness of individuality. In contrast to this was the high cultural level of the *ritsuryō* state, within which former clan chiefs moved away from family ties and into roles as members of an official aristocracy. Among some members of the group there was certainly a humanistic enlightenment nourished by the literature and thought of China. Perhaps also the new political structure defined and encouraged a consciousness of self in those most affected by the legal system. Whatever the case, it was in poetry that private feelings were expressed and where we find the soliloquy and eventually individual expression as literature. Interestingly, as contradictions in the *ritsuryō* society became critical, with growing urbanization and social tensions in the capital, expression of individuality also became more varied and revealed all those emotions born in the self-conscious man. This was the milieu in which individual creative consciousness first appeared in Japanese literature, and as lyric poetry it came into full blossom with the *waka* of the aristocrat-poets of the *Man'yōshū*.

We should be aware that epic or narrative poetry and folk song or folk poetry also contributed to the growth of individual lyricism. We describe the latter, individual lyricism, as emerging within the aristocratic class apart from the common people. But what we might term the folk song counterpart to this, the area of communal feeling, rooted in the life of the common people, and not claiming to express individual emotion, flourished over a wide area at the time of the *Man'yōshū,* to judge from the many poems of unknown authorship scattered through the collection. Clan chiefs who became the officials and aristocrats of the *ritsuryō* state had, until late in the period, close connections with their native regions, retaining their provincial identification and sharing in the world of folk literature. In the early development of individual lyricism, the new aristocracy still drew inspiration from the old world of folk song, and from time to time we see in that world a strength which actually hindered the development of individuality. Then, as they became urbanized, as a new social group formed, the aristocracy left folk song and their expression turned to lyricism. Indeed the *waka* of the *Man'yōshū* aristocracy may be viewed as the definitive movement of that group away from the world of folk song, the plebeian society. In the *Man'yōshū* the conditions we have described are time and again made explicit in the emotion and style of the poems themselves.

We have suggested already the possibility of something close to heroic epic poetry in the period of oral transmission. Among the aristocrats of the Court of Emperor Temmu we notice the emergence of a new ethnic spirit concurrent with the formation of the national state. There was a considerable mood of romanticism surrounding the Asuka-Fujiwara Court of the seventh century which in some degree was expressed through the writing of histories. The myths and legends preserved in the *Kojiki* and *Nihon shoki* are distorted, however, and preserve only a faint trace of the epic quality. That the epic spirit of the age failed to realize its literary potential probably was due to the authoritarian structure of the *ritsuryō* state and to inherent contradictions between the epics and the development and rationale of the state. Here too are the causes for the qualitatively different development and later decline of the long poem (*chōka*) in contrast to the *waka* of the *Man'yōshū*, and the *ritsuryō* state in the same way may have stimulated the emergence of individual lyricism in the *waka* form.

Individuality, folk song, epic poetry, and literacy are, of course, inseparable as the major elements in the evolution of individual lyric poetry which comes to full flower in the *ritsuryō* period with the collection known as the *Man'yōshū*.

The *Man'yōshū*

The twenty scrolls of the *Man'yōshū* record approximately 4,500 poems. In addition to the dominant forms of *chōka* and *waka* there are sixty-two *sedōka*, one poem in the Buddha's footprint-stone poems form (*bussokuseki katai*), and one linked verse (*renga*). The *Man'yōshū* was not compiled as a unified whole and there is some diversity in its editorial style. Basically the poems fall into three types: miscellaneous (*zōka*), love poems (*sōmonka*), and elegies (*banka*). Further classification can also be made through differentiating poems that are direct statements of emotion, those which dwell on some object, allegorical poems, travel poems, question and answer poems (*sedōka*) and also the style and attitude of expression. There have been various theories about the compilation of the work, but in its original form it seems to have been assembled by Ōtomo no Yakamochi (d. 785), who added his own poems and those of his choosing in scrolls 17 through 20. After Yakamochi the collection was revised to its present form, but we cannot yet make a definitive statement concerning the date of the work except to say that it belongs to the late Nara period, sometime after 759, the date of its latest poem. The title of the collection has been read variously as *Man'yōshū, Mandai no shū, Yorozu no koto no ha* (meaning either *Collection for a Myriad Ages,* or *Collection of Ten Thousand Leaves*), but the question of which is correct is still not settled. We know from statements in the work itself that various older poetry collections were drawn upon in compiling the *Man'yōshū:* the

Kokashū, Hitomaro kashū, Kasa no kanamura kashū, Tanabe no sakimaro no kashū, Takahashi no mushimaro no kashū, and so forth (kashū meaning "private collection").

In the Man'yōshū the technique for recording Japanese language by means of Chinese graphs was to use the Sino-Japanese pronunciation of the graphs and also, at times, the native Japanese word equivalent to the Chinese graph: sometimes the meaning of the graph (from Chinese) was significant, sometimes the graphs were only used as phonetic symbols. There are also instances of a playful use of the graphs, as in writing five Chinese graphs which together meant "on top of a mountain, another mountain," but which are to be understood as indicating another graph which in fact looks like one mountain on top of another and means "depart" (deru in modern Japanese). Details of the technique vary from one scroll to another, but in scrolls 5, 14, and 17 to 20 the primary writing technique is phonetic, one Chinese graph representing one syllable of Japanese, without regard for the meaning of the graph. This technique is known as man'yōgana (Man'yōshū syllabary) and was an effective if laborious writing system before the development of the simplified forms of kana in the ninth century.

The Man'yōshū was compiled from a variety of sources and its various scrolls embody different characteristics. Scrolls 1 and 2 are the oldest and most regular in style. As was the case with some later collections of poetry, the chokusenshū, scrolls 1 and 2 may have been compiled by imperial command. Scrolls 3, 4, 6, and some other scrolls are thought to have been assembled by Yakamochi. In scroll 5 the greater part of the poems are by Ōtomo no Tabito, Yakamochi's father, and Yamanoue no Okura, dealing with Dazaifu (Kyūshū). In scrolls 8 and 10 the poems are classified according to their association with one of the four seasons, and in 9 there are many poems from such private collections as Takahashi no mushimaro kashū. Scrolls 7, 10, 11, 12, 13, 14, and part of 16 have poems by anonymous writers and we find many poems from the realm of folk song. Scroll 13 especially is rich in old songs linked to the Kojiki and Nihon shoki. In scroll 14 there are mostly azuma uta which are regarded as songs of the eastern provinces. Scroll 15 contains poems by members of the mission to the Korean kingdom of Silla and love poems between Nakatomi no Yakamori and the daughter of Sanu no Chigami. Scrolls 17 to 20 contain the poems of Yakamochi, in chronological order and generally in the style of a poetry diary. In scroll 20 also there are about one hundred poems of the soldiers from eastern Japan who were garrisoned in distant Kyūshū; they are known as sakimori no uta, poems of the frontier guards.

The authors of the Man'yōshū poems and songs come from

every level of society and the work preserves many poems of the nameless commoners. The collection deals chiefly with the Yamato region, the area of Nara, but all the other districts are represented and many poems are heavy with regional flavor. Those various qualities are special to the *Man'yōshū* and are not found together in poetry anthologies of later times.

The oldest poem of the *Man'yōshū* is supposedly that by Iwa no Hime, consort to Emperor Nintoku. However, from the time of Emperor Nintoku to the reign of Empress Suiko, from about 313 to 628, the poems of the *Man'yōshū* retain a strong traditional quality which cautions us against uncritically accepting their dates and attributions. The period, therefore, which may rightly be termed the "Age of the Man'yōshū" is approximately the 130 years following the Court of Emperor Jomei (r. 629–41), continuing to the middle of the eighth century. For our examination this period may conveniently be divided into four parts.

The first period, the early *Man'yōshū,* is the forty years from the time of Emperor Jomei to the Jinshin Rebellion of 672. That was a time of political upheaval directed against the extension of imperial authority. The folk-song tradition of the *Nihon shoki* came to an end at that time and poetry began moving toward *waka* and *chōka* as individual lyric expression. The aristocratic class, which was then trying to establish order within its own ranks, for the most part was restricted by the limitations of older poetry, but still managed to express a good deal of lively human feeling. The clear and sturdy tones of their expression indeed led to statements of individual feeling which were the first emergence of the new literary aesthetic. From those years there are outstanding poems by Emperors Jomei, Saimei (r. 655–61), Tenchi (r. 661–71), Prince Ōama (later Emperor Temmu), Prince Arima, and others. But of special importance is one of the female poets of the *Man'yōshū,* Nukada no Ōkimi. Despite the times and her personally tragic life, her work reveals a brilliant talent for pure lyricism that combined intellect and passion to produce the earliest flowering of the courtly *waka.*

The second period of the *Man'yōshū* is the forty years following the Jinshin Rebellion down to the establishment of the capital at Nara; that is, from the establishment of the *ritsuryō* system to the first symptoms of its decline. From that time until the end of the *Man'yōshū* period the emperors of Japan were descendants of Emperor Temmu (r. 673–86), and the aristocratic *waka* poetry was caught up in the "Jinshin energy" which began with Emperor Temmu and his court. The era was characterized by the absolute imperial authority resulting from Emperor Temmu's victory, but aesthetically the aristocratic class retained in abundance the spirit of romantic and epic poetry out of its feeling for and background in the folk tradition. After the completion of the Taihō Code in 710, there emerged a period of unprecedented stability in Japanese political life which must have encouraged the development of Court poetry. The conditions of the time seem to have brought to *waka* considerable romantic vigor, expansion of subject matter, refinement of technique, and finally the completion of the *waka* form itself. Public or official poems were also created as expressions of the emotions of the courtiers—songs of praise (*sanka*) and elegies (*banka.*) The way to personal lyric poetry was further extended by that consciousness of individuality which was part of the maturing aristocratic society. Especially toward the end of the period, however, the public epic verse mode declined as most Court poetry found its way to personal lyricism. Generally speaking, the greater part of the aristocratic society of that period was conscious of a literary aesthetic at least by virtue of certain aspects the poetry shared with traditional and folk poetry, but it had not yet reached a clear awareness of form. Perhaps we should say that the essential quality of poetic style in those years was eclecticism and the unsophisticated expression of vigorous emotions.

Among the courtly poets were Emperor Temmu, Empress Jitō, Princess Oku (661–701), Prince Ōtsu (663–86), and Prince Shiki (716–?), but the most representative poet of the time was Kakinomoto no Hitomaro. We know almost nothing about that man's life except that he was a minor official at court, that he was appointed to a job in the provinces, and that he died in the early years of the Wadō period, 708–15. Both the quality and number of his poems in the *Man'yōshū* are quite remarkable. Hitomaro's intense subjectivity was suited to the temper and genius of the times, and his writing went right to the heart of his subject matter. His poetry is notable for its suppleness achieved through free and imaginative use of expressive vocabulary; in long poems, *chōka,* the feeling is that of a great orchestra of words. As an embodiment of the age in which he lived, Hitomaro's style was a continuous blending of opposite qualities: the non-individual and the uniquely individual; the folk songs of the commoners and the self-conscious art of the aristocracy; the epic and the lyric; the traditional and the fabricated. Nonetheless, with the poetry of Hitomaro there is a sudden heightening of romantic emotion which not only brings to light his incomparable gifts but also provides the key to the unfolding of aristocratic *waka* in the next period of the *Man'yōshū.*

In addition to the *Man'yōshū* poems we have the *Hitomaro kashū* (*Hitomaro Collection*) which, because of its many poems close to the area of folk songs, is important to any consideration of Hitomaro's style. The poet Takechi no Kurohito (dates unknown) worked in the general area described by Hitomaro's work but was inclined even more to individuality and deliberately fabricated lyricism without reaching a specifically self-conscious voice. His poems are fresh and lucid and though we have from his brush only eighteen *tanka* (including five of doubtful attribution), there is visible in his work a new style of mediation on nature which anticipated the later work of Yamabe no Akahito. Because Kurohito's work brought to rhythmical expression that reflection of the inner man which we call individuality in literature, he is particularly significant to the gentle if unself-conscious flowering of individualism which led to the next period of the *Man'yōshū*. In the second period too we should note the names of Naga no Okimaro and Kasuga no Oyu, both of whom were important in their own times and later.

The third period of the *Man'yōshū* is the twenty-three years from the establishment of the capital at Nara to 733, that is, the early period of the Nara court. It was the time of the consolidation of the national government and the creation of a capital city, Nara (then called Heijō), which was said to be "like the fragrance of blossoming flowers." At the same time, however, contradictions within the *ritsuryō* system were being intensified and the capital was frequently the scene of political intrigues among the aristocracy and particularly the Fujiwara clan. There was a deepening social unrest along with considerable increase in the sufferings of the common people. Nonetheless there was an awakening to the inner world among members of the aristocracy which led to awareness of the many variations of the human spirit, and this was realized in literature. Aristocrats and officials had long led urban lives quite separated from the scene of folk literature. Then too from an early time continental education—that is, Chinese literature—which had increasingly become part of the life of the court, contributed to the individualization of members of an intelligentsia which had already become critical and introspective. Out of the awareness of poetry as an expressive medium grew the poet's sensitivity and taste. In this period qualities which were intimate to the poetry of Hitomaro recede into the background and another mode, a self-conscious one, begins to be felt in literature. What emerges at that time is the full blossom of individual, lyrical court poetry, aware of itself and its form. We may say without exaggeration that the poetry of that period reflects every nuance of the society that created it.

The courtier Yamabe no Akahito turned his back on the mundane life around him and found a passionate interest in the beauty of nature, in many of his poems bringing about a delicate fusion of the subjective and the objective modes through his sensitive grasp of the natural scene. He creates a world of pure, lucid and elegant beauty, at times fused with a lyrical surface. Akahito has been called a poet of nature and as such he is the founder of a tradition in that mode. If we examine only his *chōka,* for example, on the subject of attending imperial journeys, those are quite obviously imitations of Hitomaro and come close to being stereotypes. However, taken as a whole, his *chōka* and *tanka* have an organic structure which stimulated literary awareness in other poets. Akahito might even be termed a writer of structure because of the delicate balance which informs nearly all of his poems.

Another courtier-poet, but one who affirmed the society of the court and prided himself on being an official of the imperial capital, was Kasa no Kanamura (dates unknown) who left several poems of outstanding style. During the period from about 725 to 750 there developed what may be called the Tsukushi poetry circle around Ōtomo no Tabito, governor of Kyūshū, and Yamanoue no Okura, governor of Chikuzen province. Most of Tabito's poetry derives from the period of his residence in Kyūshū. As the eldest son of a prominent aristocratic family, it is not surprising to find in him a man of refined character and intellect, schooled in Chinese literature and especially the thought of Lao-tse and Chuang-tse. However, he was subject to pressure from the Fujiwara clan and even as a man past sixty years of age he was assigned to a district far from the capital where, burdened with official duties, he also suffered the loss of his beloved wife. Most of his poetry was written in those later years. Longing for home, thoughts of his wife, and the solace of wine are the topics of his poetry—with an occasional touch of decadence; and yet there is something quite refreshing in the lyricism which he brings to expressing in plain language the feelings of his personal life. While Tabito sentimentalized human existence and looked to elegant and surreal realms as the source of literature, perhaps for him that was an inevitable reaction to life and a reaction in which he revealed a peculiar quality of the lyrical poet. In Tabito we may find a certain frivolity and escapism, but with Okura there is certainly a deep regard and affection for humanity. Okura was an intellectual who began his studies with Confucianism and Buddhism and subsequently broadened his interest to all areas of Chinese learning. He was without official rank when he was chosen as one of the secretaries of a mission sent to China in 701. Later he achieved recognition as governor of Hōki and tutor to the Crown Prince, and in his late sixties he became governor of Chikuzen. In contrast to Tabito, his intellect and personality were formed under conditions of adversity and great personal effort and invariably he found the materials of his poetry in the immediate conditions of human life. His social consciousness and intellectual qualities find a high moral intensity when he writes about the contradictions of society and the suffering and hardship which was the general lot of humanity. Most of his writing left to us dates from after his residence in Chikuzen. There is a good deal in his character quite the opposite of Tabito and it is quite a remarkable thing in the history of literature that a man should reveal so much sympathy for the world in his later years. The matter of content in his poetry must not obscure the fact that the value of his poetry rests securely on Okura's talent for literary structuring. We know in addition, by way of a note in the *Man'yōshū,* that Okura was editor of the *Ruijū karin* (*Classified Forest of Verse*), an early collection no longer extant.

In a totally different world from Okura was Takahashi no Mushimaro, a poet who turned his back on reality and created a new realm through the romantic beauty of his poetic structure. He has been called a poet of legends for his considerable use of legendary material and a narrative poet because of his tendency to use minutely realistic descriptions, but the apparent realism of his work is due rather to its structure and his forte is the dramatic form he brings his material. Undeniably there is an echo of decadence in his poems which tend to a rather morbid loneliness.

Among the female poets of the *Man'yōshū* the one whose work appears most often is Lady Ōtomo of Sakanoue, younger sister of Tabito. Her *chōka* are excellent and she displays great skill in handling a wide variety of subject matter. Her work extends into the next period of the *Man'yōshū* as well. Among the many other poets whose work is noteworthy are Kasa no Maro, known as "Manzei," Kuramochi no Chitose, and Yuhara no Ōkimi.

The fourth period of the *Man'yōshū* is the twenty-five years from 734 to 759, a time of decline in the aristocratic society and the *ritsuryō* system. Outwardly those were the renowned years of "Tempyō culture," but within that society the failures and contradictions of *ritsuryō* politics were intensified, social unrest became increasingly violent, and there were frequent political struggles and intrigues revolving around the Fujiwara and Tachibana clans. At that time there was a feeling of having come to the end of the energy of the Jinshin period reforms begun by Emperor Temmu. One reflection of the condition is that the *waka* generally lost the intensity of earlier years. The wellspring of lyricism was drying up and the form tended to be a pastime or merely a device of refined social correspondence. Totally separated now from their basis in folk song, *waka* soon became urbane and aristocratic, and for the most part these qualities were inherited by the aristocratic *waka* of later times. One of the representative poets of the fourth period is Ōtomo no Yakamochi (718–85), son of Tabito. Yakamochi contributed the largest number of poems to the *Man'yōshū.* He led a busy political life, first as a court official in charge of the palace guards, then as governor of Etchū and later governor of Inaba Province. However, not a single poem remains from the last twenty-six years of his life. Yakamochi came from a prominent family, but he was still under the shadow of the Fujiwara clan to the end of his days. From his youth we have some magnificent love poems (*sōmonka*), but life in Etchū opened his eyes to nature and to a broader sense of human life which was reflected in his poetry. Embroiled in stifling political struggles after his return to the capital, he explored what was then a new field of poetry by conveying his personal loneliness and anguish in a sentimental but highly polished style. Further, within a traditional form, the *waka,* Yakamochi pioneered a new style and reached in his work a realm of purity and lyricism through his serene contemplation of nature. The last flowering of *Man'yōshū* courtly *waka* appears in his poem welcoming the first day of the new year 759. That poem was composed at a time when he had been summarily assigned to the governorship of the remote province of Inaba and the first hemistich of his poem evokes the sad exile of deposed Emperor Junnin (r. 758–64) to the island of Awaji. In that final period of the *Man'yōshū* there is a burst of lyricism in a pathetic tone by way of the love exchange poems (*zōtōka*) between Nakatomi no Yakamori and the maiden Sanu no Chigami. A number of fine love poems remain from Lady Kasa and other women associated with Yakamochi. Of interest also are the many *chōka* left by Tanabe no Sakimaro (dates unknown) and the poems of the emissary to the Korean kingdom of Shiragi on the topic of the loneliness of travel and yearning for home.

As the *waka* of the *Man'yōshū* aristocracy were achieving a separate and individual style, the folk-song world of the common people continued its vigorous activity throughout the period of the *Man'yōshū*. In the books of anonymous poems there are many pieces rich in folk-song qualities and those, as song-poems, continued to develop in a folk milieu without a fixed date of composition or individual authorship. With some exceptions, the "songs of the east" (*azuma uta*) of Book 14 were songs of the common people of the eastern provinces and are generally about the emotions of love. They all frankly express the feelings of people close to the life of the land, are filled with a robust tone, and through use of dialect evoke the flavor of a particular region. Simply because the songs were produced out of a broad spectrum of life and out of the communal work of the people, they give voice to common emotions through non-individual, stereotyped expressions. Thus, even with a change of locality the songs created were of similar kinds. They were not fabricated songs but were rather born of human living before the awareness of literature as art. In contrast, however, the "eastland guard" poems (*sakimori no uta*) collected in Book 20 originate from the same area as the *azuma uta,* but are the compositions of various individuals telling of the life of the frontier guard. Such poems are quite different in expression from the songs of the natives of central Japan, producing a sparkle of emotion close to the vigor which informs the *azuma uta.* As we have mentioned, in Book 13 there are *chōka* of the shorter variety which have equivalents in songs from the ancient period; and in Book 16 there are folk songs of northern Japan and other regions. Also especially notable are love songs from the Noto district, Ishikawa Prefecture, poems from the commoner class written out of their daily and otherwise nonliterary existence. From that region too are a few examples of children's songs. In the *Hitomaro kashū* there are many compositions from the realm of folk song, and in Books 11 and 12 of the *Man'yōshū* we have considerable material of folk-song quality from the region around Kyōto, Nara, and Ōsaka. The large quantity of folk-song material recorded in the *Man'yōshū* is, of course, an important legacy from oral literature, but it is also evidence that the world of courtly *waka* had not completely broken its ties with folk literature as a basic undercurrent to its poetry. Even in later times when *waka* poetry of the Court was far removed from the world of folk song it was still able to draw on that source as a spring of literary inspiration—a point of significance in drawing the relationship between the two realms.

Writing in Chinese

The entire literature of the early ancient period was written down by means of Chinese graphs. The *ritsuryō* state in taking as its model the political organization of Sui and T'ang China strove to transplant the written documents of the continent and in fact made practical use of Chinese texts from an early date. As a social refinement Chinese literature became the literature of the Japanese court, and at the imperial university a collection known as the *Monzen* (*Anthology of Literature; Wen Hsuan* in Chinese)—thirty scrolls edited by Prince Shao Ming of the Liang Dynasty—was as highly regarded as the Confucian classics. In short, Chinese literature was not only the motive force behind written literature in Japan but, in the early ancient period, also had enormous bearing on the Japanese view of the nature of literature. The influence of Chinese literature from Han to early T'ang is apparent in the *Man'yōshū* not only in the use of Chinese script but also in the editing of the collection and in the compositions of such poets as Tabito and Okura. Through modern comparative studies the details of this influence are becoming clear and in general we may say that while Chinese literature was an influence on the thought of Japanese poets, the influence was even more pronounced in style and in rhetorical devices. Actual writing of Chinese in Japan began with the composition of poems during the Ōmi Court (667–73). From Ōmi through the Nara period composition of poetry in Chinese increasingly acquired political significance through its prestige in court society and many of the poets of the *Man'yōshū* must also be counted as poets in Chinese. However, only two works survive from the Ōmi period and they are compositions by Prince Ōtomo (648–72).

The *Kaifūsō* (*Fond Recollections of Poetry*), assembled in 751, is the oldest anthology of poems in Chinese by Japanese writers of the Ōmi and Nara periods. The editor is unknown, although such men as Ōmi no Mifune, Fujii no Hironari and Isonokami no Yakatsuku have been suggested as possibilities. The anthology contains one hundred and twenty poems by sixty-four poets: Prince Ōtomo, Prince Ōtsu, Fujiwara no Umakai, Isonokami no Otomaro, Ōtomo no Tabito, and so forth. The poems, with five graphs per line, are modeled on the Six Dynasties examples dealing with attendance at a banquet, accompanying the imperial carriage, festive gatherings, sightseeing, and similar topics—some being variations on poems in the *Monzen,* others based on a kind of poem usually composed on a set topic. The influence of ideas from Lao-tse and Chuang-tse is pervasive and the poems are as lacking in individuality as in aesthetic value, all remaining imitative. Poetry in Chinese—in ·contrast to *waka*—was preeminently an activity of the court, and it is a comment on the degree to which the aristocracy looked to China culturally that such poetry should have become an instrument of social life within the court.

From the early period too we have the *Kakyō hyōshiki* (*Standard Poetic Forms*), a work patterned after instruction books on the composition of Chinese poems, which attempts to discuss form and style in *waka* by borrowing Chinese principles of poetry. It was composed in 772 by Fujiwara no Hamanari and has the flavor of being a translation of some work on Chinese poetry, but it is still noteworthy as the first book attempting a study of Japanese poetry and marks the appearance of critical consciousness.

Late Ancient Period

A.D. 794 TO 1185

by

ABE AKIO

The Heian Period

THE LATE ANCIENT PERIOD refers to the four centuries from 794 to 1185 during which Heian, the present city of Kyōto, was the political and cultural center of Japan. The titles "middle antiquity" or "Heian Period" are also used to designate these years, and there is, of course, room for argument concerning appropriate limits of the period. We shall define the period as beginning with the transfer of the capital from Nara to Kyōto and ending with the destruction of the Taira family in the battle of Dan no ura in 1185. In terms of literary history, of course, there is good reason to distinguish the period of the *Kojiki,* the *fudoki,* and the *Man'yōshū* from that of the *Kokin wakashū, Kagerō nikki, Makura no sōshi, Genji monogatari, Konjaku monogatarishū,* and the *Shinkokin wakashū.* We also must differentiate this period from the medieval literature represented by the *Heike monogatari,* Nō drama and the comic interludes called *kyōgen,* linked verse, and medieval novella which are more closely associated with the general population than was Heian writing.

The late ancient period may be divided into three phases: the early period being the 140 years from the transfer of the capital (794) until 935, the supposed date of the *Tosa nikki (Tosa Diary)*; the middle period covering the 150 years from the compilation of the *Goshūi wakashū (Later Collection of Gleanings,* the fourth imperial anthology) to 1085, the end of the reign of Emperor Shirakawa; the late period covering the remaining one-hundred years.

Generally speaking, the early years produced a shift from *waka* to composition of prose literature, probably stimulated by a greater knowledge of Chinese prose and poetry. During the middle period the emerging prose forms reached maturity as diaries, essays, tales, anecdotes, and historical narratives, all of which were accompanied by a deepening sense of individuality. In the late period, prose literature, as the literature of the aristocratic class, came to a standstill,

39

while interest in *waka* re-emerged and led to such collections as the *Senzai wakashū* (*Collection of a Thousand Years,* the seventh imperial anthology) and the *Shinkokin wakashū* (*New Collection of Ancient and Modern Times,* the eighth imperial anthology).

Two points of particular significance in the literature of the late ancient period are the birth and development of prose literature written in the *hiragana* syllabary, and the fact that the literature was the creation of an aristocracy resident within the boundaries of the Heian capital. There was, of course, prose composition in Japan of ancient times, but with the important distinction that it was written in Chinese rather than Japanese. At the time of the composition of the *Kojiki* there was great potential for prose expression, but techniques of writing were still too immature to record the full range of Japanese with sufficient ease. The emergence of prose literature is one of the most important events in the literature of the period, and *waka* too was bound up with the evolution of prose and was transformed by it.

Within the *ritsuryō* system the aristocracy were persons of third rank or above, and by this definition the aristocracy of the late ancient period was limited to the officials of high rank. However, the authors of this period were by no means restricted to those lofty strata of official society but included persons from the fourth and fifth ranks of nobility (*shodaibu*) and acting or deputy governors (*zuryō*), many of whom were descendants of high officials, who may be called the middle-rank aristocracy. The audience too for the literature of this period was made up of members of the middle and upper levels of aristocratic society, and there seem to have been few readers from the lower ranks of officials. There is no trace at this time of the literary audience extending to the commoner level of Japanese society. It would seem, then, that a literary consciousness, which we take as fundamental to the writing of that time, derived from the official, aristocratic class, and quite justifiably that literature has been called aristocratic literature.

To say this does not imply that there was no literature of the common people. Obviously, such literature as songs, anecdotes (*setsuwa*), and performances, such as *sarugaku* and *dengaku,* were current among the common people of Japan, but the general population had no means of writing, not even the *kana* syllabaries. The people were involved in music, dance, dramatic posturing, and acting, but such activities were orally transmitted and followed in their evolution the traditional literary forms. Because nothing was written down we are now hard pressed for even a general knowledge of the popular area outside of an extremely small number of works. What knowledge is available comes from those works selected and written down by individuals from the aristocratic class. When we examine that scanty material we find evidence of only the slightest interaction between popular literature (the oral tradition) and aristocratic literature, the process being quite slow and reflecting no trace on the popular level of the rise and decline of the aristocratic writing. Popular literature at that time belonged to its own separate world and did not undergo the intense transformations experienced by aristocratic literature. Later we will need to analyze again the condition of popular literature, but the outstanding quality which marks the literature of the late ancient period is that it was the product of a narrow and limited social class.

Among the literary remains of that time are a few rare works like the *Shōmonki* (or *Masakadoki; The Revolt of Masakado*) of 940. It is thought to have been written by a monk of the eastern provinces, far distant from the Heian capital; it is an idiosyncratic work telling of the life and thoughts of a provincial warrior. Despite its provincial origin, the *Shōmonki* expresses the culture and views of Heian aristocratic society. Again, we can say of such works as the *Kanke koshū* (*Later Poems in Chinese of Sugawara no Michizane,* ca. 903), *Higaki no ōnashū* (*Collection of the Dancer Higaki no Ōna;* thirty-one poems), and part of the *Sarashina nikki* (*Sarashina Diary*) that they were written while the authors were living in the provinces, but in content they are typically aristocratic. The significance of "provincial" in describing these works is in no way as great as in the *azuma uta* and the *sakimori no uta* of the *Man'yōshū.* We may say again that the literature of the late ancient period was the literature of the aristocracy of the capital city, Heian, and the most profound awareness in that writing is of the history, geography, the political, economic and social life of the city. To study the course of literature in that period is to observe the changes which occurred within that particular consciousness of place and which, while bound up with the history of *waka,* center on the creation and development of prose literature.

Writing in Chinese

While the late ancient period immediately followed that brilliant collection of Japanese poetry, the *Man'yōshū,* we must begin the history of the period with an account of writing in Chinese, for Japanese poetry, the *waka,* casts scarcely a shadow at that time. We know from the *Shoku nihongi* and later histories that there was composition of Japanese poetry on public occasions during the reign of Emperor Kammu, 781–806, but by the time of the reign of Emperor Saga from 809 to 823, only such Japanese poems were recorded as were composed incidentally, for amusement, during imperial gatherings for the composition of Chinese poetry. In 814 the first imperial collection of poems in Chinese was made, the *Ryōun shinshū* (*New Collection Surpassing the Clouds*), and subsequently the *Bunka shūreishū* (*Collection of Magnificent Prose*), 818, and the *Keikokushū* (*Collection of State;* a collection of prose and poetry in Chinese), 827, were produced by imperial command. Representative of collections of individual authors are such works as the *Shōryōshū* (*Pure Soul Collection*) with the poems of Kūkai (774–834) and the *Yashōkōshū* (*Country Councilor Collection*), now lost, with the poems of Ono no Takamura (802–52). Important poets of the period 810 to 833 were such men as Emperor Saga, Kaya no Toyotoshi, Kūkai, Ono no Takamura, Sugawara no Kiyokimi, Yoshimine no Yasuyo, and Prince Uchiko. Chinese writers who were natives of the continent all but disappear in Japan at that time.

Writing in Chinese then included a variety of poetry and prose forms: the *fu, hsü,* and examination answers; but by far the greater quantity was poetry, and in poetry the most prominent form was the seven-word line, four-line poem called *zekku* (*chüeh chü* in Chinese). Also a form which mixed lines of varying lengths, (3,4,5,7, etc. graphs per line) reappeared. The subject matter in those poems often dwelt on sightseeing and festive occasions, but through the influence of the *Monzen,* historical poems and poems on subjects within the traditional classification (in Chinese, *yueh fu ti:* topics of the song collection) grew most numerous. There were also compositions which took as their topics the landscapes of Chinese painting, and these in turn led to *waka* on topics suggested by the scenes painted on Japanese standing screens. Though few in number, there were also poems on Buddhist themes. Generally speaking the attempt in most of the poetry of that time was to adhere to the styles of early and mid-T'ang China, the seventh and early eighth centuries.

From the Jōgan era through the Engi era, between 860 and 922, no imperial anthologies were commissioned; instead we have numerous collections of the works of individual poets. If anything, there was more writing being done at that time than during the first three decades of the century, a situation which reflects the increasing degree to which written Chinese had become a prerequisite in official society. Talented men appeared one after another between 859 and 884. The following are but a few of the most prominent: Haruzumi no Yoshinawa, Ōe no Otondo, Sugawara no Koreyoshi, Miyako no Yoshika (834–79), Tachibana no Hiromi (838–90), Shimada no Tadaomi (828–91), and Ōkura no Yoshiyuki. Between 890 and 922 such men as Sugawara no Michizane (845–903), Ki no Haseo (845–912), and Miyoshi no Kiyotsura (847–918) were prominent. The important collections from that time are: *Toshi bunshū* (*The Miyako Writings*) by Miyako no Yoshika; *Denshi kashū* (*The Shimada Writings*) of Shimada Tadaomi; *Tachibana-shi bunshū* (*The Tachibana Writings*) of Tachibana no Hiromi; *Kanke bunsō* (*Sugawara Miscellany*) and *Kanke koshū* (*Later Poems in Chinese of Sugawara no Michizane*) of Sugawara no Michizane; *Kike shishū* (*The Ki Poetry Collection*) and *Zoku-kike shishū* (*The Ki Poetry Collection Continued*) of Ki no Haseo; *Zenkeshū* (*The Miyoshi Collection*) of Miyoshi no Kiyotsura. Along with the influence of the easy but elegant style of the *Hakushi monjū* (*Collected Works of Po Chü-i*) we find also influences from the intricate verse of the late Six Dynasties. The approach to poetry found here is also basic to the style of the *Kokin wakashū,* and in some ways these poems in Chinese are very close to *waka* in spirit.

Among the writings in Chinese surviving from the late ancient period, the following titles are especially important.

Histories:
: *Shoku nihongi* (*Continuation of the Chronicle of Japan*), 797; covers the years 697–792. Principal writer: Sugano no Mamichi (d. 814).
Nihon kōki (*Latter Chronicle of Japan*), 840; covers the years 792–833. Principal compiler: Fujiwara no Otsugu (773–843).
Shoku nihon kōki (*Continuation of the Latter Chronicles of Japan*), 868; covers the years 833–50. Presented to the throne by Fujiwara no Yoshifusa and Haruzumi no Yoshitada.
Nihon montoku tennō jitsuroku (*True Record of Emperor Montoku*), 879; covers reign of Emperor Montoku, 850–58. Presented to the throne by Fujiwara no Mototsune (836–91) and others.
Nihon sandai jitsuroku (*True Record of Three Reigns*), 901; covers the reigns of Emperors Seiwa, Yōzei, and Kōkō, the period 858–87.
Ruijū kokushi (*National History Topically Gathered*), 892; the history of Japan arranged topically, rather than chronologically as were the *Rikkokushi* (*Six National Histories*). Edited by Sugawara no Michizane (845–903).

Legal Works:
: *Kōnin kyaku shiki* (*Laws and Regulations of the Kōnin Era*), 820; covers laws and regulations from 701 to 819.
Engi shiki (*Regulations of Engi*), 907; a summary of the preceding codes.

Medical Works:
: *Shinsen yakkyō taisō* (*New Elements of Medical Principles*), 799; compiled by Wake no Hiroyo.
Daidō ruijuhō (*Topically Arranged Medical Techniques of the Daidō Era*), 808. The first medical book compiled in Japan; 100 scrolls (no longer extant).

Dictionaries:
: *Tenrei banshō meigi* (*Names of All Things, in Seal and Square Graphs*), ca. 830; edited by Kūkai.
Shinsen jikyō (*New Mirror of Chinese Writing*), 830.

Travel:
Nittō guhō junrai kōki (*Ennin's Diary: Records of Buddhist Pilgrimages to China*), 847; compiled by Ennin.
Gyōrekishō (*Travel Notes*), 858; by Enchin.
Other:
Shinsen shōjiroku (*New Genealogies*), 814.
Nihonkoku genzaisho mokuroku (*A List of Books at Present in Japan*), 891. That work records 1,579 titles and 16,790 volumes (scrolls).
Hifuryaku (*Selection of Treasures*), 831; compiled by Shige no Sadanu-shi. A vast anthology, in 1,000 scrolls, from Chinese writing; all but a fraction now lost.

The flourishing of Chinese prose and poetry in the late ancient period is a reflection of the current tastes of the official and aristocratic writers. Prose composition in Japanese left nothing that might be called creative and in *waka* of the time we have only the anonymous poems collected in the *Kokinshū,* the first imperial anthology, dated 905.

After the Taika Reform, Japan adopted the legal system of China, the *ritsuryō,* and under that organization experienced a period of cultural prosperity benefiting from the achievements of T'ang China. The capital was moved from Yamato province to Yamashiro where the city of Heian was built, and in the reign of Emperor Kammu—who is said to have been inspired to a renovation of national government by his father, Emperor Kōnin—enormous energy was expended in bringing the material and intellectual culture of T'ang China to Japan; those efforts began with the study and composition of Chinese prose and poetry. And yet even by the end of the Nara period the Japanese, who had long been accustomed to an outlook conditioned by the family system, had still failed to adopt those patterns of legalistic thinking necessary to the implementation of the Taika Reform and the creation of a bureaucratic state on the Chinese model. Political reforms instituted under Emperor Kammu seem to have been an attempt to discipline the aristocracy of Nara (who had learned only the manners of T'ang) to ways of thought which were the real foundation of T'ang culture. It was indeed this attempt to learn again from China, in order to effect a change in thinking, that produced in Japan the age of Chinese prose and poetry. Emperor Kammu's vigorous reform of the university and his encouragement of scholarly and literary activities were for precisely the same motive; he believed that without such rebuilding of the intellectual foundation it would be impossible to make the *ritsuryō* system work. The imperial anthologies of Chinese poetry from the Kōnin and Tenchō periods, from 810 to 834, were also part of this effort. Writing in Chinese was then called a "great enterprise of statecraft, a thing of imperishable grandeur," and was a skill indispensable to political thought itself.

Having undergone this literary experience which was part of government policy at the beginning of the late ancient period, the Japanese of later times undoubtedly acquired an outlook on the world quite different from the people of the Yamato period. After the Jōgan years (859–77) poets were also members of the bureaucracy, yet there were relatively many who rose to official position out of poverty: for example, such men as Miyako no Yoshika, Ki no Haseo, Sugawara no Michizane, and Miyoshi no Kiyotsura. Writing in Chinese extended to the lower ranks of officialdom and to the provincial bureaucracy whose members, while not invited to submit compositions for inclusion in the imperial anthologies, were changed enough in their thinking to write poems in Chinese on their own and leave collections of such work to their heirs. We should remark too that the lower ranks of officials who were editors of the *Kokinshū* were also well acquainted with the Chinese literature of their time, a fact that accounts for the common characteristics of their poems in Chinese and the poems of the *Kokinshū*. One can hardly discuss the poetry of this collection without taking into account writing in Chinese at the beginning of the late ancient period.

The middle years of Heian saw no cessation of writing in Chinese by courtiers and officials. While no imperial anthologies were compiled, there were privately edited collections of Chinese prose and poetry as well as collections of writing by single individuals. Possibly, however, as a result of the growing body of prose forms in Japanese at that time, we have nothing like the quantity of Chinese writing which appeared during the first hundred years of Heian, a time when there was really no other means of expression than the Chinese script. There remain a number of works from the middle and late periods—by such men as Miyako no Yoshika, Sugawara no Michizane, Minamoto no Fusaaki (d. 939), Sugawara no Koretoki (899–981), and Minamoto no Shitagō (911–83). Much of that writing is indirectly critical of the government and society, but on the whole it is imitative and reveals little more than the prestige of writing in Chinese.

In the area of prose and poetry collections we have the *Honchō monzui* (*Choice Literature of the Realm*), compiled by Fujiwara no Akihira (989–1066). It was modeled on the *T'ang Wen-ts'ui* (*Choice Literature of T'ang*), a one-hundred scroll collection compiled during the Sung dynasty. It brings together 427 selections of prose and poetry from the years 809 to 1036 and arranges the material under thirty-eight categories ranging from poetry and biographies to sealed documents containing political opinions and suggestions (*ikenfūji*) and documents issued by the Great Council of State. Along with the men noted above, contributors to the anthology include Ōe no Asatsuna (886–957), Ōe no Koretoki (888–963), Prince Tomohira (964–1009), Ki no Tadana (966–99), Minamoto no Tamenori (d. 1011), Ōe no Mochitoki (955–1010), and Ōe no Masahira (952–1012). Among the collections of poetry were: *Fūsōshū* (*The Japan Collection*), sixteen scrolls compiled about 998 by Ki no Tadana; and *Honchō reisō* (*Fine Verse of the Realm*), two scrolls compiled in 1009 by Takashina no Moriyoshi. There is also a collection of the poems of Ōe no Masahira titled *Kōri hōshū* (*Classified Poems of Masahira*). The *Wakan rōeishū* (*Collection of Chinese and Japanese Verse*) was compiled in 1013, by Fujiwara no Kintō. It is a collection of fine verse, including some *waka,* later used as a handbook for reading and composition.

The late Heian period also produced works of interest in Chinese: *Chōya gunsai* (*The National Anthology*), thirty scrolls edited by Miyoshi no Tameyasu; *Honchō mudaishi* (*Untitled Poems of the Realm*), 1163; and *Honchō zokumonzui* (*Choice Literature of the Realm Continued*), ca. 1150, editors unknown; and *Shinsen rōeishū* (*New Collection of Rōei*), ca. 1142, compiled by Fujiwara no Mototoshi. Ōe no Masafusa (1041–1111) and Minamoto no Tsunenobu (1016–97) were poets in Chinese who were also known for their *waka.* Individual collections of the period include the *Hōshōji-dono goshū* (*Collection of the Monk of Hōshōji*) by Fujiwara no Tadamichi (1097–1164). Other works contain passages which touch on the lives of the common people: *Shinsarugakuki* (*New Record of Sarugaku*) by Fujiwara no Akihira, and Ōe no Masafusa's *Yūjoki* (*Women Entertainers*), *Kugutsuki* (*Puppets*), and *Rakuyō dengakuki* (*Dengaku of the Capital*). Also from this period is Akihira's *Meigō ōrai* (*Akihira's Primer*), a collection of letters which became models of style and a text for popular education (the genre being called *ōrai-mono,* meaning "primer") in use from the Kamakura period to Meiji times.

In the late period, writing in Chinese followed the pattern established in early Heian, but as the aristocrats and officials became more familiar with Chinese prose and poetry individual works appeared in the various genres with marked Japanese adaptations and innovations. In the mid-Heian period Yoshishige no Yasutane, author of *Chiteiki* (*Notes of the Pond Arbor;* an essay in Chinese and possibly the model for *Hōjōki* of early Kamakura), composed *Nihon gokuraku ōjōki* (*Notes from Japan on Easy Rebirth in Paradise*), and Minamoto no Tamenori produced *Sambō ekotoba* (*Illustrated Stories of the Three Treasures*). From late Heian, however, we have similar works which touch on the lives of the common people rather than merely redoing the traditional topics of Chinese essay writing. There was indeed a shift to writing in Chinese about all classes of Japanese society, and at the same time with the appearance of collections like *Meigō ōrai* we discover the creation of an original Japanese epistolary style in the medium of written Chinese. From imitation of the *Wen hsuan* and the writings of Po Chü-i, Japanese writing in Chinese gradually achieved an independent form to become a style of Japanese writing known as *kambun* (meaning "prose in Chinese").

Imperial Anthologies of Japanese Poetry (*Waka*)

Literary activity of the early part of the late ancient period centered on Chinese prose and poetry. When we turn to *waka* of that time we must direct our attention primarily to poems of unknown authorship in the *Kokinshū* (officially titled *Kokin waka shū: Collection of Ancient and Modern Poetry;* the word *waka* is frequently omitted before *shū,* "collection").

According to the Preface to the *Kokinshū,* the poetry of the early part of that period lay obscure and forgotten in the private love notes of romantic people and did not blossom forth in public. Poetry had become the intermediary between men and women, a private affair. Among the anonymous poems found in the *Kokinshū* are some dating from near the time of its compilation. Out of a total of 1,100 poems in the collection the anonymous poems come to 431, a ratio which seems to indicate that poems of the period following the *Man'yōshū* were often composed in situations of private life. Some poems have a clear echo of the folk-song style, slightly antique and reminiscent of the *Man'yōshū.* From their content and notes in the text we know them to be compositions of people in the Nara capital.

The period from about 860 to 925 saw the end of imperial anthologies of compositions in Chinese and also the assimilation of Chinese writing down to the lower ranks of officials. This was also the time of the emergence of six outstanding poets in *waka* (called the *rokkasen:* Six Poetic Geniuses): Henjō (816–90), Kisen, Ariwara no Narihira (825–80), Ono no Komachi (flourished ca. 850), Ōtomo no Kuronushi, and Fun'ya no Yasuhide. *Waka* began to be composed then on public occasions and, in contrast to the poetry of the *Man'yōshū* and the anonymous poems of the early Heian period, *waka* now were written by poets who had undergone a tempering of sensitivity and intellect through exposure to Chinese literature. Their work reflected a more mature sensitivity to the intellect and feelings of themselves and others.

During the first quarter of the tenth century, poetry composing contests known as *uta awase* were held at court. In *uta awase* the poets were divided into two sides, the right and left, each side composing poems, supposedly extemporaneously, which were then judged and graded, with points awarded (win, lose, and draw). The contest is said to have originated with similar competitions in composing Chinese poetry (called *tōshi* or *shiawase*). Such contests seem to have helped restore *waka* to a position of respect in the literary arts of the court and official circles. Poems offered during the *uta awase* contests became the materials of the *Shinsen man'yōshū* (*The New Man'yoshu*) by Sugawara no Michizane, a collection which matched *waka* with Chinese versions in the seven-word, four-line style. Following that work was a collection of *waka* based on lines from poems in Chinese; this was the *Kudai waka* (*Waka on Couplet Topics*), 894, by Ōe no Chisato. There was then a growing awareness of Japanese poetry (called *yamato no uta*) as something distinct from—but not inferior to—Chinese poetry (*kara no uta*). From that period also are two *waka* collections known by the identification titles *Akihagishū* (*Autumn Bush Clover Collection*) and *Tsugishikishishū* (*Colored Paper Collection*). Quite likely there existed individual collections by such men as Narihira and Henjō, since the Preface to the *Kokinshū* mentions that private collections were requested for use in its compilation. The thirty-one syllable *waka* in fact seems to have come to be regarded as the only literary art of Japan comparable to Chinese poetry.

The date 905 appears in the Chinese Preface to the *Kokinshū* but among the poems are some dated 907, 908, and 913. From this evidence we may suppose that the collection was finished sometime in 913 or 914. The editors of the collection were officials of relatively low rank, such men as Ki no Tomonori, Ki no Tsurayuki, Ōshikouchi no Mitsune, and Mibu to Tadamine, but they were nonetheless voices of authority in *waka* of the time. The *Kokinshū* was compiled by order of the Emperor to select outstanding poems of past and present poets, excluding poems already included in the *Man'yōshū*. Drawing on individual collections of poetry the work of 124 poets known by name was selected, their work, together with anonymous poems making 1,000 poems in all. The poems are arranged under thirteen categories: Spring, Summer, Autumn, Winter, Congratulatory, Partings, Travel, Names of Things, Love, Laments, Miscellaneous Subjects, Miscellaneous Forms and Poems of the Bureau of Poetry. Most texts of the *Kokinshū* have Prefaces both in Chinese and Japanese, but some lack one or the other. The structure of the *Kokinshū,* with twenty scrolls or volumes and the poems arranged by subject matter, became the model for subsequent imperial anthologies and other collections of Japanese poetry.

Among the 124 poets those represented by a conspicuously large number of poems are: Ki no Tsurayuki (99 poems); Ōshikōchi no Mitsune (60 poems); Ki no Tomonori (44 poems); Sosei (36 poems); Mibu no Tadamine (35 poems); Ariwara no Narihira (30 poems); Ise, daughter of Fujiwara no Tsugikage (22 poems); Fujiwara no Toshiyuki (19 poems); Ono no Komachi, Kiyowara no Fukayabu, Henjō, and Fujiwara no Okikaze (17 poems each). In this collection the number of poems written by men contemporary with the compilers is particularly large.

The poems as a whole belong to three periods. The early period is characterized by the work of anonymous poets, there being 431 poems of this type. The middle period is the time of the Six Poetic Geniuses, circa 875. The late period is the time contemporary with the editors of the *Kokinshū*. The poems of the late period lack the directness and candor of the earlier poems, presenting an oblique view of their subjects and always rather self-conscious about their own thoughts and feelings. They tend to be analytical, quite artificial and intellectual. The language of the poems has also changed. Instead of fixed epithets, the pillow words (*makura kotoba*) of earlier poetry, we find frequent use of pivot words (*kakekotoba*) and associative words (*engo*). The pivot word is one that produces two or more meanings in a line depending on how the word is parsed or cut; the associative word is one that echoes and expands the idea of a preceding word, as "thin" or "frail" might be *engo* in a poem where the word "thread" is a topic word. Poems in the *Kokinshū* make frequent use of abstract nouns, such as "thing" (*koto* and *mono*) and "person" (*hito*), and the use of particles becomes conspicuous. There is not, however, much variety in the vocabulary. Many complex nouns, verbs, and abstract modifiers appear, but the language is most often traditional and conservative. On the whole the collection is delicate and elegant as well as abstract and indirect in expression. The poets of the *Kokinshū* had adopted Chinese modes of thought and in consequence their work reflects a good deal of theory which, in a complicated emotional setting, only distorts the free expression of the writer's feeling. The tendency to intellectualize emerges so strongly with the editors of the *Kokinshū* that had they attempted any further explication of their ideas the expression would have required prose.

Among the poets of the *Kokinshū* several merit special attention: Henjō, Narihira, Tsurayuki, and the women poets Ono no Komachi and Ise.

Henjō, son of Yoshimine no Yasuyo, editor of the *Keikokushū,* was head of the imperial archives under Emperor Nimmei and was a talented administrator well familiar with Chinese intellectual disciplines. He became a monk (Henjō is his religious name) and is said to have lived a scholarly life on Mt. Hiei, near Kyōto. Many of his poems are playfully witty, but underlying his lightness of touch is a serene intellect.

Ariwara no Narihira, whose father was Prince Abo, is portrayed as a great lover involved in many romantic affairs, and noted for his pure poetry filled with the violent emotions of his life. In contrast to the scholarly Ki no Tsurayuki, Narihira's talent was preeminently poetical.

Tsurayuki's skill as an editor brought to the *Kokinshū* its qualities of elegance and symmetry. At times Tsurayuki produced work that was intimidating in its complexity, but his mastery of poetic technique, in which he could also be playful, led to fresh starts and new directions which were in part a characteristic of his contemporaries who were discovering the sophistication of Chinese poetry and prose. Tsurayuki's ideas on poetry anticipated an art that would combine external, formal beauty with depth of feeling. In addition to his achievements in poetry, his Preface to the *Kokinshū* and Preface to the collection (no longer extant) of *waka* ordered by Emperor Uda in 907, he is the author of a pioneering work of prose literature, the *Tosa nikki* (*Tosa Diary*). From his brush we also have the *Shinsen wakashū* (*New Selection of Poetry*), an anthology of 360 poems drawing chiefly on the *Kokinshū,* which he produced for Emperor Daigo about 930.

Ono no Komachi is supposed to have been the daughter of a governor of Dewa province, but little is known about her life. She seems to have had a great many love affairs and most of her poetry deals with the emotions of love. Indeed, at times her poetry falls victim to the strength of her emotions and reads like a hastily composed first draft.

Ise was the daughter of the governor of Yamato, Fujiwara no Tsugikage. She was in attendance at court and suffered abandonment by her lover, Fujiwara no Nakahira. Later she bore a son by Emperor Uda. Her writing is rather too full of mannerisms, but her love poetry is quite distinguished.

Following the *Kokinshū* is the *Gosenwakashū* (or *Gosenshū, Later Collection of Waka*), ordered in 951 by Emperor Murakami. This work in twenty volumes was compiled by members of the Bureau of Poetry: Kiyowara no Motosuke, Ki no Tokibumi, Ōnakatomi no Yoshinobu, Minamoto no Shitagō, and Sakanoue no Mochiki. Compared with the *Kokinshū*, the *Gosenshū* has many love exchange poems and a number of long headnotes (*kotobagaki*) wherein the author of the poem is referred to in the third person. The collection has no preface or introduction. The *Gosenshū* was compiled during the early period of the emergence of prose literature and so it has been suggested that aspects of the work reflect a compromise in the direction of the prose tale or *monogatari*. We can in fact observe the same tendency in the private individual collections of *waka* from this time. One criticism of the *Gosenshū* has been that for an imperial anthology it was somewhat carelessly assembled, and some doubt has been raised as to whether or not the manuscript reached a finished form. It may even be that the editors intended to leave the work unfinished.

Among individual collections of poetry from the late ancient period, the first half of the personal collection of Fujiwara no Koretada is of particular interest. Under the pen name Kurahashi no Toyokage, supposedly a lowly official, his *Toyokageshū* (*Toyokage Collection*) tells of his affair with a certain woman. With varying degrees of success other personal collections took approaches similar to that of the *Toyokageshū*. The following collections are representative of this type:

> *Motoyoshi shinno gyoshū* (*Collection of Prince Motoyoshi*)
> *Atsutadashū* (*Collection of Fujiwara no Atsutada*)
> *Motozaneshū* (*Collection of Fujiwara no Motozane*)
> *Saneakirashū* (*Collection of Minamoto no Saneakira*)
> *Nakatsukasashū* (*Collection of Lady Nakatsukasa*)

The authors of collections such as these were usually from the upper-class aristocracy, as were, for example, Minamoto no Shigeyuki (d. 1000) and Taira no Kanemori (d. 990). The poems in these collections are not basically different from those of the *Kokinshū,* and yet in the *waka* on secret love affairs there is a freedom not found in the *Kokinshū* which in that area maintains discretion appropriate to an imperial anthology.

Concerning the *Shūishū* (*Collection of Gleanings*), the third imperial anthology, in twenty volumes, there is some question whether it or the *Shūishō* (*Draft of the Shūishū*) was composed first. Current opinion favors the *Draft,* edited by Fujiwara no Kintō, as the earlier, dating from about 996. The later version was completed between 1005 and 1007 by the retired Emperor Kazan. The *Shūishū* contains 1,351 poems and includes poets of the *Man'yōshū,* the *Kokinshū,* and the *Gosenshū,* such as Ki no Tsurayuki (107 poems), Hitomaro (104 poems), and Ōnakatomi no Yoshinobu (922–91; 59 poems). The collection has a new flavor, however, given to it by poets writing during the decade around the year 1000. The work of Sone no Yoshitada (fl. ca. 985) and Lady Izumi Shikibu (ca. 970–1030), however, had not yet achieved much critical regard. In style the poems of the *Shūishū* recapture the elegance of the *Kokinshū,* but the strong rhythms of the older collection are lost despite a fine unity of spirit and language. Many poems in the anthology were composed on themes suggested by picture screens; such poems were known as *byōbu no uta*.

Fujiwara no Kintō (966–1041), a high ranking member of the nobility and one of the cultivated men of his day, was leader of the court poetry circle in the period of the *Shūishū*, but his talent as a poet was not as exceptional as his position and advantages might suggest. In his *Shinsen zuinō* (*New Elements of Poetry*) and *Waka kubon* (*Nine Grades of Waka*) Kintō asserts that while the language and spirit of a poem must be compatible, a poem must also be suggestive and give an aftertaste. Sone no Yoshitada (930–1003?) is regarded as a heretic from the poetry style of his time, having composed in a realistic vein on everyday subjects freely and occasionally colloquially. Indeed he brought a fresh breeze to poetry which was fixing its horizons by the first three imperial anthologies. His personal collection of *waka* is called *Sotanshū* (*Collection of Sone in the Province of Tango*) and is in one volume.

Lady Izumi Shikibu (d. 1030) is known for the many romances in her life and indeed she seems to have been high-strung and sensual to an unusual degree. She speaks wistfully in her poetry of her own person and of "a body that was no match for the heart's emotion." Of her work we have the *Izumi shikibushū* (*Izumi Shikibu Collection*) and the *Izumi shikibu zokushū* (*Izumi Shikibu Collection Continued*) as well as her *Izumi shikibu nikki* (*The Diary of Izumi Shikibu*)—albeit there is some slight doubt about its authorship—which gives a detailed account of her life during the last eight months of the year 1003. Proper evaluation of the three poets just mentioned did not appear until the end of the Heian period and the creation of a new style in Japanese poetry.

After the *Kokinshū* Japanese poetry found a fresh start through contact with Chinese writing, but the development of *waka* reached a plateau about the time of the *Shūishū*. The reason for this lay not in *waka* itself but rather in the spectacular growth of prose literature. The critical opinion of aristocratic society nonetheless remained fixed in holding *waka* still to be the heart and soul of Japanese literature.

Prose Literature

Diaries and Fiction

The major development in literature of the late ancient period was the emergence of narrative prose written in the *kana* syllabary. The literature originated in anecdotal stories called *setsuwa*, in poem-tales (*uta monogatari*), and in diaries—represented by such works as *Taketori monogatari, Ise monogatari,* and *Tosa nikki.*

The *Tosa nikki* (*Tosa Diary*), written in fact by a man, opens with the words: "Diaries are things written by men, I am told, but I am writing one to see what a woman can do." We do not know when the Japanese began to write diaries, but in the *Nihon shoki* we find a quotation from the diary of Yuki no Hakatoko which leads us to suppose the practice may have started about the time of the Taika Reform, the mid-seventh century. Thereafter and throughout the early Heian period diary keeping was an official office (known as *naiki* and *geki*), and it was continued to the end of the Heian period. Besides public diaries, private diaries are found from the Nara period, and in Heian we have imperial diaries as well as travel diaries, such as *Nittō guhō junrai kōki,* about 847, the account of Ennin's journey to China, and *Gyōrekishō* (*Travel Notes*) by the monk Enchin who describes his pilgrimage to China about 859. Those works were written in Chinese or in a highly Japanized style of Chinese called *hentai kambun.* Also, they were primarily records of fact, events and ceremonies, not descriptions of the writer's feelings and thoughts.

Prose writing in the *hiragana* syllabary seems to have developed through letters written to accompany *waka* at the time when *waka* were being composed as love poems. The letters were written by both men and women who would have been aware of the effectiveness of the form in revealing their most intimate feelings, but the men, though praising writing done in *kana,* had taken up written Chinese as their literary medium and seem to have felt that the syllabary was inferior. They inclined to the opinion that the cursive syllabary, *hiragana,* was a medium more suitable for women than men. Even Ki no Tsurayuki, who wrote the *kana* Preface for the *Kokinshū,* felt it necessary to add a Chinese Preface to his *Shinsen wakashū.* Nonetheless, Tsurayuki was quite sensitive to the uses of *kana* prose, realizing that the *kana* syllabary, in which he could easily write his own language and express his personal feelings, was the most appropriate medium for the travel diary. In his *Tosa nikki* he tells of the journey by boat from the province of Tosa on the southern shores of Shikoku, around the eastern end of the island, to the Heian capital. Under the pretense that the diarist was a woman, Tsurayuki felt free to write outside of his role as Court official and used the diary as a vehicle for his personal expression. The diary is cast in the special form of a journey by boat, and yet we should not expect from it a factual account of the journey but rather the personal reactions evoked by that experience. The basic materials of the diary are: continuing sadness arising from Tsurayuki's loss of his young daughter in Tosa; the writer's views on poetry as editor of the *Kokinshū;* and the writer's humor and irony in his view of the world and human affections. As an early work in *kana* prose, the *Tosa nikki* demonstrated the literary possibilities of the *kana* writing system, but in comparison with later works this diary is monotonous in expression and not yet able to create a significant mood of individuality in observation or experience.

Taketori monogatari (*The Tale of the Bamboo Cutter*) brings together various *setsuwa* and legends to create a new dimension in Japanese literature. A variety of extant *setsuwa* (from *Konjaku monogatarishū,* for example), if taken separately or in limited combinations, will give us the general outline of *Taketori,* but the *monogatari* was not simply the product of writing down a series of brief incidents or *setsuwa.* The idea of an extended prose narrative was a necessary precondition on top of which the material of the story had to be formed to the outlook of the Heian aristocratic society. The "princess" of the story is called Kaguya. She is a magical being whose parents dwell with their race on the moon, but for some transgression Princess Kaguya is reborn on earth, inside a stem of bamboo, and is raised by an old man and his wife. She grows to maturity in a short time and brings wealth to her foster parents. Eventually five suitors present themselves. The girl wishes to reject all her suitors, but to please her foster father she agrees to marry the one who fulfills the (impossible) tasks she demands as proof of the man's devotion. When all the suitors fail, the emperor himself asks for Kaguya, but by this time the people from the moon come to reclaim the girl from her exile, and despite the effort of the earth people, they take her home to the sky. The story has intriguing psycho-mythical dimensions, but the various *setsuwa* elements—the trials of the suitors, the foundling story, and a typical *setsuwa,* an explanation of the origin of the name of Mount Fuji—are not well connected and do not give over-all structure. We can only speculate about the earlier forms of the *setsuwa,* since it is obvious that *Taketori* underwent a number of writings even before the time of the *Kokinshū.* The present version seems to have emerged between 939 and 956. The history of its authorship is unknown, although such names as Minamoto no Shitagō and the priest Henjō have been associated with it. In *Genji monogatari* (*The Tale of Genji*) *Taketori* is discussed as the archetype and parent of all *monogatari.* Clearly this *monogatari* form, distantly related to *setsuwa,* provides the basic pattern of later fictional tales. The later *monogatari* associated with *Taketori* include *Utsubo monogatari* (*The Tale of the Hollow Tree*), *Ochikubo monogatari* (*The Tale of Lady Ochikubo*) as well as *Genji monogatari* and its successors. A separate type which developed out of *setsuwa* was the poem-tale (*uta monogatari*) of which *Ise monogatari* (*Tales of Ise*) is the prototype.

Ise monogatari in the "popular edition" (*rufubon*) is composed of 125 stories and 209 poems. Most of the stories center on Ariwara no Narihira (825–80) and many of the poems are his, although the hero in the *Ise* stories is simply referred to as a certain man. Other versions of *Ise monogatari* contain varying numbers of stories and poems, but they generally maintain the arrangement of the popular version which begins with the story: "Once a man, having attained his majority and possessing an estate at the village of Kasuga . . ." (the first phrase, *mukashi otoko*, "once [there was] a man," or a close variation of it, begins each story) and ends with the poem on death: "That it is a road along which we all have to go at last. . . ." There are many extant versions of *Ise* and there are various theories concerning its composition, including the very plausible idea that it was written by someone in Narihira's family. The popular edition is thought to date from the first half of the tenth century, but almost certainly the work was revised thereafter. Each story presents in prose the circumstances of the composition of the poems, drawing not only on Narihira's personal collection of poetry but also from other collections such as the *Man'yōshū* and the *Kokinshū*. There is no attempt in *Ise* to represent the *monogatari* as true stories, nor is any attention paid to whether or not the poems were those of Narihira or another poet. The aim of the collection is to present the full range and flavor of the *waka* by means of prose settings precisely tailored to the poems, as though the poetry had been turned into prose. It is this blending of poetry and prose that creates the distinctive mood of *Ise*. The following is Section 91 of *Ise*.

Once a man, who was already sad about the time that had passed since he had met his beloved, composed this poem on the last day of the third month:

> Indeed, but
> I regret this evening,
> Last of the days of spring.

Simple and brief as they are, the *Ise* stories do not merely expand on the poems as marginal notes or as the headnotes of a poetry collection. With an anthology only the poems are important as literature, but in the poem tale, prose and poetry combine to produce a single, unified piece of writing which is imbued with the flavor of *waka*. Thus, in contrast to such tales as *Taketori monogatari* where the movement of events is of most importance, the poem tale takes as its subject the lyrical mood and emotions behind the composition of poetry. Both forms of the *monogatari* share the lineage of poetry and *setsuwa* which had been maturing in Japan since the early ancient period, but *Ise* retains aspects of the Heian aristocratic society free of the influence of Chinese writing, and this quality was to be an important part of subsequent *monogatari* literature.

Yamato monogatari (*Tales of Yamato*) is a *setsuwa* collection composed of 173 stories built around 294 poems. Named characters recur throughout the work, but without the continuity of atmosphere and personality that is maintained with the romantic hero in *Ise monogatari*. Little skill is evident in structuring the work, but it is notable for the reportage quality of its stories. While only certain parts of the collection reach the aesthetic level of the poem tale, it is still of considerable interest for the stories it tells about the circumstance of poetry composition, especially in the second half of the collection. With the exception of a few late additions at the end, *Yamato monogatari* dates from about 951, with some stories having been added during the second half of the century.

Utsubo monogatari is another of the few surviving *monogatari* out of the many that seem to have been contemporary with *Ise, Taketori, Yamato monogatari* and the *Tosa nikki*. The *Utsubo monogatari* is thought to date from between 970 and 983. It exists in twenty scrolls or volumes. The author remains unknown, although one hypothesis offers the talented Minamoto no Shitagō as the writer.

The story begins with Kiyowara no Toshikage, son of the emperor, setting out for China. After encountering a storm his ship lands him in Persia where he learns to play the koto under a famous master, returning to Japan with a koto, or harp, of marvelous quality. Thereafter the focus shifts to Toshikage's descendants: his only daughter and her son, Fujiwara no Nakatada, and the daughter known as Inu no Miya born to Nakatada and his wife Ichi no Miya. The skill and lore of the koto is transmitted through four generations and the story is complicated by rivalries and a power struggle centered on the Crown Prince. In content and treatment the first half of *Utsubo* is fantastic and unreal, but as the story progresses it becomes a concrete and realistic narrative. In the case of *Ochikubo monogatari* also the author is unknown, but it is thought to date from about the same time as *Utsubo*, 980. Ochikubo is the daughter of Chūnagon Tadayori and, badly treated by her stepmother, she must live in a cellar (the room called *ochikubo* from which the heroine acquires her name). Eventually the son of the Minister of the Right hears of her and courts her. After many complications the two marry and are successful at Court, while appropriate fates are assigned the good and evil characters of the story.

Ochikubo sets its story against a realistic background of aristocratic society in the Heian capital and at no time does it slip into the fantastic. Its characters are drawn with great clarity and the story has a logical, natural progression. Even though the writing is not particularly skillful, it has the merit of conciseness. Occasional lapses in taste are mitigated by the considerable humor developed in the story. Further, the business of Shōshō, the hero, remaining faithful to Lady Ochikubo throughout the story was for its time a striking invention.

Another story from that time dealing with maltreatment of a stepchild is the *Sumiyoshi monogatari* (*Tale of Sumiyoshi*), but the extant work is a revision dating from the early medieval period.

The *Kagerō nikki* (*Gossamer Diary*) was produced about the same time as *Utsubo* and *Ochikubo* and is thought to have taken its final form about 974. It is the diary of the daughter of Fujiwara no Tomoyasu, Governor of Ise. In it she tells of her marriage and life with Fujiwara no Kaneie during the twenty years following 954. The diarist notes that it is a record of things that actually happened to her, in contrast to the fabricated events set down in the various popular *monogatari*. She records her resentment and jealousy of Kaneie, who seldom visited her (she was the second of his wives). As an auto-biography and factual record, this work, of course, succeeds as realism beyond the usual level of the *monogatari* of its day, although the writer was doubtless too hasty in her accusations against Kaneie who was more burdened with duties of government than romance. The ~~he had many other affairs!~~ free use of prose found here was a great step into the dimensions of a personal literary medium which until then for women writers had been limited to *waka*. With *Kagero nikki* confessional literature appears for the first time and through this kind of writing women particularly found a way to express their thoughts and feelings in detail and without constraint. After *Kagero nikki* a succession of works appeared (now known as "feminine diaries") which were emotional confessions of women from the middle ranks of aristocratic society. Such writings give an inside portrait of Heian society which could hardly have been set down in the literature created by men.

The *Murasaki shikibu nikki* (*Diary of Lady Murasaki*) from about 1010 draws a vivid contrast between people at the center of power and those on the fringes, the author belonging to the latter group as daughter of a provincial governor. The *Izumi shikibu nikki* (*Diary of Izumi Shikibu*), also from the eleventh century, records the writer's love for Prince Atsumichi and how they were separated by their respective social positions. The *Sarashina nikki* (*Sarashina Diary*) from about 1059 describes the melancholy of an ordinary woman who still has many dreams. The *Sanuki no suke nikki* (*Diary of Sanuki no Suke*) records the sympathy and devotion of a woman for the man who was emperor and whom she served until his death. Generally the language of these diaries is unexceptional, but their content was often the basis for further public writings in the forms of *waka* and *monogatari*. Besides the works just mentioned, we have a number of compositions which would more appropriately be called *monogatari* than feminine diaries, despite their form. These include *Takamura nikki* (*Takamura Diary*), *Takamitsu nikki* (*Takamitsu Diary*), and *Heijū monogatari* (*Tale of Heijū*) which date from the later Heian period and were by writers who took their materials from the lives of such figures as Ono no Takamura (early Heian poet and scholar of Chinese), Fujiwara no Takamitsu (*waka* poet), and Taira no Sadabumi (*waka* poet, d. 901).

The Pillow Book of Sei Shōnagon

Makura no sōshi (*The Pillow Book*) is a work of considerable renown, but we know little about the circumstances of its composition. Its author was the lady known as Sei Shōnagon (probable dates: 965 to 1024), daughter of Kiyowara no Motosuke and later wife of Tachibana no Norimitsu, by whom she bore a son, Norinaga. The marriage did not last long and Shōnagon became attached to another man. In 993 she went into the service of Empress Sadako and remained at the palace until Sadako's death in 1000. It is thought that *Makura no sōshi* was written during those years at the end of the tenth century. It is composed of about 325 brief notes or sections—the exact number varies with the manuscript—which may be roughly classified as follows: (1) names of things, such as mountains and rivers; and cataloguing, such as "beautiful things," "humorous things," and so forth; (2) random thoughts on palace life, human affairs and nature, without reference to any particular occasion; (3) diaristic and narrative sections, chiefly concerning the author's experiences at the imperial palace. The various manuscripts arrange the sections differently—some classifying the sections by subject, others with no apparent order—and we cannot yet say how they were arranged by Shōnagon herself.

Shōnagon's strong point was not in setting down ideas in a lineal, connected style, and so in this book it is nearly impossible to come away with any general concepts expressed by the author. Rather, *Makura no sōshi* is valuable as an exposition of Shōnagon's superb talent for observation of people and nature and her vividness of expression, of which the following provides a sample:

In the Fifth Month I love going up to a mountain village. When one passes a marsh on the way, a thick covering of weeds hides the water and it seems like a stretch of green grass; but if anyone gets out of the carriage and walks across one of these patches, the water spurts up under his feet though it is quite shallow. The water is incredibly clear and looks very pretty as it gushes forth.

Where the road runs between hedges, a branch will sometimes thrust its way into the carriage. One snatches at it quickly, hoping to break it off; alas, it always slips out of one's hand.

Sometimes one's carriage will pass over a branch of sagebrush, which then gets caught in the wheel and is lifted up at each turn, letting the passengers breathe its delicious scent.

Makura no sōshi, Section 200

In the diary sections of *Makura no sōshi* Shōnagon occasionally boasts of how she overwhelms the young nobles and people of the palace with her learning in Chinese literature, thereby gaining considerable popularity and reputation. Where the actual incidents are recorded, however, we find that she has somewhat exaggerated matters. Shōnagon doubtless offered the Empress spiritual support and probably entertained the few young noblemen who visited the Empress when she was quite ill. Shōnagon, however, did not hold views or opinions remarkably out of style with her time. Her awareness of beauty led her to record precisely the feelings expressed by people around her, but seldom more than that. But she created expressions, such as "dawn of spring" and "evening of autumn," which, as epithets with seasonal associations, became part of the standard of aesthetic cliches in later *waka* and *monogatari*. Shōnagon's talent was for prose writing and almost none of her brilliance is visible in her poetry.

[handwritten margin note: it depends by whom, does it not?]

The *Tale of Genji* and other *Monogatari*

Murasaki Shikibu (978–ca. 1016), author of *Genji monogatari* (*The Tale of Genji*), was, like Sei Shōnagon, from the middle rank of the aristocracy. The daughter of Fujiwara no Tametoki, she married Fujiwara no Nobutaka, a man twenty years her senior, by whom she had one daughter before Nobutaka died. It seems that she began to write only after she became a widow. Obviously, she was gifted with outstanding intellect and tenacity, and we may suppose that tragedy in her own life, the death of her beloved husband, heightened her sensitivity to those around her. In contrast with Sei Shōnagon, she seems to have been quite reserved in her personal life, and in the fictional world of the *monogatari*, Murasaki seems to have found solace and understanding for her melancholy.

The first half of *Genji*, the chapters "Kiritsubo" through "Fuji no Uraba," tell of Prince Genji's youth, his remarkable talent and beauty, the fateful steps of his life as prophesied by the Korean fortuneteller, his adversity and recovery—all, of course, woven through with the complexities of the young man's love affairs. In the next part of the book, from "Wakana" through "Mirage," Prince Genji stands at the pinnacle of splendor. He is termed "incomparable" in his attractiveness, yet he loses one by one the women he loves until at last he retires from society to become a monk. The last chapters of the book, "Niou" through "The Bridge of Dreams," take up the life of Kaoru, (said to be *[handwritten: illegitimate]* Genji's son but who actually is not) and Genji's later loves. The story ends without any clear resolution of Genji's life, or the lives of those close to him.

The first half of *Genji* is told in the style and form of the traditional *monogatari*, realistic in detail and somewhat detached in its observation of various aspects of society. The second half of the story, however, abandons the old form. The action is no longer removed in time but rather seems to deal with a world that is immediately before the writer's eyes, the reality of palace society of the early eleventh century. The change in approach is a singular statement of Murasaki's development and consciousness as a writer. She succeeds in fusing together in *Genji* many of the finest literary developments that went before her, not only in prose fiction but also in *waka,* ballads, and writing in Chinese, while creating above all a mature medium in prose for the expression of her own individuality.

With the appearance of the new and mature *monogatari* created by Lady Murasaki in *Genji,* succeeding works found a model for their interpretations of the psychology of Heian aristocracy and indeed were unable to create a new point of view, even though many attempted a degree of originality through fanciful plots, exotic settings, or sensuality. Such stories include: *Sagoromo monogatari* (*The Tale of Sagoromo*), composed between 1045 and 1058; *Hamamatsu chūmagon monogatari* (*The Tale of the Middle Councilor Hamamatsu*), of about 1058; *Yowa no nezame* (*Midnight Awakening*), probably after 1058; *Torikaebaya monogatari* (*The Tale of Would That They Were Exchanged*), a Heian tale, although the extant version is from an early medieval revision. Works of this kind occasionally produced passages of delicate, dream-like beauty, but they were essentially quite far removed from the inspiration of reality, and seemed quite spiritless. One collection, however, is unique for this period, the *Tsutsumi chūnagon monogatari* (*Tales of the Middle Councilor of the Embankment*). It is a collection of finely structured short stories, each presenting a vignette of life rather than the exhaustive detail of the long *monogatari*. The collection had no successors and the courtly aristocratic society from which the stories originated itself lost its vital significance.

Historical Tales

Still another side to the *monogatari* is represented by the historical tales (*rekishi monogatari*) which were really histories in narrative form rather than the chronological-categorical style of Chinese historiography. The *Eiga monogatari* (*Tale of Splendor*), probably dating from the mid-eleventh century, is a history of the 200 years from Emperor Uda to Emperor Horikawa, roughly the tenth and eleventh centuries. The narrative, though generally based on fact, contains a number of fabrications. Its central focus is aristocratic society and particularly the glory of Fujiwara no Michinaga, but its praise of Michinaga is only partially successful and the voice of the writer, or writers, remains weak. The *Ōkagami* (*Great Mirror*), another historical tale, describes the same general period as *Eiga monogatari,* beginning with Emperor Montoku (r. 850–58) and ending in 1025 during the height of the power of Michinaga. The form of *Ōkagami* includes some question-and-answer dialogue between a young samurai and the two very old men (140 and 150 years old) who are the narrators of the tale. The differing versions of history provided by the two old men plus the critical opinions of the samurai combine to offer a sharp portrait of the era of the Fujiwara regencies. The history was written between 1118 and 1123 and the author may have been Minamoto no Masasada (d. 1162). Continuing this form of history writing, the *Ima kagami* (*Mirror of the Present*), covering 1025–1170, was completed in 1170. Then in the medieval period we have *Masu kagami* (*The Clear Mirror*), possibly by Nijō no Yoshimoto, and *Mizu kagami* (*Water Mirror*), which covered the history of Japan from the age of the gods to the period in which *Ōkagami* begins. These later works were not particularly successful.

With the beginning of the period of cloistered emperors in 1086, the realities of aristocratic life noticeably differ from life in the time of Michinaga as recorded in *Genji* and *Makura no sōshi,* and fiction which tried to imitate *Genji* could not help but fail. Perhaps because it reached out for new subject matter and a new grasp of reality in the lives of monks, soldiers, and commoners, the stories in the *Konjaku monogatarishū* (*Tales of Modern and Ancient Times*) succeeded. The name of Minamoto no Takakuni (1004–77) has long been associated with the collection, but the text contains material from after Takakuni's death. *Konjaku monogatarishū* is a collection of more than 1,080 stories, *setsuwa,* the whole being divided by geographic areas (India, China, Japan) with most of the stories from Japan. In the *setsuwa* style the narrative is simple and the language unpolished and heavy with Chinese influence. Earlier *setsuwa* collections of the Heian period—works such as *Nihon ryōiki* on Buddhist themes—dealt with limited subjects, but in *Konjaku* we have for the first time a collection that deals realistically with every area of society. Through such collections as *Gōdanshō* (*Selections From the Ōe Family*), ca. 1107, and the *Hōmotsushū* (*Collection of Treasures*), on Buddhist themes, the *Konjaku* was succeeded by a number of *setsuwa* collections in the middle ages which drew on it as a primary source.

Poetry and Poetic Theory

For eighty years after the completion of the *Shūishū* no imperial anthologies of poetry were made. During that period a number of private collections of poetry were assembled and public composition as social amusement (*uta awase*) was popular, but most of the poems we have were created in the service of social communication, products of the upper levels of aristocratic society and ready-witted dialogue. Akazome Emon (ca. 957–1045), wife of Ōe no Masahira, composed a great number of such social poems and in her time was considered to be the leading poet, but when we reach the *Goshūishū* (*Later Collection of Gleanings*), the fourth imperial anthology, completed in 1086, Izumi Shikibu seems to have been more highly regarded, having sixty-seven poems in the collection to thirty-two by the older poet.

The *Goshūishū* was begun in 1075 by order of Emperor Shirakawa. Compilation was in the hands of Fujiwara no Michitoshi (1047–99) and the twenty scrolls with 1,220 poems were presented to the throne in 1086. The political power of the Fujiwara clan had been declining from the early part of the century and the provincial-governor class emerged as its successor. In the period of cloistered emperors which began in 1086, the governors exercised independent authority as "lords of the retired emperor." Michitoshi, a conservative in poetry, gave prominence to writers of the *kampaku* or regency period, such as Izumi Shikibu, Lady Sagami (fl. ca. 1050), Akazome Emon, Nōin (998–1050), and Ise no Tayū (ca. 987–1063), but he also included earlier love poems which had not found a place in the first three imperial anthologies.

During the next forty years, until the compilation of the *Kin'yō-shū,* both Michitoshi and his poetic rival Minamoto no Tsunenobu (1016–97) died and the leading positions in poetry came to be held by Minamoto no Toshiyori (known as Shunrai, 1055–1129), Fujiwara no Akisue (1055–1123), and Fujiwara no Mototoshi (1056–1142). By order of Emperor Horikawa, in the first years of the twelfth century, Shunrai, Mototoshi, Ōe no Masafusa, Akisue and a dozen other poets composed the model hundred-poem sequence (*hyakushu uta*), known as the *Horikawa-in ontoki hyakushū waka* (*Hundred Poems of Emperor Horikawa*), which prompted the *Horikawa godō hyakushū* (*Second Horikawa Hundred Poems*) in 1116, under cloistered Emperor Shirakawa.

By order of Shirakawa, the fifth imperial anthology, the *Kin'yō-shū* (*Collection of Golden Leaves*), was assembled under the editorship of Shunrai and the ten scrolls were presented in 1127. This collection was guided by the personal tastes of Shunrai which were often contrary to Emperor Shirakawa's own ideas on poetry. It is the shortest of the anthologies and contains a number of descriptive poems. The *Shikashū* (*Collection of Verbal Flowers*), the sixth anthology, was the work of Fujiwara no Akisuke (1089–1155), founder of the Rokujō school of poetry. It is a respected collection and like its predecessor also known for its attempt to introduce a new style in *waka*.

An interesting development beginning about the time of the

Goshūishū in the late eleventh century is the appearance of a succession of studies of poetry and essays on poetic theory which sometimes became quite caustic in their critical remarks. The earliest of those works was *Nan goshūi* (*Errors in the Goshūishū*) by Fujiwara no Tsunenobu who attacked what he considered to be the gross faults of the *Goshūishū*. Other polemic studies include: *Shūi kokon* (*Gleanings Past and Present*) by Fujiwara no Norinaga (fl. ca. 1145–60) and the *Kōyōshū* (*Later Leaves Collection*), both written in opposition to the *Shikashū;* the *Bokutekishū* (*Shepherd's Flute Collection*) by Fujiwara no Kiyosuke (1104–77), a counterattack on the *Kōyōshū*. Interpretive works, studies, indexes and so forth were produced and they formalized differences of opinion, leading to the major opposing views of the Nijō and Rokujō schools. The following titles are notable in this genre:

Toshiyori kuden (*Teachings of Toshiyori*), by Minamoto no Toshi-yori (known as Shunrai, 1055–1129).

Kigoshō (*Notes on Poetic Language*), by Fujiwara no Nakamitsu.

Waka dōmōshō (*A Primer of Waka*), by Fujiwara no Norikane (1107–65). A dictionary of *waka*.

Okugishō (*Secrets of Waka*), by Fujiwara no Kiyosuke.

Fukuro sōshi (*Pocket Book of Waka*), ibid.

Waka shogakushō (*First Book of Waka*), ibid.

Shuchūskō (*Pocket Notes*), by Kenjō. Composed about 1187.

Korai fūtaishō (*Notes on Poetic Style Through the Ages*), by Shunzei. A pioneer history of poetry.

The critical trend represented by such writings moved away from the poetic mood of the first three anthologies and toward the establishment of a new style in *waka*. The first attempts to realize this new poetry sought novelty in vocabulary and expression as well as in exploring unorthodox subject matter, but when it came to assembling imperial anthologies the compositions of such mid-Heian poets as Sone no Yoshitada, Izumi Shikibu, and Ōe no Masafusa were again pressed into service. The inheritor of this crisis was Fujiwara no Toshinari (1114–1204), known to poetry as Shunzei, who was able to unite important elements in the old and the new styles and revive the aesthetic of the *Kokinshū*. Through a manner that owed much to *Genji monogatari,* he found a touchstone of value in that mystery and depth called *yūgen*. To create poetry with the quality of *yūgen,* Shunzei held, it was necessary above all for the poet to refine and discipline his own mind.

Five months before the Heian capital was destroyed by the Taira armies in 1183, Shunzei received an imperial commission to compile the seventh imperial anthology titled *Senzaishū* (*Collection of a*

Thousand Years), but the twenty scrolls and nearly 1,300 poems were not presented to the throne until 1187. That great wars had been fought meanwhile between the Taira and the Minamoto clans mattered little to Shunzei who found life's worth and meaning in the poetic instant when a man dwelt in the realm of *yūgen* and could crystalize that essence of life in a thirty-one syllable poem. Thus in the anthology he could display the work of Minamoto no Toshiyori (a political enemy of his teacher Fujiwara no Mototoshi) more frequently than any other poet—and explain himself with the remark that "while Shunrai himself is hateful, his poems are not."

The world which confronted Shunzei and the people of his time was quite different from the world of the Heian aristocracy as it existed up to the early twelfth century. The prose forms of Shunzei's age could not deal in the aesthetics cultivated by courtly society from the beginning of Heian. If any part of the old aesthetic standard was to continue in the later twelfth century the only choice was to embody it in lyric poetry rather than prose, for prose already had become the literary medium of the warrior class and the common people whose voice had achieved new strength in national life. Poetry, *waka*, was all that remained to the surviving aristocracy of Heian. Until mid-Heian the aristocrats could find in their daily lives adequate materials to form a sense of beauty, an aesthetic life which served as their poetic theory. But from Shunzei's time, simply because of circumstances into which they were born, poets of the new style required a theory, a formalized and explicit Way of Poetry (*uta no michi*). They could no longer compose in the style of poets of the first three anthologies; *waka* after Shunzei was a refined discipline. Only those who underwent special training or disciplehood as "men of poetry" could claim to write poetry as a fine art. And only they could judge poetry as art. In a sense such poets deliberately ignored the vastly changed reality of life between antiquity and the end of the Heian period. For them it was supremely important to reach for an imperishable ideal beauty rather than mundane reality. The man who carried this approach to its furthest development, devoting himself to the creation of purely sensuous beauty in language, was Shunzei's son Fujiwara no Sadaie, known as Teika (1162–1241), and in the *Shinkokinshū* (*New Collection of Ancient and Modern Times*) of 1206 his aesthetic ideals became the foundation of an imperial anthology.

One of the important poets in the purist school was the monk Saigyō (1118–90) who occupies a special position in the *Skinkokinshū*, to which he contributed more poems than any other single poet. Saigyō began his career as a warrior of low official rank and went on to become well known in the aristocratic circle which included Teika among other renowned poets. His life as a monk, however, and especially his experiences of travel and the natural scene, heavily color his poetry and in this regard set him apart from the idealists or purists among these who were self-consciously poets.

Ballads

Another area of poetry at that time was that of songs or ballads which, since they were orally transmitted, included many that are lost to us today. A few were preserved, however, written down by members of the aristocracy who from time to time even tried composing in the ballad style. Ballads were one of the foundations of written literature and are important for the contribution they made to *waka* and the *monogatari.*

Kagura, or *kamiasobi* as they were originally called, were Shintō music and dance ballads performed in worship of a deity. They seem to have been of ancient origin, but we cannot accurately set a date for their composition. There is a record of what seems to have been *kagura* performed in 859 at the Seisō Hall within the imperial palace, and from 1002 until the present the function has continued in the Naishi-dokoro, the Hall of the Sacred Mirror. The repertory now consists of about eighty songs and a performance begins with pieces known as *Niwabi* and *Achime no waza.*

Folk songs known as *saibara* (literally "horse-readying" songs) are mentioned in 839 and later these were adapted to the koto and performed at the imperial court. Another designation, difficult to distinguish from *saibara,* was *fuzoku uta* or folk songs; these are identified with the eastern provinces. The name appears during the Nara period, in 717, associated with the southern-most provinces of Kyūshū. During the Heian period the songs became part of the repertory of the Ōutadokoro, the Court Bureau of Music. Later the music found a place in Buddhist temples, but by the end of the Kamakura period, early in the fourteenth century, the, music was forgotten. A kind of *fuzoku uta* called "eastern dances" (*azuma asobi* or *azuma odori*) was also performed in the eastern provinces and in the Heian period they became dances for religious occasions. The name appears in 861 in conjunction with festivals at the Kamo Shrine and Iwashimizu Hachiman Shrine.

During mid-Heian songs known as *rōei, wasan,* and *imayō* were performed. *Rōei* were song versions of Chinese poetry, prose, and, later, Japanese *waka.* They were being performed by 969 and two collections are extant: the *Wakan rōeishū* (*Collection of Chinese and Japanese Rōei*) and the *Shinsen rōeishū* (*New Collection of Rōei*). *Wasan* are hymns in Japanese language praising Buddha. They originated in such things as the Buddha's footprint-stone poems and passages of the Lotus Sutra. The famous Heian period monk Genshin (d. 1017) composed a number of *wasan: Gokuraku rokuji san* (*Six Daily Hymns of Paradise*), which presents matins, mid-day hymns, sunset hymns, etc.; *Tendai daishi wasan* (*In Praise of Tendai Daishi*), hymns in praise of the Chinese founder of the Tendai school of Buddhism, Chih-I (531–97). These hymns are the core of the genre which was later taken up by the Buddhist Pure Land sect (Jōdoshū) and which survived into the middle ages. Such ballad literature as we have discussed was collected in a work known as the *Ryōjin hishō* (*Secret Selection of Songs*), a fragment of the collection by Emperor Go-Shirakawa (r. 1155–58) which was discovered in 1911. In this work also were recorded popular songs called *imayō uta*, "songs in the present style" (in contrast to the old style of *kagura* and *saibara*). Some differentiation in the early period can be made among Buddhist *shōmyō* (hymns of Indian origin), religious ceremonial songs, and popular songs, but later these blended with court ballads and were called simply "miscellaneous *imayō*." Such songs were also performed by professional entertainers, such as dancing girls (*yūjo*), shrine maidens (*miko,*) puppeteers (*kugutsu*) and the vaudeville called *sarugaku*. Specialists in the kind of *imayō* called *shirabyōshi* also appeared among the dancing girls.

Medieval Period

A.D. 1185 TO 1600

by

NISHIO KOICHI AND TESAKI MASAO

The Kamakura and Muromachi Periods

THE CONCEPT of a "medieval literature" is based on the three-part division of history into ancient, medieval, and modern, and medieval literature is viewed as growing out of a feudal society, closely associated with that society's ruling military class. Medieval literature too is deeply colored by Pure Land Buddhism of the Heian period and the new Buddhist teachings of the Kamakura period.

On the pattern of European history, some Japanese writers set the time of the beginning of the medieval period early in Heian and classify Tokugawa or Edo literature as medieval on grounds that the Tokugawa period was also feudal in its social structure. Again, some literary historians characterize this period with such epithets as "warrior literature," "recluse literature," "religious literature," or "folk literature." Some attempt to characterize it in terms of the development of a particular form or with the emergence of aesthetic ideals, such as *yūgen* (mystery and depth), *sabi* (loneliness), and *wabi* (subdued taste). Various theories also attempt to define a beginning date for medieval literature in conjunction with changes in the social background. For example: at 1087, the beginning of Cloister government (*insei*); 1156, the Hōgen Rebellion; 1185, the fall of the Taira clan; 1192, the beginning of the military dictatorship of Minamoto no Yoritomo; 1221, the Jōkyū disturbances. But the question still remains as to how we define the general idea of medieval literature and what kind of break it made with the literature of antiquity. The terminal date of the period is debatable too and is related to other issues, such as our perspective on modern literature; the treatment of Azuchi-Momoyama period (1579–98); as a political and aesthetic unit, the end of the Imagawa clan in 1560; Nobunaga's construction of Azuchi Castle in 1576; the Battle of Sekigahara (1600); or the inauguration of the *bakufu,* the military government, in Edo in 1603.

In this discussion we shall follow the most common approach, that which takes medieval literature simply as the literature of the Kamakura and Muromachi periods, roughly from 1185 to 1600, and recognizes Tokugawa literature as a separate entity. We may keep in mind too that only since 1868, the beginning of Meiji, has the literature of Kamakura and Muromachi been viewed as a body of writing distinct from the Heian period.

The connotations of the term "medieval literature" have been defined only vaguely in the past, but some progress has been made through focusing on individual authors and works, and various studies have gradually illuminated the values and distinguishing qualities of the literature in general. We may say that medieval literature, out of its negation and rejection of ancient society and aristocratic literature, gradually formed a new and independent outlook on the world and in turn produced a uniquely medieval image of man and nature. Our realization of such qualities in the outlook of medieval writing is thus leading to more intrinsic standards of evaluation.

The period we have defined by the dates 1185 and 1600 falls roughly into two parts, separated by the end of the Kamakura shogunate, the military government, in 1333. The medieval period was complicated and tumultuous. It instituted rule by military government, acquired a feudal social pattern, and was subject to tensions due to the lingering influence of the old aristocracy. It suffered wars and uprisings in the sixteenth century, but withal saw the development and spread of new schools of Buddhism, literature of recluse writers and of the theater, and the emergence of a popular literature as well.

If we may venture a general characterization of medieval literature, then we should say that it is a literature of transition, from antiquity to the modern world, and consequently embodies characteristics of a period of rapid change. And during those four hundred years great changes took place in Japan: the Cloister government declined and disappeared; great wars were fought between the Minamoto and the Taira clans; the Kamakura government was established with accompanying transformations of the political and economic structure; wars were fought between rivals to the throne, the Northern and Southern Courts; internal disputes of the Muromachi *bakufu* were followed by the Ōnin War from 1467 through 1477, and then the century of civil war known as *sengoku*. In reflecting the changing society literature constantly wavered between preserving and altering its traditional standards. In the Kamakura period there still remained in literature's creative consciousness and attitude, as well as in form and content, a great deal of the Heian period, an adherence to the halcyon years of courtly writing and attempts to revive and maintain those qualities. But at the same time much of the population had turned its attention to the eastern provinces of Japan, away from the old capital, and groups there were amassing new economic and military strength. During the Kamakura period there was a split in the political control of the country, but eventually it was due to the warriors of eastern Japan, men who became the military and economic leaders, that the medieval literary world emerged. Medieval literature began with military tales and discovered new literary materials, forms and expression suitable to the new age and a broader national society where the warriors themselves appear conspicuously in a good deal of the writing. Another powerful influence on medieval literature was the new Buddhism which emerged in the Kamakura period. The new Buddhist sects were stimulated by the instability of society and the uncertainty of individual life which resulted from the wars. These faiths, as they spread among the wider population, gave a significantly Buddhist coloration to the content and concept of literature.

From the end of the Kamakura through the Muromachi periods the currents we have indicated gradually blended and produced such new literature as *renga* (linked verse), Nō drama, and *kyōgen* (comic interludes of Nō). To take a broad view of our subject, it seems that the form and style of every genre that became independent in medieval literature was latent, though undifferentiated in *setsuwa* literature from the end of the ancient period to the beginning of the middle ages. The *setsuwa* themselves were in fact a basic genre in medieval literature and within a brief time stimulated the composition of war tales which were the new and major literary vehicle of the age. *Waka* and *monogatari,* the traditional literary forms of the Court, had greatly declined, but with such collections of poetry as the *Shinkokinshū* we find in the medieval style of symbolic poetry a mode that recaptures the brilliance of Heian. In the area of the *monogatari,* a form that had almost totally lost its creative energy, the tale or narrative was reborn as the medieval *sōshi* (novella), and indeed the *monogatari* itself re-emerged later in the novels of the Tokugawa period. The essays, diaries, and travel accounts of Heian reappeared in forms ranging from Buddhist *setsuwa* collections, sermons and the literature of the Five Mountains (Zen Buddhist inspired), to poetry theory and linked verse. In the latter the period produced a vein of critical writing filled with Buddhist ideas. Having once discarded imitation of antiquity as a standard, the middle ages could bring a fresh poetic voice to its own world and feelings.

Stories: *Setsuwa*

From the end of the ancient period through the early middle ages those brief stories called *setsuwa,* which earlier had been orally transmitted, were most actively recorded. Many of the stories found in *setsuwa* collections can be traced to written sources, but it seems clear that for the most part *setsuwa* lived as folk literature or folk stories and may perhaps be defined by those terms.

Following such late Heian compilations as *Konjaku monogatari-shū, Uchigikishū,* and the *Kohon setsuwashū,* a number of general collections of *setsuwa* appeared during the Kamakura period which contributed a great deal to the war tales and other medieval forms. For convenience we shall list the major collections:

Kojidan (Tales of Antiquity), 1212–15; compiled by Minamoto no Yorikane; historical and biographical anecdotes, written in Chinese.

Zoku kojidan (The Tales of Antiquity Continued), 1219; modeled on *Kojidan,* author unknown.

Ujishūi monogatari (Tales of the Uji Collection), early 13th century; editor unknown (details discussed below).

Jikkinshō (Summary of the Ten Precepts), 1252; editor unknown. Exemplary stories from China and Japan, closely related to the next collection.

Kokon chōmonjū (Tales New and Old), 1254; edited by Tachibana no Narisue. An assemblage of Japanese *setsuwa* from various collections—such as *Konjaku monogatarishū, Ujishūi,* and *Kodanshō.*

Yotsugi monogatari (Tales of the Generations), date and compiler unknown; tales of Heian and Kamakura periods.

Ima monogatari (Tales of the Present), compiled after 1239, possibly by Fujiwara no Nobuzane. Brief stories of medieval poetry, customs, love, humor, and so forth.

Hōmotsushū (Collection of Treasures), date unknown; an interpretive collection of Buddhist stories by Taira no Yasuyori.

Hosshinshū (Religious Awakenings), before 1216; edited by Kamo no Chōmei. Stories of conversion to Buddhism.

Kankyō no tomo (Leisure's Companion), 1222; possibly by the monk Jien. Thirty-one stories on Buddhist themes.

Senjūshō (Selected Stories). Stories of monks and marvels, attributed to Saigyō (1118–90).

Shishū hyakuin'enshū (Personal Collection of Karmic Tales), 1257; 147 Buddhist stories from India, China, and Japan.

Shasekishū (Sand and Stone Collection), 1279–83; a collection of Buddhist stories, in conversational style, by the monk Mujū (1226–1312). There is considerable humor in the collection, which may have been used as the basis for Buddhist sermons.

Zōdanshū (A Miscellany), 1305; compiled by Mujū.

Several thousand old *setsuwa* have survived in writing to the present day. Their forms and contents are varied, but their range stays within clearly set limits and the same story may appear virtually unchanged in a number of collections. Indeed the world of *setsuwa* in the Kamakura period may be regarded as having been defined by the materials in the above collections. We think of *setsuwa* as stories which were part of the lore and daily life of every class from nobility to commoners. Looking over the whole field in terms of concept and materials we can recognize three areas of stories.

The first area is that of stories about life among the courtiers and aristocrats. The authors of those stories were members of the aristocracy who undertook to record, somewhat nostalgically, the refined life of the preceding age. The second group of stories expresses the new conditions of life in medieval Japan. Such *setsuwa* draw on popular material or matters of local interest. The third group is that of Buddhist *setsuwa*. Those were collected in order to provide simplified explanations of Buddhist doctrine, but they also capture a wide spectrum of social phenomena associated with religion.

Until recent years *setsuwa* literature was regarded as naive, non-individual, and of little aesthetic value. However, we have come to recognize the genius of those popular stories which vividly and dynamically delineate the variety of human existence, and this awareness has led us to re-evaluate the literary importance of *setsuwa*. Considering the three main areas of prose literature in the Kamakura period, the *setsuwa* of popular and local origins are particularly significant as the basic materials of later medieval literature.

The quality of freshness in the *setsuwa* collections of late Heian appears strikingly in the *Konjaku monogatarishū* and it is frequently present also in the Kamakura period collections through *setsuwa* which grew directly out of the oral folk tradition. The *Ujishūi monogatari* (*Tales of the Uji Collection*) trades heavily in the written tradition of *setsuwa*, drawing from such collections as *Konjaku monogatarishū* and *Kohon setsuwashū*, yet many of its stories seem to have been recorded directly from oral literature. They require our special attention. Of the 197 stories in the collection many seem to treat the *setsuwa* as a short *monogatari*, using colloquial language freely and including lively conversational dialogues. Some eighty *setsuwa* more or less repeat stories from the *Konjaku* collection, but in the *Ujishūi* versions superfluous explanations detailing people and places are omitted, and the *Konjaku's* peculiar style, which mixes Chinese and Japanese, is softened into the pseudo-archaic sentence style characteristic of works influenced by *monogatari* of the Heian period. The strong and wild beauty of *Konjaku monogatarishū* is softened, giving expression to the talent and humanistic outlook of the author through subtle descriptions of people and events. The collection is further set apart from *Konjaku* through what we feel as the writer's eye in observing events and the presence of a single creative hand at work in the text. This quality is especially present in such stories as: "How the Buddhist Nun Adored Jizo" (No. 16), "How Kūsuke Offered the Buddhist Memorial Service" (No. 109), "How a Gambler Wins a Bride" (No. 113), "What Tokugyō Perpetrated at Lake Sarusawa" (No. 130), and "How a Bonze Made His Watery Way to Heaven" (No. 133). In such stories as "How the Ogres Removed a Wen" (No. 3) and "How the Sparrow Remembered a Kindness" (No. 48), we have examples of classical forms of popular stories that continue in the oral tradition even today. The *Ujishūi* also reveals the medieval taste for levity, quite distinct from *Konjaku monogatarishū,* in the attention it gives to oral humor, and in a number of stories, such as "How the Little Boy Slept During the Rice Dumpling Dinner" (No. 12) and "Why the Country Boy Cried When He Saw Cherry Blossoms Fall" (No. 13) we have fine portraits of the character of youth. Inevitably we find here and there in *Ujishūi* a very conscious didacticism, but on the whole the collection is charged with the unknown author's lively concern for the *setsuwa* form. It is a rewarding work of literature which also mirrors the emotional life of a time and society; without passing moral judgement, the stories succinctly portray the variety of the human heart.

    Setsuwa of considerable literary interest are also found in other general collections, such as the *Kokon chōmonjū* of 1254 and the *Jikkinshō* of 1252, and occasionally in Buddhist *setsuwa* collections, such as *Hosshinshū, Kankyō no tomo,* and *Senjūshō.* In the *Shasekishū* and the *Zōdanshū* the priest Mujū exercised his penchant for combining *setsuwa* and *monogatari* with exemplary Buddhist stories which drew on his wide reading and personal experience. Mujū's two collections include interesting folk traditions which we may suppose the priest himself collected during his long residences in distant provinces, setting them down in the remarkable collections of religious *setsuwa.* Stylistically, Mujū followed in the steps of the writer of the *Ujishūi stories,* while his broadly sympathetic attitude is reminiscent of Yoshida Kenkō's *Tsurezuregusa* (*Essays in Idleness*).

War Tales

    In the *Heike monogatari* (*Tales of the Heike*), Book 11, it is told that Minamoto no Yoshitsune sent word of his victory over the Taira clan in the battle at Dan no ura and of the return of the sacred emblems to ex-Emperor Go-Shirakawa: "The retired Emperor along with the various Lords were greatly pleased. His majesty invited Hirotsuna inside the palace and inquired about the details of the battle." This incident is also mentioned in the Kamakura period history *Hyakurenshō* (*Attic Notes*) and we may suppose that the story of the terrible destruction of the Taira clan and the boy Emperor Antoku must have been deeply moving to many listeners. It seems likely that from the time of the Hōgen, Heiji, and Jishō periods (ca. 1156–80) tales of warfare recited by men who had themselves participated in the fighting found interested and sympathetic audiences among all classes of people and in all areas of Japan. The battles, too, focusing on Kyōto and the nearby provinces, bespoke in harsh and immediate terms the change from antiquity to the middle ages. Thus in the tradition of oral *setsuwa* on military subjects there was gradually formed the heroic image of the warrior, the *bushi,* an image that first coalesces in the *Hōgen monogatari* (*Tales of the Hōgen Period*) and *Heiji monogatari* (*Tales of the Heiji Period*) and which came to all but dominate the age. With the *Heike monogatari* (*Tales of the Heike*) of somewhat later date the new genre of war tales takes on the dimensions of epic poetry and stands as one of the brilliant literary achievements of the early medieval period.

The new image of man reflected in the war tales was, however, a gradual literary creation. Among the sources of the war tales are such works of reportage from the Heian period as the *Shōmonki* dealing with the revolt of Taira no Masakado in the years 935–40, and the *Mutsuwaki* (*Records and Stories of Mutsu*), about the battles of Minamoto no Yoriyoshi in the northernmost provinces of the main island. Perhaps equally influential is the kind of military reporting we find in Book 25 of *Konjaku monogatarishū*. The debt there is not simply to the prose style, which is a mixture of Chinese phrases in Japanese sentences, but to the new character portraits in stories about "the majesty of warriors" and "the soldier's spirit." In *Konjaku* too even stories of thieves and pirates (in Book 29), go beyond good and bad deeds and become tales worthy of those who have real power to wield in society. As *setsuwa* in a period of rapid change, the tales vividly drew the potential cultural power of the new class of warriors. Further, as a literature close to the oral tradition, the war tales matured in the same milieu as the *setsuwa,* the general life of the Japanese people at that time.

The *Hōgen monogatari,* which dates from the early Kamakura period, and *Heiji monogatari* are each in three scrolls and seem to be by the same author. They recount the Hōgen and Heiji period rebellions against their social backgrounds, and in doing so describe the rise of the warrior class. The central figure in *Hōgen monogatari* is Minamoto no Tametomo. On the basis of his experience as a warrior, Tametomo proposed a night attack in one battle, but he was forced to defer to the wishes of the Great Minister of the Left Yorinaga.

As a result Tametomo's forces in turn were subjected to a night attack by the enemy, and he laments: "This very thing is what I,
Tametomo, have advocated a thousand times." Indeed the Hōgen
war ranged parents, children, and brothers between the opposing
sides, and though Tametomo fought valiantly, he realized his cause
was lost. In the end he was taken prisoner, but his life was spared
because of his bravery and he was exiled to the island of Ōshima.
In creating the heroic and pathetic literary image of Tametomo, exaggeration is, of course, part of the author's technique, and the author's grasp of his subject is perhaps more intellectual than otherwise.
We should recognize that the popular *setsuwa* tradition also tended to
idealize its characters and that that feature contributed to the heroic
figures described by the war tales.

   In the *Heiji monogatari,* Minamoto no Yoshihira (known as
Akugenda, "the fierce eldest son") is drawn to heroic scale, and both
Yoshitomo of the Minamoto clan and Shigemori of the Taira clan
are presented as brilliant leaders of fighting men. We are given the
image of Fujiwara no Mitsuyori, a nobleman renowned for his physical strength, and others who at conference offer their arguments without hesitation. This admiration for men of ability who can act decisively
at critical moments is a literary premonition of the coming new age.
In another mood, tragedies of defeat—such incidents as the death
penalty for a child of Minamoto no Tameyoshi, in *Hōgen monogatari,*
the suicides of the wives of noblemen, and the story of Tokiwa Gozen
(mother of Yoshitsune) in *Heiji monogatari*—are described with
sympathy and the sad vicissitudes of history are properly dramatized.
In short, many literary qualities of the *Heike monogatari* were already
a part of these two early war tales, and their subject matter too left a
profound mark on later literature.

   Heike monogatari not only stands first among the war stories but
also is one of the first-rank classics in Japanese literature. The story
begins with the words: "In the sound of the bell of the Gion Temple
echoes the impermanence of all things. The pale hue of the flowers of
the teak tree show the truth that they who prosper must fall. The
proud ones do not last long, but vanish like a spring night's dream.
And the mighty ones too will perish in the end, like dust before the
wind." Long after the lutes of *Heike* reciters had stilled, the music of
this language, with its fateful rhythms, reached deep into the soul of
the people.

   The story of the Heike or "Taira clan" opens with a description
of the prosperity and the tyranny of Taira no Kiyomori, describes
the strife among powerful Buddhist monasteries in Nara and on Mt.
Hiei, and at last introduces the discovery of the political intrigues
among the men gathered around ex-Emperor Go-Shirakawa. The

scene then shifts to the Minamoto clan, gathered in full force under Minamoto no Yoritomo, and the assault on the Kyōto capital by the armies of Kiso no Yoshinaka, followed by the pursuit of the Taira by Yoshitsune's army. The tale ends, in beautiful and powerfully rhythmic prose, with the successive defeats of the Taira, the destruction of their forces, and the death of the boy Emperor Antoku who was drowned in the sea at Dannoura. From beginning to end *Heike* maintains a sense of the transiency of existence, not only in connection with the Taira clan whose power faded after the death of Kiyomori, but also in dealing with the lives of such men as Saikō, Narichika, Shunkan, Yoshinaka, and Yoshitsune whose personal fates are made to reflect the Buddhist principle that all earthly things are transient, that those who prosper must fall. Transience itself may well be called the first theme of the story, but the whole work embodies a complex variety of other qualities.

We should notice first of all that, as befits a war tale, *Heike monogatari* vividly narrates the scenes of combat involving the Minamoto, the Taira, and the soldier-monks. In the Heian period stories, warriors were looked down on as being vulgar and barbarous, but in the Kamakura period such men are idols of the nation, and brilliant, heroic figures in literature. In such scenes as the famous Battle of the Bridge, the defeat of Kurikara, the advance attack at Uji, the battles of Ichinotani, Yashima, and Dan no ura—quite apart from the key Buddhist theme of transiency—we are given glowing portraits of vital and powerful individuals in passages of remarkable beauty. Apart from the scenes of battle we find admirable characterizations of men of intellect and spirit (such as Tadamori, Shigemori, Saikō, and Mongaku) living in a tumultuous age. To be sure, they are literary idealizations of the warrior figure, and in the language describing their battle gear, or their boasts of pedigree before the enemy, there is much stereotyped expression. Such passages are still impressive and beautiful, effectively presenting the warrior figure as the second major theme of *Heike monogatari*. In this dimension *Heike* might be termed an epic-hero poem, for by that time in the middle ages the idealized image of the warrior was already fixed in the *setsuwa* tradition, and out of that tradition grew the *Heike monogatari* itself.

The story is unsparing in its sympathetic treatment of the defeated Taira and their supporters, for behind the superb descriptions of battle there lies the story of the tragic deaths of the victims of war and the grief of their families intertwined with the fall of Heian aristocratic culture. We find a third theme which, in contrast to the scenes of warfare, weaves into the tale the subtle qualities of the Court literature. In drawing the tragic fate of young men of the Taira such as Tadanori, Atsumori, and Koremori, all of whom had been raised to aristocratic culture and accomplishments, the effect is like that of a long picture scroll in contrasting refinement and the tumult of battle.

The greater part of *Heike monogatari* deals with the story of the defeated Taira clan. It explores the misery of war and the pain of separation, but it also examines the value and meaning of an aristo-cratic tradition and its accomplishments in poetry and music. On another level *Heike* is a story of religious awakening and the reli-gious meaning of death, and to illuminate this concern exemplary *setsuwa* from Chinese literature and Confucian teachings were added to the main story. In such incidents as that of Koremori who left the wars to become a monk on Mount Kōya, finally taking his own life by drowning; Kumagai no Naozane who killed Atsumori—a youth who might have been his own son—and, bitterly lamenting his profession of arms, entered religious life; and Kenreimon'in, the mother of Emperor Antoku, whose strange and tragic life finally allowed her a peaceful death—we find in *Heike monogatari* moments of victory and defeat of the warriors and nobles transcended by the force of Buddhism creating its own image of man's existence.

Although we do not know who the author of the original *Heike* may have been, a work of such diversity obviously underwent a long development during its recitation by the professional lute-playing story tellers known as *biwa hōshi*. Their elaboration and refinement of the story for popular entertainment produced the various groups of texts extant today. Scholars point out that there was a great surge of sympathies among both the audience and the creators of *Heike,* from those who felt the inevitability of history's changes in the success of the Minamoto cause, and reflected this in their admiration for the vigorous warrior leaders, to those who heard of the Taira defeat and destruction with regret and pity for the tragic fate of the vanquished. Doubtless there were some too who consoled their own misfortune and grief by hearing these stories and resolved their own lives through religious devotion. It would seem that *Heike monogatari,* the repre-sentative Japanese classic of the early middle ages, achieved this wide popularity and brilliance, whether as reading or recitation, through its beautiful fusion of those three themes which were central to the broad current of medieval literature: religion; the warrior; aristocratic culture.

Another work dealing with the wars between the Minamoto and Taira clans is the *Gempei seisuiki* (*Record of the Rise and Fall of the Minamoto and Taira*) in forty-eight scrolls. Written in the late Kamakura period, it dwells on the Jishō years, 1177–81, and seems to be in effect a composite of several versions of *Heike.* Although dealing with the same subject as *Heike,* the work is somewhat long-winded, poorly structured, and lacking in descriptive vividness. By contrast too the *Gempei seisuiki* has the quality of a work composed to be read rather than one tuned to the needs of dramatic recitation.

The *Taiheiki* (*Chronicle of Grand Pacification*) is a war tale describing the vicissitudes of the years from 1318 to 1367, particularly the struggles between the Northern and Southern Courts. Little can be guessed about its authorship or date except that it was probably complete by about 1370. The standard text in forty volumes falls into three main parts. The first centers on disturbances of the decade following 1324, the battles of such men as Prince Morinaga, Nitta no Yoshisada, Kusunoki no Masashige, plus the defeat of the Hōjō family and the movement by Emperor Go-Daigo that culminated in the Kemmu Restoration. The second part (v. 13–21) takes up the struggle between the Ashikaga and Nitta, the revolt of Ashikaga no Takauji against the throne, and the death in battle of the Kusunoki brothers, Nawa no Nagatoshi, and Kitabatake no Akiie, and finally the death of Emperor Go-Daigo. The central theme is the breakup of the restoration government and the civil war between the Northern and Southern Courts. The third part of the work relates the internal struggles of the Ashikaga government and the confusion of shifting alliances, the counter offensive by the Southern loyalists, and finally the assumption of stewardship of the realm by Hosokawa no Yoriyuki, as adviser to the young shogun, Yoshimitsu.

Compared with the *Heike* the *Taiheiki* draws a far more complicated and confused scene and it lacks the unity provided by *Heike*'s lyricism and by the theme of transiency. It offers on one side men who will give their lives out of loyalty to the throne or their lords, and on the other those who are forever involved in conspiracy and betrayal for the sake of their own fortunes, positions, and greed for political power. We feel a certain fragmentation resulting from the forced way in which the *Taiheiki* demonstrates the Buddhist principle of cause and effect, but there appear in the work new types of men, hitherto unknown in literature: the mountain priests (*yamabushi*) and freebooters who, in small groups, briefly occupy the stage by virtue of their wit and courage. The *Taiheiki* successfully portrays the new kind of men who live to fulfill their personal desires—a type not found in *Heike monogatari*. It is much to the credit of the *Taiheiki* that it should have created this image or prototype of the samurai who appears during the Sengoku period (the "Age of the Country at War," 1490–1550) and remains into the early Tokugawa period.

Two well known stories are usually counted among the *gunki* or war tales, even though they differ from the *gunki* in structure and style and deal with biography rather than the broader social scene. These are *Gikeiki* (*Record of Yoshitsune*), in eight scrolls, dating probably from early Muromachi, and *Soga monogatari* (*Tale of Soga*) from about 1340, in twelve scrolls. For neither is the author known. Stories about the Soga brothers and about Minamoto no Yoshitsune were current during the Kamakura period as hero-legends in the oral tradition, and during the Muromachi period these were collected and fused into tales of individual tragic heroes that found great popular sympathy. If the tales are weak in creative individuality, they are still significant indicators of popular taste in literature.

Essays, Travel Accounts, Buddhist Sermons

The medieval period in Japan was a time of upheaval. We may well consider to what degree social unrest and tumultuous personal life impressed the Buddhist principle of *mujō,* the impermanence of life, on the minds of the people. Perhaps the clearest statement on this point lies in the vigor with which the Buddhist faith spread among the common people. After the spiritual decline of aristocratic Buddhism during the Heian period, there arose during the Kamakura period various new schools of Buddhism which were closely tied to the life of the ordinary citizen. In literature a new era of strong Buddhist influence began in *setsuwa,* essays, diaries, travel accounts, and sermons which were part of the fabric of life and thought in Japan and which achieved their own literary distinction. Whether in the novel, in poetry, or in the theater, Japanese literature is generally weakest in structuring ideas. There is a strong tendency to find expression through emotional lyricism and indeed this quality defines the main weakness as well as the distinction of Japanese writing. But in the medieval period the forms we have mentioned are outstanding for their intellectual qualities, and it is proper to note too that they were all produced out of an intensely religious context.

One feature of the Buddhist *setsuwa* collections is that apparently they were assembled as partisan and exemplary sermons. Such collections flourished after the middle Heian period and are known to us through such sketch-like stories as those in the *Uchigikishū* (*Word for Word Collection*) and the *Kanazawa bunkohon bukkyō setsuwashū* (*Buddhist Setsuwa Collection of the Kanazawa Library*). Considered as Buddhist literature, these collections reach only the level of superficial records of religious events and are weak in their feeling for religious life—yet there is non-Buddhist material of interest in the stories. One work in the genre, the *Hōmotsushū,* adopts a dialogue form in the style of the *Ōkagami,* bringing together sketchy, anecdotal *setsuwa* in order to present simplified explanations of Buddhist doctrine. On the other hand, the collections *Kankyō no tomo* and *Senjūshō* expand into the area of the writers' own feelings and opinions which, when combined with the *setsuwa,* create an effect rather like that of the essay. With collections such as these in which it is no longer sufficient merely to transmit the stories, we obtain a clear view of the deep religious feelings of the writers—emotions which have been sparked by the *setsuwa*—and at the same time we are able to view the development of *setsuwa* material into the full essay form.

With the establishment of the government in Kamakura at the beginning of the medieval period communication between eastern and western Japan enlarged considerably. As a result men with leisure made many journeys all over the country—and left to posterity a great number of diaries, travel accounts, and essays. The following are among the principal works of the many and varied writings in the travel essay genre.

Iseki (*Journey to Ise*), by Kamo no Chōmei.

Minamoto no ienaga nikki (*The Diary of Minamoto Ienaga*), late Heian.

Kenshunmon'in chūnagon nikki (*The Diary of Shunzei's Daughter*), completed in 1219; an informative work on customs, politics, and literature.

Utatane no ki (*Sleepy Journey*), by the nun Abutsuni, author of *Izayoi nikki;* the first half is a diary, the second half a travel account.

Izayoi nikki (*The Diary of the Waning Moon*), by the nun Abutsuni, previously wife of the poet Fujiwara no Tameie (1198–1275); diary and account of her journey to Kamakura from Kyōto.

Ben no naishi nikki (*The Diary of Lady Ben*), date and authorship uncertain, but probably by a woman at the court of Emperor Go-Fukakusa (r. 1246–59). The diary covers the years 1246 to 1252, touching on ceremonial affairs and including some poetry.

Asukai masaari no nikki (*The Diary of Asukai Masaari*), ends in 1280.

Nakatsukasa no naishi nikki (*The Diary of Lady Nakatsukasa*), begins in 1280 and ends in 1290; touches a variety of affairs at court and ends with a pathetic retirement of Nakatsukasa due to illness.

Takemuki ga ki (*The Diary of Lady Takemuki*), covers the period 1329–49, being the diary of the daughter of Hino Sukena. The extant version is considerably less than the original, but it is a rare work for its time.

Miyako no tsuto (*Keepsake of the Capital*) is a poetry travel diary from early Muromachi by Taira no Munehisa; the work is considered a forerunner of Bashō's *Oku no hosomichi*.

Kōya nikki (*The Mount Kōya Diary*), by the monk Ton'a (d. 1372).

Ojima no kuchizusami (*Ojima Improvizations*) is a travel diary by Nijō no Yoshimoto from the year 1352.

Michiyukiburi (*Snow on the Road*) is a travel diary by Imagawa Ryōshun (d. 1420).

Nagusamegusa (*Consolations*) is a travel diary by the poet Shōtetsu (d. 1459) written about 1421. It included a good deal of discussion of poetry, *renga,* and the *Tale of Genji.*

These works, which include many travel accounts, were written as unpretentious personal memoirs and most are weak in literary structure, but they present vignettes of the authors' times and the consolation that Buddhism brought to men's hearts. Readers have found some of the works quite moving.

Kamo no Chōmei (1153–1216), author of *Hōjōki* (*An Account of My Hut*), was born to a family which held priestly office at the Kamo Shrine in Kyōto and he was personally noted for his accomplishments in poetry and music which earned him the recognition of retired Emperor Go-Toba and frequent participation in Court poetry recitals and competitions. Despite his inherited position, Chōmei does not seem to have been inclined to the Shintō priesthood, and he eventually retired from official life to become a Buddhist monk. From his brush we have such works as *Hosshinshū, Iseki, Mumyōshō* (*Nameless Selections*), and a personal collection of poetry. His most renowned work now is the *Hōjōki,* written in 1212 at his hermitage on Mount Hino. The first lines of that work are particularly famous:

'The flow of the river is ceaseless and its water is never the same. The bubbles that float in the pools, now vanishing, now forming, are not of long duration: so in the world are man and his dwellings.'

He then proceeds to tell of the Great Fire of Angen, in 1177, which destroyed the capital, of earthquakes, famine, moving the imperial palace to Fukuhara, and other important events of the late 12th century. And he sighs, "All is as I have described it—the things in the world which make life difficult to endure, our own helplessness and the undependability of our dwellings." He explains the feelings which led him to become a monk and carefully describes the hut, barely ten feet square, which he had built on Mount Hino, and how excellent was the quiet life it allowed him. He may have felt a sense of delusion in his attachment to the quiet life, for he ends with the words: "All I could do was to use my tongue to recite two or three times the *nembutsu,* however unacceptable this is from an impure heart." The compact structure of the work (it is only twenty-two pages in modern type) seems especially appropriate to emphasize the

meditative theme and the hermit's life through which Chōmei sought
to escape the uncertainties of human existence. The essay is also outstanding for the vividness it achieves through a mixture of Chinese
and Japanese in its prose.

In the conduct of his own life Chōmei examined the problem of
how man should live; ultimately he centered his examination on his
own heart and mind and there sought the reality of his being. *Hōjōki*
begins from the viewpoint of a Buddhist recluse acutely aware of life's
impermanence, then moves to a reflective critique on the life of the
aristocracy. In this he brings a freshness and depth which was lacking
in the old, traditional literature. Indeed his essay became a favorite
of readers in later periods who suffered the uncertainties of the
world. However, we may find in *Hōjōki's* view of the transience of
life a lyricism that is overly sentimental. Chōmei lived during a period
of great change in Japan, from 1155 to 1213, but failed to note such
upheavals as the wars between the Taira and the Minamoto clans,
or the importance of the *bakufu,* the new military government in
Kamakura, and those limitations were certainly the result of his
negative and resigned outlook on the times.

The collection known as *Tsurezuregusa* (*Essays in Idleness*) was
probably composed between 1330 and 1332 during the time of the
struggle between the Northern and Southern courts. It has been suggested that the essays existed earlier in the form of notes and a diary.
The author of the *Tsurezuregusa* was Yoshida Kenkō (1283–1350),
his name coming from his residence at the Yoshida Shrine in Kyōto.
Kenkō (also known by his lay name, Urabe no Kaneyoshi) retired
to the Buddhist clergy in 1324 and from that time, just after the
death of Emperor Go-Uda, whom he had served, he lived as a recluse,
despite having been a popular poet at the imperial Court. Kenkō thus
would have been about forty-eight when he wrote *Tsurezuregusa.*

The collection offers 243 comments and short essays, ranging
from a few lines to several pages in length and touching on a variety
of topics: manners, the arts, affections, religion, custom, nature, and
so forth. It has been a favorite book of taste and instruction since
the middle ages and clearly the work is a classic statement of Japanese
life, traditions, and ideals. While the collection seems self-contradictory
on occasion, it reveals Kenkō as an extraordinarily perceptive man
with a view over a wide range of human experience. The *Essays* also
encompass a subtle view of the psychic life of the individual.

One of Kenkō's personal concerns is for the past, a yearning that
sees in the fashions of his own day increasing debasement of former
standards. Yet he notes that while people speak of the times as de-
generate, the final phase of the world in Buddhist terms, the refined
atmosphere of antiquity still prevailed within the palace walls. Indeed,

Kenkō was ill at ease with the vulgar and common tastes of his day, and he looks admiringly at the Heian courtly tradition in life and literature. He was one of the last representatives of the old Court. As a poet he was counted among the very best of the period and his personal collection of verse reflects a supple and natural expression. His outlook was also greatly influenced by the Buddhist feeling for the transience of the world, but his feelings about the quality of evanescence are quite contrary to those of Kamo no Chōmei for he discovers beauty and delight as he calmly studies man and nature and finds a new reality beneath all the aspects of change. Kenkō's aesthetic has the changlessness of Buddhist enlightenment. He admonishes one to pursue religious discipline with almost monastic zeal, but his sensitivities are those of a worldly man with great insight into human nature. *Tsurezuregusa* is a superb handbook on man and society—a work admirably objective, from a Buddhist point of view, and quite appropriate coming from this monkish writer. The few negative qualities of the *Essays* are over-balanced by a positive outlook that offers a fresh view of society and nature. Its prose style, while frequently ambiguous, is notably smooth and elegant and has long been a model of fine writing.

As the main exclusively Buddhist literature of the medieval period we have the writings of the founders of new sects or schools and the prose and poetry by the Zen priests of the Five Mountains (*gozan*), the collective name for the three Zen temples at Kamakura and the two in Kyōto. The new religious leaders were reformers and innovators, and while they wrote new interpretations and doctrine their followers and disciples met the general public and laity with more personal expressions of their individual faith. The men who preached the new Buddhism spoke their belief with fervor and out of the depth of their sincerity they produced a literary expression of their individuality and inspiration that seems to transcend mere recorded words. Among such works are: *Wago tōroku* (*The Doctrine in Japanese*) by Hōnen (1133–1212); *Mattōshō* (*Last Instructions*), collected in 1289, and *Goshosokushū* (*Epistles*) by Shinran (1173–1262); and *Tannishō* (*Consolations*), a collection of Shinran's sayings by his disciple Yui Enbō. In these works the simple style of Japanese, making considerable use of the *kana* syllabary, carried the teachings of Buddhism to the reader with intimacy and warmth. In contrast, the ninety-five volumes of the *Shōbō genzō* (*The Eye of the Good Law*) by the Zen monk Dōgen (1200–53) are written in a special style of Sino-Japanese which substitutes Chinese in place of the syllabary, suitable perhaps as a vehicle for the clear austerity of Dōgen's profound religious experience. Nonetheless, his writings were warmly received for the reverential spirit with which he treated the sages of antiquity in his almost unique style of writing. With Nichiren (1222–82), in such works as *Risshō ankokuron* (*A Treatise on the Establishment of Righteousness and the Peace of the Country*), 1260, and *Minobusan gosho* (*The Book of Mount Minobu*), the intellectual tone is abandoned and his writing is full of direct appeal to the reader's emotions. From the time of the attempted Mongol invasion onward, Nichiren's writings become alive with the strength of his proselytizing spirit.

Aside from the religious writings of such teachers, there exist various kinds of documents worthy of literary study from the brushes of priests in every sect, but among the most outstanding are works of prose and poetry in Chinese produced by Zen Buddhist monks of the Five Mountains' monasteries. The writing is known either as *gozan bungaku* (Five Mountains literature) or *zenrin bungaku* (Zen temple literature). Among the Zen priests of the medieval period were many who had studied in China or who were Japanese residents of Chinese origin; consequently, the Chinese coloration in this literature was of major importance and it may even be regarded as a kind of imported writing. Zen literature, being the point of contact between Zen and the general literary world, mediated in the development of the unique qualities in medieval Japanese literature and was in the development of medieval culture. *Zenrin* writing began in the Kamakura period and matured during the years of the Northern and Southern courts and early Muromachi, coming to a complete end with the beginning of the Tokugawa period in 1600. There was considerable variety in the writing which included aphorisms, poetry and prose collections, diaries, travel accounts, biographies, and epistles. The following men are representative authors of the early and mature periods: Issan Ichiin (d. 1317), Shiren Kokan (d. 1346), Sesson Yūbai (d. 1346), Chūgan Engetsu (d. 1375), Gidō Shūshin (d. 1388), and Zekkai Chūshin (d. 1405). From about the middle of Muromachi period, the end of the fifteenth century, *zenrin* literature declined as the monasteries themselves fell into the role of serving the government as a state religion. The driving force was lost along with traditional Zen discipline and in the later years only the comic writing of Ikkyū Sōjun (d. 1481)—an apostate from the Five Mountains—kept a spirit of freshness and vitality.

Poetry

Waka and *Renga*

The tradition of imperial anthologies of *waka* originated with the *Kokinshū*. The seventh imperial anthology, the *Senzaishū* (*Collection of a Thousand Years*), completed about 1188, marked the transition from antiquity to the middle ages, and with the eighth anthology, the *Shinkokinshū* (*New Collection of Ancient and Modern Times*), the tradition reached its zenith.

The editor of the *Senzaishū* was Fujiwara no Toshinari (1114–1204) who is known by his religious name of Shunzei. At the age of ten he lost his father, Toshitada, and spent the rest of his youth as an adopted child, remaining conscious that he was descended from the great Fujiwara no Michinaga and aspiring to continue the poetic tradition of his family and even recapture past glories. With the death in 1177 of Fujiwara no Kiyosuke, the pre-eminent figure in the Rokujō family which was famous for its poetry studies, Shunzei received the patronage and protection of the Regent Kūjō no Kanezane and was thus confirmed officially as well as by virtue of his talent as leader of the Court poetry circle. The *Senzaishū* was commissioned by Emperor Go-Shirakawa in 1183 and was presented to the throne in 1187. In editing the *Senzaishū,* Shunzei returned to the tradition of the *Kokinshū.* Thus in contrast to the two preceding anthologies, *Kin'yōshū* (*Collection of Golden Leaves*) and *Shikashū* (*Collection of Verbal Flowers*) which were each in ten volumes and without prefaces, the seventh imperial anthology included a Preface and was arranged in twenty volumes. Shunzei offered as his standard of selection the principle of "thinking only of the poetry and not of the writer" (remarked in his *Korai fūtaishō* [*Notes on Poetic Style Through the Ages*]). It was Shunzei's aspiration to bring about a return to the "true way" of Japanese poetry. At the center of his views on *waka* is the idea of mystery and depth called *yūgen*. In a collection of poetry and critiques called *Jichin ōshō jikaawase* (*Abbot Jien's Personal Poetry Competition*), of 1221, Shunzei wrote: "It is not necessary that a poem always express some novel concept or treat an idea exhaustively, but . . . it should somehow . . . produce an effect both of charm and of mystery and depth. If it is a good poem, it will possess a kind of atmosphere that is distinct from its words and their configuration and yet accompanies them. The atmosphere hovers over the poem, as it were, like the haze that trails over the cherry blossoms in spring. . . ." The idea of *yūgen* was quite influential among young poets at that time and to a considerable extent was inspiration for the golden years of *waka* known as the period of the *Shinkokinshū*.

While the first steps in the compilation of the *Shinkokinshū* were taken by Shunzei, it was retired Emperor Go-Toba (1180–1239) who became the actual motivating force in the project. Go-Toba was a born poet of great ability and when the cloistered government began with his abdication in 1198 the young retired sovereign became the center of a renaissance in poetry. In 1201 Go-Toba revived the Wakadokoro, the court Bureau of Poetry, and in the same year ordered compilation of the eighth imperial anthology under the direction of six men: Minamoto no Michitomo (1170–1227), Fujiwara no Ariie (1155–1216), Fujiwara no Teika (1162–1241), Fujiwara no Ietaka (1158–1237), Asukai no Masatsune (1170–1221) and Jakuren (d. 1202). In response to the order for the anthology a great poetry competition, *utaawase,* was held, out of which were produced the twenty volumes titled *Sengohyakuban utaawase* (*The Fifteen-Hundred-Round Poetry Contest*), containing 3,000 poems (a *ban* or "round" producing two poems). The scale of this *utaawase* was the greatest in the history of *waka* and involved thirty poets, each contributing one-hundred poems. At that time too there were experiments in one-hundred-line poems. The *Shinkokinshū* was, as we have mentioned, arranged in twenty volumes, the whole having two Prefaces, one in Chinese and one in Japanese which was mostly *kana* with few Chinese graphs. The editing was largely completed in 1205, but thereafter Go-Toba himself continued to work over the collection.

The wide range of sources in the *Shinkokinshū* is indicated by a line in the *kana* Preface which says, "We have neither excluded poems of the *Man'yōshū* nor drawn only from poems collected in the seven anthologies since the *Kokinshū.*" About sixty percent of the *Shinkokinshū* is composed of ancient *waka,* including poems from the *Man'yōshū,* with the remainder coming from poets contemporary with the collection. It would in fact be appropriate to describe the work as a representative history of *waka* from antiquity to the beginning of the middle ages. Each poem in the collection was, of course, carefully chosen, but further there is considerable influence from the one-hundred-line poems which were quite popular at that time. Great care was taken with the arrangement of the poems to create sequences and progressions in mood and time, while overall the collection maintains a unity through the aesthetic ideal of *yūgen*. The nucleus of the *Shinkokinshū* is found in the *waka* written by poets of the period. The most important of the poets, along with the number of poems they contributed to the collection, are:

Saigyō (1118–90), 94 poems
Jien (1155–1225), 90 poems
Fujiwara no Yoshitsune (1169–1206), 79 poems
Shunzei, 73 poems
Princess Shokushi (d. 1201), 49 poems
Fujiwara no Teika, 47 poems
Fujiwara no Ietaka (1158–1237), 43 poems
Jakuren, 40 poems
Retired Emperor Go-Toba, 34 poems
Daughter of Shunzei (dates unknown), 28 poems
Asukai no Masatsune, 22 poems
Fujiwara no Ariie, 19 poems

Minamoto no Michitomo, 17 poems
Fujiwara no Hideyoshi (1184–1240), 17 poems
Lady Kunaikyō (daughter of Minamoto no Moromitsu, d. 1207), 15
   poems
Lady Sanuki of Retired Emperor Nijō (known as Nijōin no Sanuki,
   dates unknown), 15 poems

Fujiwara no Teika (1162–1241) was the son of Shunzei. He
maintained in his own ideals and in practice Shunzei's concept of
yūgen, emerging as the most renowned and advanced poet of the
Shinkokinshū period. In 1178 when Teika was seventeen years old,
we find his name among the twelve poets who participated in a poetry
composition with Emperor Go-Tsuchimikado, that being his debut as
a poet. Shunzei himself was by then in his sixty-fifth year, a time when
his position was secure as the doyen of the Court poetry circle, but for
Teika the road ahead was by no means without challenges. In opposition to the new *yūgen* style criticism gradually developed within conservative poetry groups, such as the Rokujō family, to the effect that
the new poetry did not follow Dharma—that it was out of keeping
with cosmic laws. The critical barbs in the struggle converged especially
on the young Teika, and the intensity of the argument was reflected
years later in Teika's *Kindai shūka* (*Superior Poems of Our Times*),
written, it is thought, for Minamoto no Sanetomo (1192–1219), which
contains the following passage:

> 'In recent times a number of poems have appeared in which the
> poets have tried to improve the vulgar style a bit, showing preference for
> old words, so that now something of the proper style of poetry, which
> had been lost since the time of Kazan, Ariwara no Narihira, Sōsei, and
> Ono no Komachi, is seen and heard again, although people who are igno-
> rant of the nature of things insist that something quite new has appeared
> and that the art of poetry has changed. Students of the art among the young
> people today seem to think that they are composing real poetry, while
> in fact they know nothing about proper style. They are vastly concerned
> with obscurity, making difficult what ought to be simple, and they string
> together all sorts of things that have no relationship to one another. They
> are all disposed to select the most inappropriate poems for their models.'

The *Kindai shūka* shows too that Teika's faith in his father's
theory of *yūgen* grew from the belief that it represented a return to
the true traditions of *waka.* The theory also found general acceptance
among medieval poets. However, the *Shinkokinshū,* which was the
embodiment of *yūgen,* does not represent the final stage of Teika's
poetic ideals, for in his effort to deepen the traditional spirit of *waka*
he came to regard the idea of *yūgen* as having certain weaknesses. It
is rather in the years after the *Shinkokinshū* that we find the gradual
emergence of Teika's own theory of intensity of feeling in poetry, the
principle which was called *ushin* and meant having feeling or "soul."
In his *Maigetsushō* (*Monthly Notes*), written in 1219 when he was

fifty-eight, Teika sets out his ideas of *ushin* with his usual persuasiveness. The ten styles of *waka,* he says, are: the "style of mystery and depth" (*yūgen yō*), the "style of universally acceptable statement" (*koto shikarubeki yō*), the "style of elegant beauty" (*uruwashiki yō*), the "style of intense feeling" (*ushin tei*), the "lofty style" (*taketakaki yō*), the "style of describing things" (*ken yō*), the "style of interesting treatment" (*omoshiroki yō*), the "style of novel treatment" (*hitofushi aru yō*), the "style of exquisite detail" (*komayakanaru yō*) and the "style of demon quelling force" (*onihishigi tei*). And he says, "Among these ten forms none has the essential nature of poetry more than the *ushin tei.*" Elsewhere he says, "The *ushin tei* surpasses the other nine forms." The *ushin* form then is both a style of *waka* and the highest ideal of *waka,* and thus is also a universal ideal. There is nothing in the theory that negates the ideas of *yūgen,* but it seems evident that Teika regarded the *ushin* concept as having advanced a step beyond the premises of *yūgen.*

In his later years, after having developed the idea of *ushin,* Teika compiled the *Shinchokusenshū* (*New Imperial Collection*), the ninth anthology, with 1,376 poems, ordered by the retired Emperor Go-Horikawa. It was completed about 1234, some thirty years after the *Shinkokinshū* and more than a decade after the Jōkyū Disturbance. Not surprisingly we find a quality in the work that reflects the medieval world and the greatly diminished vigor of the Court. The collection of *waka* known by the title *Ogura hyakunin isshu* (*The Ogura Book of One Hundred Poems by One Hundred Poets*) was probably first arranged by Teika.

Compared to the *Shinkokinshū* poems those of the *Shinchokusenshū* seem desiccated, a quality which was to characterize most of medieval poetry. The ninth anthology also reflects the trend of the age with its many poems by warrior poets. Nonetheless, we find a singular splendor in the *waka* of Minamoto no Sanetomo who is represented by some twenty-five poems in the collection.

Fujiwara no Tameie (1198–1275) was the son of Teika. We find in his book *Eiga ittai* (*The Form of Poetry*), which sets out his views on *waka,* a carefully orthodox transmission of Teika's later theories, but with particular emphasis on the craft of language and vocabulary, and the necessity to study old poetry and maintain purity of poetic language—points which Tameie took as his ideal. We find a tendency toward conservatism and loss of individual flavor or feeling (what Teika called *kokoro*). Still, in Tameie's time descendants of the imperial house were established as poetry masters by the shogun, and in 1251 Tameie completed the *Shokugosenshū* (*Later Collection Continued*) and in 1265 took part in compiling the *Shokukokinshū* (*Collection of Ancient and Modern Times Continued*), the tenth and eleventh imperial anthologies, respectively.

After Tameie's death three of his sons established the families known as Nijō, Kyōgoku, and Reizei—the Nijō branch, descended from Tameuji (1222–1286), representing the conservative tradition, while the Kyōgoku family, descended from Tamenori (1226–1279), and the Reizei, descended from Tamesuke (1263–1328; son of Abutsuni, the later wife of Tameie and author of *Izayoi nikki*) represented the innovative side. Compilation of the imperial anthologies thereafter remained mostly in the hands of the conservative Nijō poets down to the twenty-first and last collection, the *Shinzoku kokinshū* (*New Collection of Ancient and Modern Times Continued*) which was completed in 1439 and is remarkable only for its preservation of convention. The *Gyokuyōshū* (*Collection of Jewelled Leaves*), the fourteenth imperial anthology, completed about 1313 by Kyōgoku no Tamekane, son of Tamenori, and the *Fūgashū* (*Collection of Elegance*), the seventeenth imperial anthology, completed in 1346 by retired Emperor Hanazono (r. 1308–18) who followed in the footsteps of Tamekane, were the last to show any creative vitality. The *Shin'yōshū* (*Collection of New Leaves*), completed in 1381 and not counted among the official imperial anthologies, contains only poems of persons attached to the Southern Court. It was compiled by Prince Munenaga (d. 1385) and is known as a lyrical and spirited collection of *waka*.

To the Nijō school belong four "masters" of poetry from the period of the Northern and Southern Courts: the monk Ton'a (1289–1372), Yoshida no Kenkō (1283–1350), Jōben (d. 1356) and Keiun (dates unknown). Their work generally was uninspired. In contrast to such orthodoxy, the Reizei school found notable adherents in men who are prominent in the history of poetic thought: Kōun (d. 1429), author of *Kōun kuden* (*Oral Tradition of Kōun*); Imagawa Ryōshun (1325–1420), who left many critical writings; Shōtetsu (1381–1459), the advocate of return to the aesthetics of Teika; Shinkei (1406–1475), famous for his linked verse and author of *Sasamegoto* (*Musings*), *Hitorigoto* (*Soliloquies*), *Oi no kurigoto* (*Mutterings of an Old Man*), and other *renga* treaties.

Toward the end of the medieval period the traditions of the Nijō school were continued through Gyōkō (1381–1455) and Tō no Tsuneyori who transmitted what were termed "secret" traditions relating to the interpretation of the *Kokinshū* to Sōgi (1421–1502), then through Sanjōnishi no Sanetaka (1455–1537) and his family to Hosokawa Yūsai (1534–1610) with whom the medieval *waka*, which had undergone great changes, came to an end. The story of the reformation of *waka* by Toda Mosui (1629–1706) and others, however, properly belongs to the Tokugawa period.

In contrast to the stagnation of *waka* poetry during the later half of the middle ages, the linked-verse form (*renga*) was extraordinarily creative. The beginning of linked verse is found in the short *renga* which were the joint compositions of two poets, one composing the upper hemistich and the other adding the concluding hemistich to make a *tanrenga* or short linked poem. Later ages rather fancifully set the origin of *renga* far in the past, describing the form as a dialogue between soldiers and the old men who built the fires in camp. *Renga* is also known as the "way of Tsukuba," from a place name in eastern Japan, and the word Tsukuba often appears in the titles of *renga* collections. The early linked verses are in the *kataula* form (two parts of 5–7–7 syllables each) and the first *renga* in *tanka* or *waka* form (5–7–5/7–7) appears in Book 8 of the *Man'yōshū*.

> Sahogawa no   With waters of
> mizu o seki agete   The River Saho
> ueshi ta o   I have tilled the field,
> karu wasa ii wa   But the early rice
> hitori narubeshi   I must eat alone.

The short linked verse form gradually becomes more frequent as we enter the Heian period and in the *Kin'yōshū*, the fifth imperial anthology, completed in 1127, there is a separate section devoted to *renga*. Beginning with the period of the cloistered emperors, in the last quarter of the eleventh century, *renga* were extended to three and four links called "chain *renga*" (*kusari renga*) and then to long *renga* of fifty to one hundred links and even some extravagant examples with thousands of lines. The great popularity of *renga*, however, began in the Kamakura period, mention being made in Fujiwara no Teika's diary, the *Meigetsuki* (*Bright Moon Diary*), one of the important sources of information on early Kamakura. Still, after the end of Heian, *renga* tended to light and witty themes and were called "free" or "comic" *renga* (*mushin renga*) in contrast to linked verse which stressed the *waka* mood as "serious" linked verse (*ushin renga*). The "serious" verse came to be regarded as the main tradition, and Teika along with other fine poets soon found value in the form. The popularity of *renga* produced an appreciation of the importance of the initial verse, the *hokku*, and simple rules were formulated concerning the way in which verses should be linked. Emperor Juntoku (1197–1242) devoted some fifteen lines to *renga* composition in his *Yakumo mishō* (*Notes on Waka*).

Even though *renga* composition was practiced by the poets at Court, *renga* remained subordinate to *waka* and writing in that form was less prestigious. But outside the Court, among commoners, composition of linked verse proceeded on its own, developing as a popular verse form and a major genre of medieval literature, known as "underground" *renga* (*chika renga*). In that area a number of masters of the art appeared toward the end of Kamakura, such men as: Jakunin,

Jakui, Dōshō, and Zen'a. Dōshō is regarded as the founder of the popular *renga* movement, while Zen'a is considered to be its best poet. Kyūsei (1281–1375), a disciple of Zen'a, along with Nijō no Yoshimoto (1320–88), edited the first collection of *renga,* called *Tsukubashū* (*Tsukuba Collection*), which was a work in twenty volumes dating from 1356. He also took part in assembling a rule book of *renga* composition, the *Ōan shinshiki* (*New Regulations of Ōan*), dated 1372. Nijō no Yoshimoto was also the author of such books on theory of *renga* as *Chikuba mondō* (*Questions and Answers on Renga*).

Renga began its rapid growth as popular poetry from about the middle of the fourteenth century. There was a brief decline in activity during early Muromachi, but around 1430 *renga* entered another period of great activity through the interest and patronage of the shogun Ashikaga no Yoshinori and the poets known as the Seven Sages of the Bamboo Grove—a group which included Takayama Sōzei (d. 1455), Chiun (d. 1448) and Shinkei (1406–75). Sōzei was the leading figure of the period and he, together with Ichijō no Kanera (1402–81), composed *Shinshiki kon'an* (*Modern Views of the New Rules*), a revision of the *Ōan shinshiki.* Following that Sōgi (1421–1502) was the central figure in *renga,* in 1476 editing the *Chikurinshō* (*Bamboo Grove Notes*), a collection of the *renga* of the Seven Sages. With Renzai (d. 1510) in 1495 Sōgi completed the twenty-volume *Shinsen tsukubashū* (*New Tsukuba Collection*). However, the finest sequence in *renga* is considered to be *Minase sangin hyakuin* (*Three Poets at Minase*), from 1488.

The tradition of *ushin* or serious *renga,* which began in the Kamakura period, reached its zenith at this time, even though comic *renga* (*mushin renga*) and composing initial verses (*hokku*) continued to be popular. Linked verse flourished until the end of the middle ages, but the form ended with the late sixteenth century. Two books of the Muromachi period prepared the way for the seventeen-syllable *haiku* which dominates the modern period. They were *Haikai no renga dokugin senku* (*One Thousand Comic Verses*), by Arakida no Moritake (1473–1549), and the *Shinsen inu tsukubashū* (*New Doggeral Tsukuba Collection*) of Yamazaki no Sōkan (dates unknown).

Fiction

Monogatari and Otogizōshi

The decline of *monogatari* literature was already visible at the end of the Heian period and by the middle ages it had quite lost its vitality. Still, stories in the *monogatari* form continued to be written and according to the *Fūyō wakashū* (*Wind and Leaves Collection*) of 1271 there were nearly one hundred *monogatari* in circulation, all presumed to be compositions of the Kamakura period. Only ten have survived in whole or part, among them such tales as *Torikaebaya monogatari* (*The Tale of Would That They Were Exchanged*), *Sumiyoshi monogatari* (*The Tale of Sumiyoshi*), *Koke no koromo* (*Robe of Moss*), and *Iwashimizu monogatari* (*The Tale of Iwashimizu*). We have in addition from that time stories, such as *Matsukage chūnagon monogatari* (*The Tale of the Middle Councilor Matsukage*), and *Sayo goromo* (*Night Robes*), as well as some of the stories in the *Tsutsumi chūnagon monogatari* (*Tales of the Middle Councilor of the Embankment*) which are thought to date from Kamakura. Characteristically the later *monogatari* attempted to follow in the footsteps of *Genji monogatari,* but they neither reached the level of *Genji* nor did they create a new approach. The mood of the court and of the court *monogatari* was better captured by *waka* aiming for the effect of *yūgen,* the feeling of mystery and depth demonstrated in the *Shinkokinshū.*

As was the case with *monogatari* of the Heian period, little is known about the authors of the stories, but we suppose that most were by men in the service of noble families or at the imperial court. However, according to the *Mumyō sōshi* (*Nameless Book*), a critique of *monogatari* literature possibly by the daughter of Shunzei, the story entitled *Ukinami* (*Rolling Waves*) was written by Fujiwara no Takanobu (1142–1205). The same source noted that Fujiwara no Teika composed a number of *monogatari* and was the author of *Matsura no miya monogatari* (*Tale of the Matsura Palace*). While the men writing in that period could indeed define a new realm of beauty in *waka,* in the area of the *monogatari* they were unable to break the mold that stamped it as feminine literature.

The inspiration and model for *monogatari* literature remained, as we have noted, the tales of the Heian period and our view of the genre is greatly indebted to the *Mumyō sōshi* mentioned above. We assume from internal evidence that this critique was written between 1196 and 1202. It begins with a scroll by scroll examination of *Genji monogatari,* its characters and descriptions, and then takes up the general area of *monogatari* in Heian after *Sagoromo monogatari* and down to *Torikaebaya* and early Kamakura tales. The critiques in *Mumyō sōshi* extend also to poetry collections and women writers, but its principal focus is the *monogatari. Genji* is taken as the best of the classical tales and is the basis of comparison for other stories. The critical terminology in this work corresponds to that used in poetry of the time of the *Shinkokinshū* and the work generally shows an attitude of acceptance toward the *monogatari* of the 12th century.

The critical terminology includes such remarks as the following: *kokoro ni shimite medetaku oboyu* (to delight by capturing one's affections), *aware ni kanashi* (bittersweet sadness), *midokoro aru* (worthy of note), *kokoro gurushi* (painfully disturbing), *en aru* (having associations), *imiji* (splendid) and *omoshiroshi* (highly attractive). In contrast to the terms of approval, things that were unlovely, ugly, or strange were criticized as *sarade mo ari nan to oboyuru koto* (a thing which one feels should be otherwise).

We must remark also on the opposition to the whole area of *monogatari* literature in the medieval period originating in a sense of sin and evil which grew out of Buddhist thought. There was a sense of uneasiness with the *monogatari* which was considered to be a medium of amusement, a vain thing of frivolous words. Even Teika, in his *Meigetsuki,* offers a sigh concerning the *kyōgen kigo* ("wild words and flowery phrases") of *Genji monogatari.* The monk Mujū, author of *Shasekishū,* found it necessary to make his apology to the effect that he is setting down this Buddhist collection of *setsuwa* because he has long been an avid reader of *monogatari* and cannot break the habit. But as he remarks in the introduction to the *Shasekishū,* the wild words and flowery phrases of vain amusement are, through karmic association, part of the Buddha Way, and through exemplifying the meanness and shallowness of the world make known the profound principles of nirvana. Such an apology for literature, peculiar to the middle ages, may in part explain the decline of *monogatari* literature.

The tradition of Heian courtly fiction, the *monogatari,* all but vanished during Kamakura and in its place, in the later medieval period, appeared the genre known as *otogizōshi,* which were short narratives or novellas. The title is an anachronism and derives from a collection of stories published in the early eighteenth century—*Bunshō sōshi (The Tale of Bunshō), Saru genji sōshi (The Tale of Monkey Genji),* and so forth, twenty-three in all. The *otogizōshi* which have survived to the present number in the hundreds. For convenience we present representative titles under the six types that account for most of the stories.

1. Stories of the Imperial Court   Theme
   Shinobine monogatari (The Tearful Voice)   romance
   Wakagusa monogatari (The Maiden Waka-
   gusa)   romance
   Ko-ochikubo (Little Ochikubo)   stepchild
   Iwaya no sōshi (The Stone Dwelling)   stepchild
   Komachi sōshi (Lady Komachi)   poem tale
   Izumi shikibu (Lady Izumi)   poem tale
2. Stories of Monks and Buddhism   Theme
   Aki no yo no naga monogatari (Long Tale of an
   Autumn Night   love between men

Matsuho no ura monogatari (*The Bay of Matsuho*)	love between men
Sannin hōshi (*Three Priests*)	religion
Takano monogatari (*Tale of Takano*)	religion
Amida no honji (*The Essence of Amida*)	previous existence
Kumano no honji (*The Buddha of Kumano*)	previous existence
3. Stories of Warriors	Theme
Shuten dōji (*The Drunken Brigands*)	heroic rescue
Onzōshi shimawatari (*Yoshitsune's Journey*)	diplomatic mission of Yoshitsune
Akimichi (*Akimichi*)	vendetta
4. Lives of Commoners	Theme
Bunshō sōshi (*The Tale of Bunshō*)	success and social advancement
Monokusa tarō (*Master Lazy*)	success
Issun bōshi (*Master One Inch*)	Tom Thumb's adventures
Ko otoko no sōshi (*The Tiny Man*)	Tom Thumb (a *honjimono*)
Fukutomi sōshi (The Tale of Fukutomi)	fame and fortune through breaking wind
Saru genji sōshi (*The Tale of Monkey Genji*)	fishmonger wins a courtesan
5. Exotic Lands	Theme
Yōkihi (*Yang Kuei-fei*)	the mistress of Emperor Ming-huang of China
6. Animal Stories	Theme
Tsuru no sōshi (*The Crane*)	crane becomes a girl and marries her rescuer
Fukurō (*The Owl*)	owl mourns his beloved bullfinch
Chōdo utaawase (*The Furnishing's Utaawase*)	inanimate objects performing
Suzume no hosshin (*The Sparrow's Conversion*)	religion
Aro kassen monogatari (*War of the Crows and Herons*)	war tale parody

The fourth category, "Lives of Commoners," is chiefly concerned with stories of getting ahead in the world and includes a good deal of humor and satire. While these stories are not the most numerous of the *otogizōshi* they are important for the view they give of dreams and realities in the life of the common man.

A few authors of the novellas are known—such men as the monk Genna (d. 1350), Nijō no Yoshimoto, and Ichijō no Kanera (1402–81)—but most of the works remain anonymous products of descendants of the old aristocracy, monks, and persons of leisure and others living in the capital. We may suppose too that the audience for such stories would more likely have heard them aloud than have read them.

Further, many *otogizōshi* were circulated in the form of illustrated scrolls. Compared to the Heian *monogatari*, the *otogizōshi* were all extremely short works, and while they were certainly not high in aesthetic value they clearly occupy an important place in the history of literature for their role in introducing literary arts to the general population and as forerunners of the books in *kana* (*kanazōshi*), which were the first new literature of the modern era.

Historical Tales

The *Ima kagami* (*Mirror of the Present*) and *Mizu kagami* (*Water Mirror*) were written in the late twelfth century as continuations of *Ōkagami* and *Eiga monogatari*. The *Ima kagami* covers the years 1025 to 1170 (the year of its writing) and adopts the dialogue and biographical technique of *Ōkagami*. The author is not known. In a similar style the *Mizu kagami* offers a chronological narrative of the entire history of Japan from 660 B.C. to A.D. 850, the point at which the *Ōkagami* begins. The narration is by an old woman who talks with a pilgrim who had heard stories of the distant past from an old hermit. The author may have been Nakayama no Tadachika (1131–95). The sources of the *Mizu kagami* include such histories as *Fusō ryakki* (*Outline of Japan*), a chronologically ordered work written in Chinese by Kōen (d. 1169), a monk of Mt. Hiei, which drew on memoirs, histories, temple records and so forth after the Six National Histories. Also from that period, in 1218, is a narrative or *monogatari* history called *Akitsushima monogatari* (*Tale of the Dragonfly Islands*)— "Dragonfly Islands" being an ancient poetic name for Japan—which gives in question-and-answer form the history of Japan from the age of the gods down to the reign of Emperor Yōzei (r. 876–84). While we may suppose that the times were receptive to that approach to history writing, the *Mizu kagami* is not remarkable as literature. In the Preface and Postface to the *Mizu kagami*, where the dialogue form is maintained, we find clear statements of the author's motive for the work, which was to have us learn from the realities of the past and present. He sees a world without limits, infinite in time, where endings are beginnings and beginnings are endings. "The fact is that in these later days, born in a small land long after the time of the Buddha, everything we see and everything we hear is evil," he says, and so "We must not praise the past and speak ill of the present"—for they are one and the same. The work attempts to alleviate the spiritual malaise of the early middle ages and is sustained, as are other *rekishi monogatari*, historical tales, by the search for some connecting principle in history. There is some question whether *Mizu kagami* was written before or after the *Ima kagami*, and there is even a case for its having been composed at the end of the Kamakura period.

A history known as *Iyayotsugi,* possibly after the appellation of its narrator, followed *Ima kagami* with a history of Japan down to where the *Masu kagami (The Clear Mirror)* begins, but this work of Fujiwara no Takanobu (1142–1205) is no longer extant. *Masu kagami* recounts the years from 1180 to 1333, when Emperor Go-Daigo returned from his exile on the island of Oki. The style is elegant and archaic, and if it is lacking in originality it is nonetheless a valuable piece of writing, especially for its sources which included diaries and official records. Probably written between 1338 and 1378, by Nijō no Yoshimoto it is thought, the *Masu kagami* managed to find a neutral viewpoint at a period when loyalties were strongly divided between the court and the Kamakura military government as a result of the rebellions of the Jōkyū and Genkō eras (1220 and 1332). The *Masu kagami* was the last of the medieval historical *monogatari* and the last of the "mirror" histories.

The broad epical view of history which was embodied in the historical *monogatari* did not extend to the war tales, and the search for a theory of history which we find in *Mizu kagami* did not develop far enough to be successful. There is a parallel, whatever the reasons, between the decline of the aristocratic *monogatari* and the disappearance of the narrative history, both having fallen off after promising beginnings. There are, however, two works in the theory of history which we should note from the medieval period: *Gukanshō (My Foolish Ramblings)* and *Jinnō shōtōki (Records of the Legitimate Succession of the Divine Sovereigns).* The *Gukanshō* was written by the poet-monk Jien (1155–1225). Jien was the son of Fujiwara no Tadamichi and was the younger brother of Kanezane, the first minister or *kampaku.* He took up religious life at the age of eleven just after his father's death, studying at Mount Hiei and there becoming head of the Tendai school of Buddhism when he was thirty-eight years old. As a youth he lived through the wars between the Minamoto and the Taira families and he began writing his interpretive history of Japan on the eve of the Jōkyū Rebellion. He was also highly critical of the historical tales, which he felt avoided confronting the real events of the past, and was led thus to his own re-examination of historical writing.

The *Gukanshō* is in seven scrolls and covers the history of Japan from the first emperor, Jimmu, down to the reign of Emperor Juntoku in the early thirteenth century, attempting a study in depth and searching for some underlying principle uniting the past and the present.

The *Jinnō shōtōki,* six scrolls, is a work on the interpretation of history by Kitabatake no Chikafusa (1293–1354), written while he was in the midst of a military campaign. Chikafusa was a central figure in the rival Southern Court, and it was while fighting for the restoration of what he considered to be the legitimate imperial line that he wrote this work in 1339 at the Oda Castle in Hitachi. The immediate motive for his writing was the death of Emperor Go-Daigo, whose cause he supported; corrections and additions to the book were made in 1343. Chikafusa was less concerned with the details of history than with expounding the mystique of imperial rule. His book was designed to encourage faith in the ultimate victory of Emperor Go-Murakami who had become heir to the throne at the age of twelve. Clearly, Chikafusa's own hopes were supported by his belief in historical necessity stemming from the divine character of the imperial line. He says that the purpose of the book is to present the truth as it has been handed down since the age of the gods, not merely to present what is usually heard. And thus the appropriate title for the work is *Records of the Legitimate Succession of the Divine Sovereigns*. Despite this clear statement of the author's intention, he is severe in his judgments of emperors and ministers who do not conduct themselves with humility before the gods. Of Emperor Buretsu (r. 498–506) he says: "His temper was bad and he allowed all manner of evil; therefore his descendents did not long endure," and of Emperor Nintoku (r. 313–99) that he "possessed saintly qualities, but his line ended with himself. Virtue lasts a hundred generations, but if the descendents are bad the line will perish, and of this there are many examples." The rationale throughout the book is that matters of government are regulated by divine will. This divine will is explained as follows: "The gods' (*kami*) fundamental pledge is to assist human beings. All people under heaven are creatures of the divine. And while we honor the emperor, heaven does not allow, nor do the gods take pleasure in, the suffering of many for the amusement of one being. And thus the beneficence of heaven is given or withheld in accord with the propriety of government." The statement is not coldly hypothetical but rather one that pours from the heart of the writer—for which reason the work is high in literary interest. Both this book and the *Gukanshō* share the search for a historical principle, a reason to history. Their outlook and occasion for writing differ, but both are remarkable as discursive, critical writings sensitive to the aspirations of the human spirit.

Theater

Nō, *Kyōgen, Kōwakamai*

The Nō drama was the most completely medieval development in the performing arts and it reached its zenith early in the Muromachi period. The antecedants of Nō include *sarugaku,* a dance form that developed from *sangaku,* which was Chinese in origin, and *dengaku,* the popular dance forms of rural Japan. From the imperial court and Buddhist temples of the Heian period such performances as the "longevity dances" also contributed to Nō. Professional entertainers gradually found a place in Japan during Heian period and often wore religious garb since they were associated with temples where they performed at festivals and at other times for public entertainment. *Sarugaku* or "monkey music" was a light, humorous kind of performance that depended on acrobatics, juggling, and conjuring tricks, while *dengaku,* it is thought, was primarily dancing. However, from early Kamakura times the two kinds of performances began to fuse and by the Muromachi period any real differences between the two had disappeared. Both then seem to have used acrobatic feats as a prelude to dramatic pieces with a story line which was the main act. In the early Muromachi period the dramatic part was known by the names *sarugaku no nō* and *dengaku no nō,* meaning the "art" or "accomplishment" (nō) of "monkey music" or "field music." After the middle of the Muromachi period and the great popularity of *sarugaku,* the performances came to be known simply as Nō. The texts of the plays are known as *yōkyoku.*

During the late fourteenth century a number of theatrical companies were performing in western Japan. Under the name of *dengaku,* two troupes were active: the main company located in Uji-Shirakawa, and a new company in Nara. In *sarugaku* four groups of Yamato-*sarugaku* (Yamato referring to the province around Nara) were performing at Kasuga Shrine and Kōfukuji, the great monastic complex at Nara. On the southeast shore of Lake Biwa three troupes of Ōmi-*sarugaku* were at Hiei Shrine. The *dengaku* performances were most popular with Hōjō no Takatoki (1303–33) and Ashikaga no Takauji (1305–58), but the third shogun Ashikaga no Yoshimitsu (1358–1408) favored the *sarugaku* performances of the troupe led by Kan'ami Mototsugu (1333–84), and under the patronage of Yoshimitsu, *sarugaku* recreated its materials into Nō. Kan'ami's son Seami inherited his father's company and defined the new drama in more than 150 plays which were elaborately literary and highly refined in their aesthetic aim. Of the approximately 240 Nō plays still performed more than half are by Seami. In addition to those librettos, Seami left some twenty essays on theory and aesthetics of Nō which served to define his school: *Kadensho (Transmitting the Flower),* *Nōsakushō (The Making of Nō), Sarugaku dangi (Lessons in Sarugaku),* and so forth.

Seami touches on many aspects of Nō—for example, the training of an actor, the theory of performance and composition—and his view of the theater is subtle and complex. But as his central motif we may take his theory of the "flower" of performing and his ideas of *yūgen*. The "flower" (an image derived from the lotus as a symbol of supreme truth in Buddhism) meant the beauty and perfection created by the actual performance. He takes as the first requirement in producing the flower the ability of the actor to capture the mind of the audience. In the *Kadensho* he says: "When the flowers of the myriad trees and grasses blossom each in their season we are delighted by their rare beauty. In *sarugaku* (Nō) too people are made aware of the rare and precious, of the soul of beauty and delight. These three—the flower, rarity, and beauty—are quite the same in spirit." The "flower" is therefore beauty, and its attributes must necessarily be rarity and loveliness. But the "flower" is also transient and its beauty fades in a moment. In his youth a performer will surely have this "flower" and with it may capture his audience, but to have the "flower" even after the decline of youth's physical beauty is the true and profound accomplishment indicated by the *tao,* the way of Nō. In this regard Seami differentiates the temporal or evanescent "flower" and the true "flower." He says: "The true flower blossoms or falls according to the talent of the individual; the true flower is long lasting." The true "flower" is the result of human achievement; that is, it is the flower of art. In this analysis is the basis for Seami's detailed explanations of his theory of strict discipline in the study and practice of the arts.

The "flower," however, is no more than the exterior, and without the essence that creates the "flower," that brings a deepening of inner beauty, the effect is empty. Here lies the motive for Seami's rationale of *yūgen*. "The inner person's *yūgen* is expressed by graceful attire. The performer must use refined speech and acquire the expressions and ways of speaking of the aristocracy so that his words are gentle at all times. This is the *yūgen* of language." The *yūgen* of music is its pleasant melody, soft and flowing to the ear. In dance *yūgen* is consummate skill and a quiet elegance of body that is moving to the viewer. And in mimicry it is to produce the impressions of age, of woman, and of the martial man all with beauty and grace. If these various kinds of *yūgen* are truly mastered, then *yūgen* will be part of the performer and no matter what role he undertakes, it will have *yūgen*. Grace of body is the essence of *yūgen*.

The heart of Seami's aesthetics is described by the "flower" and *yūgen,* and only by meticulous pursuit of these qualities is the art of Nō brought to perfection. Still, at the end of the quest neither the "flower" nor *yūgen* are required, for there is an element which is not in *yūgen* but which exists with it. That is the area of perfect beauty which Seami called the "highest attainment" (*taketaru shin'i*). At the highest stage of accomplishment, the actor may deliberately make use of faulty technique which, by contrast and novelty, will serve to remind the audience cf his superb skill. This area is described in detail in Seami's *Shikadō* (*The Way of the Highest Flower*).

The points we have mentioned indicate the center of Seami's aesthetics, but this much is only a fragment of his whole philosophy of the actor's art. Indeed it is appropriate to remark that Seami's aesthetics is one of the finest creations of the early fifteenth century in Japan.

The reasons behind the adversity that befell Seami in his later life are not clear, but in 1434 he was exiled to the island of Sado on the northwest coast of Japan. His nephew On'ami (1398–1467) enjoyed the patronage of the sixth shogun Ashikaga no Yoshinori (1393–1441) and became leader of the Kanze Nō troupe of Seami, but otherwise unremarkable. However, Seami's theory of Nō was adopted and further developed by his son-in-law Kaneharu no Zenchiku (1405–65). Zenchiku wrote several outstanding plays, such as *Ugetsu* (*Rainy Moon*), a play in which the poet Saigyō is the central figure, and *Tamakazura,* about the daughter of Yūgao in *Genji monogatari.* After the Ōnin wars of the decade 1467–78, Kanze Kojirō Nobumitsu (1435–1516), the son of On'ami, was the most prominent figure and is noted for plays, such as *Funa benkei* (*Benkei and the Boat*), which use startling effects and give a particularly active role to the deuteragonist (*waki*), an innovation in Nō drama which from Seami's time had specialized in the protagonist (*shite*) role. No outstanding personality appeared after Nobumitsu and in general, although new plays were written throughout Tokugawa, the Nō theater did no more than preserve tradition.

We have little certain knowledge about the early history of *kyōgen,* the comic interludes of a Nō program, but they seem to have gradually taken form along with the Nō plays. Seami says: "The number of plays in a program of *sarugaku* used to be four or five, but now in benefit performances for a temple, or similar occasion, three true Nō plays and two *kyōgen* are given to make up the program." We gather, therefore, that at least from Seami's time the practice of alternating Nō and *kyōgen* existed, but the texts of *kyōgen* now available were only written down during the Tokugawa period. Our source here is the *Kyōgen no hon* (*Book of Kyōgen*) by Ōkura Toraaki (1597–1662), dating from 1643. Toraaki transcribed the *kyōgen* then being performed, but none of them can be traced back further than the end of the Muromachi period. In his study of *kyōgen,* called *Warambegusa* (*Young Grasses*), written in 1660, in which he brings together all he could discover about the plays, Toraaki criticizes the art as it existed in his own time: "By common repute *kyōgen* is a lot of formless fussing, wild and senseless, silly face-making, wide-eyed and gape-mouthed, children making unseemly gestures . . . but this is surely not the *kyōgen* of Nō. Indeed, it would be difficult to call this the *kyōgen* of *kyōgen*." Caustic as this is, it may represent the state of *kyōgen* as it had survived from the middle ages. In advocating tradition, Toraaki says: "*Kyōgen* is a simplification of Nō, like the thing and its parody. For instance, Nō is like *renga*, serious in content, and *kyōgen*, using jocular language, is like *haikai*. But still, the form of *kyōgen* is that of Nō." The source for this may be Seami's argument in his *Shūdōsho* (*Book of the Discipline*) in which he finds the quality of *yūgen* in *kyōgen*. "We say that there is pleasure in wit, that it is a feeling of delight. The *kyōgen* performance is quite in accord with this. When this feeling is produced in the audience, then the performer has indeed achieved a high degree of this very attractive *yūgen*." We may be sure that in the early *kyōgen* the actors followed only a very general plot and, depending on the particular circumstances, speeches and other business were changed or improvised. The Nō theater was a theater of dance, centered on the *shite* or protagonist who was masked and who usually represented a well-known character from literature, legend, or history. In contrast, the *kyōgen* brought the common man to the stage as hero; it was a theater of comedy based on humorous dialogue, and it aimed at light amusement rather than the transcendent mood of *yūgen*. *Kyōgen*, in the form of written texts through which it could be transmitted in fixed plays, dates only from Tokugawa and the emergence of three schools: Ōkura, Izumi, and Sagi.

The "Kōwaka dance" (*kōwakamai*) or "ballad drama" has certain resemblances to Nō and is thought to have developed about the same time, the tradition being that it was invented by Momonoi Naoaki (ca. 1393–1470), his boyhood name being Kōwakamaru, from which the dance name was created. Naoaki is said to have recited the *sōshi* called *Yashima no ikusa* (*Battle of Yashima*) to a melody he devised. The performance was well received and Naoaki was even encouraged by Emperor Go-Komatsu to develop other pieces. We may assume that dance or dramatic posturing accompanied the recitation. Of the thirty works used in *kōwakamai* as it is known today, more than half are about military figures, either the Soga brothers or Yoshitsune. The performance was popular among warriors during the late medieval and early Tokugawa periods, but the performance sharply declined during the seventeenth century and today only vestiges remain in Ōe village in Fukuoka Prefecture.

In the area of songs and ballads we should recall the *imayō* or "present style" songs of late Heian since they continued to be performed during Kamakura. The most representative ballads of the early medieval period, however, were the *enkyoku* (literally, "party music") which originated with Buddhist monks and were long series of alternating five-seven syllable lines on a variety of themes—the seasons, travel, history of China and Japan, etc. According to the *Enkyokushū* (*Collection of Enkyoku*) manuscript, a collection of more than 170 *enkyoku* lyrics, the most prolific writer seems to have been the monk Meiku (ca. 1240–1306). The religious ballads called *wasan* continued and in the Kamakura period were adopted by new sects of Buddhism, principally Jōdo, as useful in teaching religion to the common people. *Wasan* are based on the *imayō* pattern of four lines alternating five-seven syllable phrases, but *wasan* are deeply religious in content, taking up doctrine and stories of monks and saints, such as Shinran (1173–1262) and Ippin (1239–98), which considerably adds to their literary interest.

During the Muromachi period a new kind of song took the place of *imayō;* this was the *kouta* or "little song." The *kouta* were various songs that grew out of earlier materials—such as *imayō, enkyoku, dengaku,* the ballads of *sarugaku,* and the short songs of *kyōgen.* It is possible to trace their antecedents in the more than 310 songs recorded in the *Kanginshū* (*Collection of Leisure Songs*) of 1518. In contrast to the long and often ponderous lyrics of *enkyoku* and recitation of *Heike monogatari* (the style called *heikyoku*), the *kouta* are brief and many songs have only a few lines. While most are love songs, in their melancholy lyrics we find a good deal of the feelings of the generation of commoners who suffered the wars of Ōnin and Bummei, between 1467 and 1487. In the Preface to the *Kanginshū* we learn that the author was a monk who had "built a hut with a distant view of Fuji, and watched the snows of a decade or more pile on the window," but beyond that his identity is unknown. The remains of the genre of *kouta* are expanded with a volume by the Zen monk Sōan and by *Kouta no ryūtatsu* of Takasabu no Ryūtatsu (1527–1611). Both works show the form of the *kouta* during the transition from the middle ages to the Tokugawa period.

Modern Period

A.D. 1600 TO 1868

by

NAKAMURA YUKIHIKO

The Edo or Tokugawa Period

THE LONG PERIOD of wars among the medieval feudatories came to a close with the battle of Sekigahara in 1600 and the two campaigns in Ōsaka against the supporters of Toyotomi Hideyori, son of Hideyoshi, in 1613–14. The victor in the struggle to rule Japan was Tokugawa Ieyasu (1542–1616) who established his center of government in Edo, modern Tōkyō, and began the national organization termed *bakuhan.* Under this system the military government, the *bakufu,* directed matters of foreign relations, national policy, and the imperial court, while the administration of local affairs, in the feudatories or *han,* was left to the daimyō. The third shogun, Tokugawa Iemitsu (1604–51), initiated the system of enforced residence in Edo (*sankin kotai*) as well as other obligations for the daimyo, but essentially the relationship between the *han* and the *bakufu* allowed the medieval feudal structure to continue while superimposing on it a kind of centralized authority typical of modern nation states. Under the closed-country policy begun in Iemitsu's time, Japan was nearly completely isolated from the changing world abroad, remaining so for more than two-hundred years until the Meiji Restoration in 1868. The Edo period is often referred to as "modern" (*kinsei*), in contrast to the period after 1868 which is known as the "recent" period (*kindai*).

The four social classes—warrior, farmer, artisan, and merchant—which gradually emerged during the middle ages were formally and rigidly divided during the Tokugawa period. Members of the warrior or samurai class held governmental posts in the *han* and in the national administration in addition to their military functions. Farmers, fishermen, and artisans were engaged in production. Merchants were concerned exclusively with the circulation or distribution of goods produced and with financial matters. Production was centered on agriculture and the warrior's income was assigned as a rice stipend. Inevitably, however, with the development of cities and the emergence

107

of the early stages of a modern capitalistic economy, real economic power shifted from rural producers to the urban merchants and artisans, the group that came to be known as townsmen (*chōnin*). The townsmen of Kyōto, Ōsaka, and Edo, places where considerable freedom was allowed, became particularly influential. Within each of the four classes differences in degree were officially recognized. Thus warriors were distinguished as "upper" or "lower"; among farmers there were landowners, small cultivators, tenants, and so forth; among merchants there were wholesalers (*ton'ya* or *toiya*), retailers (*kouri*), and so forth. Standing apart from the four classes were members of the court aristocracy and the Buddhist and Shintō clergy, while at the bottom of the social scale were those who belonged to an outcast group. Generally speaking, people of every class and degree passed on their occupations to their descendants. Buddhism, which was by now mixed with Shintō, had dominated the religious and intellectual world of Japan since the early middle ages and was now protected by the government's anti-Christian policies in which the Buddhist clergy sometimes took part. In the daily life of the four classes Buddhism along with Shintō was the sustaining faith, but leadership in intellectual matters shifted to Confucianist teachers. By both the *bakufu* and the *han,* Confucianism was made the foundation of official educational policy. The teachings of the great Sung dynasty Confucianist Chu Hsi (Shushi in Japanese) were consistently supported by the *bakufu,* but other Confucian schools, such as the "school of ancient studies" (*kogaku*) and the philosophy of Wang-ming (1473–1529), whose theories were known as *yōmeigaku* in Japan, found advocates from time to time. Whatever the school, it was clearly Confucian studies that held the highest prestige, and in the form of a movement to unite the "three religions," Buddhism and Shintō sought a place in the ascending constellation of the new Confucianism. The ethical spirit of the personal practice of "the five principles" (the duties and roles of lord, spouse, parent and child, elder brother, and friend) which centered on Confucian filial piety was the standard of social life throughout the Tokugawa period. It was in such a context that the literature of the time developed.

As Tokugawa society was a mixture of the medieval and modern worlds, so too was its literature. It was composed in part of the waning traditions represented by *waka* and the *monogatari,* the Nō theater and *kyōgen.* Another area was defined by the rise of Confucianism and the accompanying popularity of Chinese poetry and prose. Closely woven with these strands of the past was the new literature in the form of *haiku* and *senryū* poetry, the puppet theater (called *jōruri* or *bunraku*) and kabuki. These were distinctly modern creations which began at the end of the sixteenth century and reached maturity during

Tokugawa. There is also the Tokugawa novel which continued to influence even the novels of recent times. Critics during the Tokugawa period paid enormous respect to tradition and its products, counting as frivolous anything that was new. Traditional literary arts were thought to be indispensable to the proper development of human beings, and the new literature which existed outside of the traditional "way" and merely entertained or informed, was considered to be at best an adulterated art. However, the new literature was gradually recognized as embodying certain pragmatic values; and, of course, the lively spirit of the Tokugawa era is most evident in the new literature rather than in writing that was confined to traditional modes. It was the new literature that provided a vital image for the new age and which in the long run proved to be of greater social and aesthetic importance.

The two areas we have pointed to, the traditional and the new, have been misunderstood at times since they pertain not to a particular class or occupation in Tokugawa society but rather to what we might best indicate through the terms awareness and education, qualities which had come to bear little relationship to social class. One reason for this condition was that literature which had hitherto been circulated in manuscript could now be reproduced in printed form. On top of this new availability of literature, the success of public education supported by the *bakufu* and the *han* had made literacy general. Given the will to obtain them, books might be available to anyone; and the leisure which economic prosperity gave to the townsmen could be directed to appreciation of works of traditional literature, just as the aristocracy and the samurai might easily enjoy the new writing. It was a situation in which both the new and the old forms were enhanced. Since the early middle ages the identity of men of letters with a particular social class had gradually shifted toward the condition we find in Tokugawa, when relatively accessible education, taste and talent defined the literati. Within a short time book publishing as a business took on most of its modern qualities. Lending libraries also were common and Japan's literary heritage spread through the towns and countryside. In a while commoners, who before had not participated at all in the world of written literature, became not only its audience but also its creators. At that point also arose the distinction between traditional and new literature, "serious" or classical as against new and popular.

The Seventeenth Century to 1688

Tokugawa Ieyasu, through Confucian scholars such as Hayashi Razan (1583–1657), established the philosophy of Chu Hsi not only as the guiding principle of education and government but also as the rationale behind the society he envisioned, one closely resembling that of Sung dynasty China. Neo-Confucianism was a worldly system of thought capable of resisting those Buddhist influences which had become an obstacle to Ieyasu and his advisers. The study of Chu Hsi was quickly adopted in the various *han* or fiefdoms, and the success of this philosophy in the society as a whole is understandable when we consider that, compared with Buddhism, it was rationalistic, and that far from taking the Buddhist view of denying the phenomenal world, neo-Confucianism in its teachings completely affirmed the final reality of the immediate world. It simply did not lie within the resources of Buddhism then to revive the power and role of the intellect which had waned during the long period of wars. Such a force was felt, on the other hand, in the new and rationalistic Confucianism. Neo-Confucianism captured the allegiance of young intellectuals who felt that its teachings were morally sound and able to set right the disordered society. Samurai and the new townsmen class who became the leaders of the new period of peace in Japan put their faith in neo-Confucianism. Rationalism, affirmation of the phenomenal world, regard for ethical standards—these concerns were characteristic of the early feeling for enlightenment in the *bakufu* and were also qualities embodied in the literature of the time. In the area of religion progressive thinkers inclined toward rationalizing Buddhism and Shintō with Confucianism, and even conservatives who previously had criticized or rejected this idea bowed to the times and found merit in combining the three teachings.

Neo-Confucianism regarded the *tao* or ethics as its first principle and thought of literature as a means of transmitting the *tao*. While the philosophy differed basically from the outlook of medieval Buddhism, it nonetheless expressed a didactic view of literature, that literature should "foster virtue and reprove vice." The enlightened, utilitarian view of the early *bakufu* also held a view of the art to the effect that if literature had no practical function, then it was merely a pastime and amusement. However, both the *bakufu* and the *han* in their civil policies regarded literature, especially traditional literature, as a desirable refinement. The three qualities—the "refinement" of traditional literature, utilitarianism or literature that taught the reader a philosophy and entertainment—marked the horizons of the time, and these elements often appear side by side in a single work.

In the area of traditional literature the phoenix-like *waka* enjoyed renewed popularity. The Nijō school of *waka* which adhered to the style of the *Kokinshū* was continued in the late sixteenth century by Hosokawa Yūsai (1534–1610) who was almost alone in teaching the tradition among the nobility and the military families of the time. But the Nakanoin and Karasumaru families, among others, successively produced masters of poetry, and Emperors Gomizuno-o (r. 1611–29), Gosai (r. 1656–63), and Reigen (r. 1663–87) were interested patrons of the art. At the same time the poetry tradition represented by Matsunaga Teitoku (1571–1653) achieved a modest popularity, and through Teitoku's disciple Kitamura Kigin (1624–1705) reached the samurai families of Edo, then through Mochizuki Nagayoshi (1609–81) was adopted by important families in Ariga and Harima provinces and later was taken up by commoners of Kyōto. The Nijō school was later continued through such men as Mushanokōji Sanekage (1661–1738) and while the tradition eventually waned it did persist, as a name at least, throughout the Tokugawa period. During those centuries, however, highly formalized verse writing failed to produce lyrics with any spark of passion except in the work of Kinoshita Chōshōshi (1569–1649) who in his leisured life took up poetry and the newly popular shamisen. He was bound by no rules in his compositions and in his *waka* made free use of slang and coined words in an attempt at what might be called realism in song. These poems along with some excellent stylized prose in the old mode are preserved in his *Kyohakushū* (*Drinking Song Collection*) published in 1649. Chōshōshi was also the initiator of a group called the Hōhenkai, a club interested in literary criticism and influential in setting the new direction in Tokugawa literature.

For the Confucian scholars in Japan *kambun,* writing in Chinese, was indispensable, but for most people literary *kambun* and Chinese poetry were merely cultural ornaments, and as such judged to be of poor literary quality. The *waka* verse form was scarcely more creative. In poetry of recluses, represented by the Chinese writing in *Shimpen fushōshū* (*New Selection of Wastepaper*), published in 1676, by Ishikawa Jōzan (1583–1672), the Kyōto Confucianist, and the *Sōzanshū* (*Grass Mountain Collection*), 1674, by the priest Gensei, founder of the Zuikōji Nichiren temple, the best work of the period is present with humor and depth of feeling. That later critics found their writing in Chinese "primitive" is due to the consistently Japanese flavor of their writing apparent in the choice of graphs or vocabulary and in the failure to adhere to conventional poetry forms.

Humorous or "playful" linked verse called (*haikai no renga*) was written and collected before the Tokugawa period by Sōgi (1421–1502), Arakida no Moritake (1473–1549) and Yamazaki Sōkan (1464–1553). Such light and humorous verse, along with the "wild poems" (*kyōka*) or humorous poems in *tanka* form, and the short, light stories which were written down during the late sixteenth and early seventeenth centuries, became part of the literary life of the Kyōto region. Matsunaga Teitoku was one of the central figures in poetry of the time and he attracted a number of poets interested in *haikai* linked verse. One of the early public gatherings for composition in this mode was recorded at the Myōmanji temple, Kyōto, in 1629. A few years later, in 1633, Matsue Shigeyori (1602–80), a follower of Teitoku, published his *E'nokoshū* (*Puppy Collection*), and Nonoguchi Ryūho (1595–1669) published his *Haikai hokkuchō* (*Book of Haikai and Hokku*), a collection of seventeen-syllable verses, the *hokku* or initial verses of *renga*. Such works marked a new stage in the poetry of linked verse as it had developed during the middle ages and it seems that suddenly nearly all the poets in Japanese were writing *haikai*. In the *E'nokoshū* some 177 names appear, but twenty years later the number of authors appearing in the *Gyokukaishū* (*Jade Ocean Collection*) soared to 658. Teitoku himself was the center for this nation-wide interest in poetry and in 1651 published *Gosan* (*The Umbrella*), a handbook of instruction and vocabulary for the composition of *haikai*. This followed two exemplary anthologies of *haikai* published in 1643 through which Teitoku sought to give examples of the style of his school. The collections are *Aburakasu* (*Soybean Cakes*) and *Yodogawa* (*The Yodo River*). The poets known as The Seven Masters of Haikai came from the Teitoku circle and the *haikai* of Teitoku's school is known as *teimon haikai,* using the first element of Teitoku's name. His rules of composition generally followed the principles of *waka* and *renga,* although with a good deal of innovative freedom. Each verse, he advised, should include *haigon,* this being the term for words, especially from the colloquial language but including Chinese and Buddhist terms, which were not part of the vocabulary of *waka* and *renga.*

Haikai poetry, in contrast with the lyrical and elegant linked verse, dealt with humorous and worldly situations. Enlightened literary men praised *haikai* as a suitable introduction to *renga,* saying: "the form is deep in feeling and makes use of humor." That meant that the form was the same as *renga* but the content less serious and demanding. In this view *haikai* was valuable as an educational tool, an introduction to traditional literature, despite reflecting the liberality, humor, and even vulgarity of the new times. Pseudo-classicism was indeed part of Tokugawa culture and the adherence to a fixed vocabulary which combined colloquial and literary expressions was a hesitant first step into the complexities of linked verse. Still, the method was exceedingly popular and in the *hokku,* the initial seventeen-syllable verse, poets toyed with odd rhetorical flourishes through use of nearly meaningless *engo* (word association) and *kakekotoba* (pivot words). The crowd of poetasters created a flood of verses that were barely poor jokes, inspired by identical ideas and techniques, while those who passed for poetry masters battled for leadership of the *renga* groups, repeating their emotional arguments and making a grotesque spectacle of half-baked poetry. But publication of linked verse continued and *haikai* eventually showed some progress in the direction of mature literature. The later years of Shigeyori and Ryūho saw a qualitative change in *haikai* when these men began to advocate *haikai* of spiritual depth.

With the encouragement of poetry schools by the Nijō family, generations of poetry in the classical tradition going back to the *Man'yōshū,* the *Kokinshū,* and the *Shinkokinshū* continued their influence and authority. In prose the old *monogatari*—such works as *Ise monogatari* and *Genji monogatari*—found attentive readers and were frequently published along with interpretations and annotations. There was also a considerable audience for printed editions of *setsuwa* and other stories from the medieval period. Indeed, an appreciation of old literature and the classics was a prominent feature of the Tokugawa enlightenment, while at the same time a new literature was being created in prose works whose form was close to the novel. We should keep in mind that in early Tokugawa Japan the level of literacy was still not very high and even published writing did not circulate widely. There was considerable activity in entertainment based on literature and advances in general education through the medium of oral narration—with the best of this material ending up in written, printed form. There is thus a close resemblance between the oral literature of early Tokugawa, a literature with many of the qualities of the *setsuwa* or short tale, and the various prose forms popular during the middle ages.

The *Seisuishō* (*Sobering Laughter*) and *Kinō wa kyō no monogatari* (*The Tale of Yesterday Is Today*) edited by Anrakuan Sakuden (1554–1642), a monk of Kyōto, are typical of humorous stories originating in oral entertainment and later set down in writing. *Musha monogatari* (*Warrior Tales*), 1654 is representative of the various collections of anecdotes about medieval military figures chiefly from the sixteenth century. Mystery and ghost stories—told at night to the successive extinguishing of lamps—were recorded in anthologies like *Inga monogatari* (*Tales of Destiny*), published in 1661. *Taikōki* (*The Life of Hideyoshi*), a twenty-two volume work from 1626, and *Kōyō gunkan* (*A Military Mirror of Kai Province*), 1656, in twenty volumes, were outstanding works on political and military science. The Zen monk Suzuki Shōzō (1579–1655) wrote various popular tracts explaining the essentials of Buddhism. Many publications also remained medieval in style, such as *Kyomizu monogatari* (*The Tale of Kyomizu Temple*), a two-volume work, dated 1638, which argued the merits of Confucianism over Buddhism, and *Gion monogatari* (*The Tale of Gion Shrine*), a Buddhist rejoinder to *Kiyomizu,* published in 1640. Such works variously argued the merits of Shintō, Buddhism, and

Confucianism in the conduct of human affairs and were rather like sermons in their colloquial, question-and-answer form. In the area of general advice on manners and society, and following the essayistic and conversational style of *Tsurezuregusa,* were such works as *Kashōki (Laughable Notes),* 1642, and *Kuyamigusa (Seeds of Regret),* published in 1647. *Setsuwa* was renewed in the wave of Confucian studies which enveloped Japan and such works as *Kanninki (Notes on Forbearance),* a long volume dated 1659 by Asai Ryōi (d. 1691), and *Chie no kagami (Mirror of Wisdom),* 1660, borrowed heavily from the story collections of China and Korea.

The prose works we have mentioned belong to the genre known as *kanazōshi,* books written in one of the syllabaries (usually *hiragana* rather than *katakana*) and containing few Chinese graphs in the text. For that reason the books were easy to read and particularly suitable to their didactic purposes. The *kana* books were enthusiastically received by the audience for the new printed literature which, even though written in a simple style, offered a substantial flavor of traditional literary qualities. The *kanazōshi* were a long way from the modern idea of prose fiction or the novel, but they gradually accumulated elements which culminated in the type of fiction called *ukiyōzōshi,* stories of the "floating world" of urban life, which appeared at the beginning of the eighteenth century. Some of the *kanazōshi,* however, were close to the old or traditional novel form, the *monogatari.* The story known as *Uraminosuke,* after the name of its hero, is a tale of tragic love, dwelling on miracles performed by Shintō and Buddhist deities and taking up historical incidents involving the *kampaku* Toyotomi Hidetsugu. *Ōsaka monogatari (The Tale of Ōsaka),* in the style of the old war tales, tells of the destruction of Osaka castle. In those as in other *kanazōshi* successive editions of the stories alter the content somewhat to suit changing tastes in literature—that is, away from purely military matters and toward the area of romance. Another successful type of *kana* book was the parody. *Mottomo no sōshi (The Just Right Book)* was modeled on *Makura no sōshi; Nise monogatari (The Imitation Tale)* describes in droll fashion contemporary Japan using the mode of *Ise monogatari.* Another influential work was *Chikusai monogatari (The Tale of Chikusai)* which describes the travels and remarkable prescriptions of a quack doctor. A number of travel books were produced, known as *meishōki* or "notes to famous places," and they offered considerable cultural as well as geographic information—often, as did *Chikusai,* in fictionalized form. The prose works in *kana* all originated between 1624 and 1644, the years known as the Kan'ei period.

Authors of the *kanazōshi* included intellectuals from the privileged class, *haikai* masters who associated with the upper class, and Confucian scholars and polemicists who were especially concerned with changes in the new society and government. Suzuki Shōzō, mentioned earlier, was a priest and wrote from the Buddhist point of view. Asai Ryōi too, though at first a *rōnin* or masterless samurai, became a priest and Buddhist advocate, and one of the most active *kanazōshi* writers. Tsujihara Gempo, the translator (from the Chinese) of *Onna shisho* (*The Four Books for Women*), and Yamaoka Genrin (1631–72) are representative of writers who lectured on Confucian and Japanese classics. Because the authors of *kana* books above all were concerned with their own times, they nearly always found their subjects in the contemporary world and their ideas were immediate and up to date. Their styles too gradually broadened to include the modern colloquial language. In two works by Asai Ryōi, *Otogiboko* (*Companion Maid*), written in 1664, and *Ukiyō monogatari* (*Tale of the Floating World*), about 1670, the *kanazōshi* reached their height with new and old elements successfully blended, and clearly anticipated the new style in fiction the *ukiyozōshi* which grew rapidly during the last decade of the century.

After the century of disruptive warfare which ended the middle ages in Japan, it is hardly surprising to find a great part of the renaissance of Tokugawa appearing in the world of entertainment. Every kind of eroticism flourished in the pleasure districts, and the song and dance performances called kabuki (meaning "frolic") reached all over Japan by way of traveling companies, such as the one led by the woman known as Izumo no Okuni. Their performances brought together various popular entertainments from the preceding centuries, combining and developing elements freely and often erotically. Women's kabuki of the kind offered by the Okuni troupe was banned in 1629 as a threat to public morals, and in 1652 its successor, the young men's kabuki, was prohibited on the same grounds. The third form of kabuki, which continues to the present, appeared in 1654 when only grown men were allowed to appear on the stage. In effect, the various government proscriptions against lewd stage performances encouraged kabuki to develop from a crude show to mature theater. In the three major cities, Ōsaka, Kyōto, and Edo, regular and permanent theaters appeared and kabuki developed its own music and, of course, found female impersonators for women's roles.

The literature of kabuki developed from skits or improvization to fixed dialogue with dramatic form. A significant phase in its growth was the conversion of earlier song and dance pieces, on the general theme of the meetings and partings of men and women, to "Shimabara numbers" which dramatized the customers' meetings with women in the Shimabara pleasure district. The plays were certainly lascivious and were prohibited in 1658, although erotic performances were not limited to plays dealing with Shimabara. Ways were sought to attract audiences without incurring government censorship and one important source of lyricism as well as humor was found in the old *yōkyoku* or Nō, including, of course, the *kyōgen* comic interludes. Thus in the earliest available texts of kabuki plays the *yōkyoku* element is quite conspicuous (in *Takayasu,* for example), and in *kyōgen* influence from such plays as *Shimbochi taiko* (*The New Drum*) and *Busshari* (*Bones of the Buddha*) is evident. Various dances were added to the plays and the contents were modernized. Further, the *kyōgen* tradition of realistic performance and the *yōkyoku* specialty of pantomine and gesture were each adapted in unique ways by kabuki. The shift from skit to drama was also closely linked with *jōruri,* the puppet theater, which competed with kabuki and from which kabuki borrowed many of its long dramatic plays. One often finds kabuki and *jōruri* plays with identical titles. Out of the combinations of the three sources, Nō, *kyōgen,* and *jōruri,* the one act *kyōgen*-kabuki grew to two and more acts in the next period of its development.

Dramatic recitation known as *jōruri* developed during the middle ages and acquired its own repertory in such pieces as *Jūnidan zōshi* (*The Twelve Part Story*). The emergence of this art as half of the modern theater of Tokugawa was due to its adoption of the singularly expressive and newly imported samisen (from China via the Ryūkyū Islands) as musical accompaniment and the combination of recitation with puppets (known as *ebisukaki* or *ayatsuri ningyō*). In its early form the recitation embodied qualities of ballads, prose literature, and the theater, but with various new additions to the story telling the theatrical element became most prominent.

The independent literature of *jōruri* recitation was not large and the art began by bringing together *bukyoku* (dance pieces) and the medieval novellas, the *otogizōshi*. Among the early reciters was one of particular renown during the first decades of the seventeenth century, the man known as Sugiyama Tango-no-jō, who performed before the shogun and was awarded official rank for his work. Slightly apart from the main stream of *jōruri* were plays on Buddhist themes, sermon plays (*sekkyō jōruri* or *sekkyō bushi*), which drew on *setsuwa* literature and told of religious miracles that took place in Japan. The story of Shuntokumaru, the tragically afflicted youth of the Nō play *Yorobōshi* (*The Stumbling Boy*) is one of the sermon plays. The puppet theater of the early decades of the century found in such stories the basic elements for its development, adding spectacle by way of the puppets to stories that were already a delight to the ear. By the middle of the seventeenth century reciters, or *tayū* as they were known, were performing essentially new works—even though the basic materials of their stories might be borrowed—refined to a higher level of theatrical presentation. Further, completely new plays also began to appear. Among the reciters of the time was the man known as Sakurai Tanba-no-jō who performed plays called *kimpira* pieces by Oka Seibei (d. 1689) and other playwrights. These *kimpira* plays dramatize the superhuman feats of the stalwart and righteous warrior sons of four ancient military heroes, the greatest of whom was Kimpira (known in legend as the son of Sakata no Kintoki, late Heian period). Such fictionalized history was criticized as nonsense, but the plays which began in Edo achieved popularity also in western Japan, the Kyōto-Ōsaka region, and with the *kimpira* plays began truly theatrical productions of *jōruri*. Emotionally charged love dramas were created in the Kyōto-Ōsaka theaters, recited by famous *tayū* such as Yamato Tosa-no-jō (dates unknown) and Inoue Harima-no-jō (1632–85). Considerable refinement was made in the literature of the new plays and in expressive manipulation of the puppets. The glory of the old *jōruri* probably reached its greatest height just after 1673 with the appearance of the famous *tayū* Uji Kaganojō (1635–1711). In Kaga-no-jō's words, "The voice of Nō and *kyōgen* is the father of *jōruri,* and the style of the *sōshi* is its mother." He was noted for the elegance of his recitation and initiated publication of *jōruri* texts in books called *marubon,* complete with musical directions. Doubtless the language of the plays was heightened through the influence of Nō, and it is said that Chikamatsu Monzaemon (1653–1724) wrote for Kaga-no-jō. In any case, Kaga-no-jō provided the foundation for the elaboration of *jōruri* achieved by Chikamatsu and the reciter he worked most closely with, the famous Takemoto Gidayū (1651–1714) of Ōsaka.

The Genroku Era: 1688–1703

The Genroku years saw the flowering of the creative developments in Japan which first emerged during the vital years of the early Tokugawa government. The continuing decades of peace brought real economic power to the townsmen and the circumstances that produced the rise of the *chōnin* or townsmen class lent a new tone of exuberance to the whole of Japanese society. The literature of Genroku, whether composed in Japanese or Chinese, for a popular audience or one erudite and refined, reached a breadth and intensity that truly expressed the spirit of the age. Part of this spirit, which grew out of the early *bakufu,* was due to what we may term the affirmation of reality, the somewhat abstract speculations of the early Tokugawa Neo-Confucianists turned into practical and personal philosophies, for example, the study of the philosophy of Wang Yang-ming (*yōmeigaku*) taught by Nakae Tōju (1608–48) and Kumazawa Banzan (1619–91) and the reinterpretation of Confucius by Itō Jinsai (1627–1705) under the name of *kogigaku* (study of the ancient meanings). Historical studies flourished in academic circles and brought new appreciation and affirmation of human nature as opposed to some ideal view of man—one result being critical writing opposed to philosophies which denied man the central place in his world. Writers were able to take themselves as a starting point and the whole literary outlook underwent a transformation.

The ideas on literature of Itō Jinsai and his followers were directly opposed to the moral theories of the Neo-Confucianists. Itō maintained that literature simply told of feelings and emotions which were the basic materials of human existence, and that these emotions were common to all men of whatever time or place. Since literature was the expression of human emotions, its first obligation was to state them truthfully. To that end a plain and direct expression of the world just as it is was preferable to elaborate embroidery of reality. That, then, was the theoretical foundation of the literature of the Genroku years, and this outlook extended through the views of such scholars of Japanese classical literature and culture as Keichū (1640–1701), who felt that in *waka* and in *monogatari* the important thing was to include the writer's fleeting emotions expressed just as they came from the heart. But, he added, outstanding works of literature provide their own justification or rationale.

What emerged from the work of such scholars as Itō and Keichū was further support for the idea held by Genroku writers that human existence itself was the reason for literature. Looked at in broadest terms, the idea of literature as a study, a discipline or art (expressed by the word *michi* meaning "Way") remained unchanged since its emergence in the middle ages. But the great transformation of Genroku was in the affirmation of human emotion as the primary source of literature and in stressing the importance of common, everyday subjects. Human feeling and sympathy, expressed in the word *jinsei,* is extensively examined by Chikamatsu and the poet Bashō. As used by them, the term expresses a good deal of what is meant by "humanism." The mood of the Genroku years was generous and its manners were sumptuous, if not extravagant, with pride assuming a new role in *chōnin* life. The amusement districts of the cities were open to all and critical guides to the gay quarters or brothel districts had been published even before Genroku. The gay quarters along with the theaters —which some considered equally opprobrious—prospered greatly in that era.

In poetry circles too new ideas and approaches grew from the work of scholars working in Japanese literature, a field covered by the term National Studies or Japanese Studies (*kokugaku* or *wagaku*). Shimokōbe Chōryū (1624–88), a disciple of the poet Kinoshita

Chōshōshi (1569–1649), was an Ōsaka *chōnin* turned scholar and specialist in the *Man'yōshū*. Among his works are two anthologies of poems by commoner poets who, following Matsunaga Teitoku and Hosokawa Yūsai, sought to continue in the Nijō tradition based on the *Kokinshū*. Chōryū published those neoclassical poets in *Rin'yō ruijinshū* (*The Rubbish Leaves Collection*), 1670, and in *Heisui wakashū* (*Pond Plants and Water Collection*), 1678. The *Rin'yō ruijushū* contained some 1300 *waka* by poets of the *jigeha* or "underground school." Other men in western Japan were active in similar work and in Edo the National Studies movement was advanced by Toda Mosui (1629–1706) who based his work on a scientific or philological approach, criticizing the theorists of the Nijō school and their claims regarding the *Kokinshū*. Toda edited a collection of new *waka* in 1702 with the title *Tori no ato* (*Birds' Footprints*) and offered the opinion that "Even for humble people there was no obstacle to undertaking the art of poetry." The *kokugaku* scholar and poet known as Keichū (1640–1701) undertook careful textual analysis of the *Man'yōshū* and other works, correcting many errors in older studies, and published the results in his *Waji shōranshō* (*Notes and Corrections to the Syllabary*) which exposed errors in Fujiwara no Teika's interpretation of ancient *kana* usage and gave a shock to poetry circles which had made a near saint of Teika.

Despite the advanced and liberal views of such men in matters of *waka* poetry, actual compositions reflect little influence from the world of Genroku and can scarcely be compared to the brilliance achieved in other areas of literature; for *waka*, tradition proved to be exceptionally strong rooted. In the field of poetry in Chinese, Kinoshita Jun'an (1621–98) brought new life to T'ang styles and Murakami Tōsen (1624–1705) developed a style in regulated verse form. Teachers of Chinese poetry also appeared in Genroku—Kasawara Kyōun, for example—but their influence was not felt until a later period.

The pretentiousness and forced humor that accompanied the full development and popularity of Teitoku's style of *haikai* led some poets of the school to abandon the style. But the pivot for change and new direction in the world of *haikai* of the mid-seventeenth century was Nishiyama Sōin (1605–82), a pupil of Satomura Shōtaku (d. 1636). Sōin first achieved prominence as a poetry master in the *renga* salon of the Temman Shrine in Ōsaka where his genius, wit, and breadth of spirit—obvious in such works as *Sōin senku* (*A Thousand Verses by Sōin*), 1673, and *Sōin gohyakuin* (*Five Hundred Poems by Sōin*), 1676—attracted many young avant-garde poets. His pupils included the novelist Ihara Saikaku (1642–93) and Okanishi Ichū (1633–1711), a student of ancient Japanese literature. Both of those men were among the nine poets who contributed to the *Ōsaka doku-*

ginshū (*Anthology of Ōsaka Poets*), a two-volume collection with commentary by Sōin, dated 1675. The poets who looked to Sōin as their mentor made up what is known as the Danrin school. Tashiro Shōi (dates unknown) and other poets of Edo about that time formed a Danrin group and produced *Danrin toppyakuin* (*A Thousand Danrin Poems*), published in 1675. In Kyōto the poet Sugenoya Takamasa (fl. ca. 1665) also joined the new style. Despite severe criticism from the Teimon poets, the Danrin school, between 1660 and 1680, achieved total dominance of the *haikai* scene. Sōin and Ichū, borrowing from the Chinese philosopher Chuang-tzu, taught their view of *haikai* through parables. Teimon critics of Danrin pointed out that the really distinguishing element in the school was "modernism" combined with considerable permissiveness in technique. This "vulgar modernism," as it was called, became prominent during the Genroku period and the accusations seem to refer to use of subject matter taken from contemporary life. "Vulgarity" meant the abandonment of the severe classicism of the Teimon and movement toward a more popular quality which was not distressed by inelegant subject matter. *Haikai* not only broke out of limitations on content; its "popular" quality was embodied in the use of *haigon* or "*haikai* language," which meant colloquial language and words of Chinese origin. Critics accused *haikai* of "debauchery," a charge not limited to poetry of the seventeenth century; by this was meant a fondness for change and novelty. "Permissiveness" or "lawlessness" were also objections raised by the Teimon against Danrin poets; the accusation there pointing to disregard of the inflexible rules of Teimon *haikai* composition. Within their own rules of composition Danrin poets produced a number of new techniques: *nukefū* was the method of indicating the subject of the poem only by inference, carefully omitting it from an obvious place in the verse; *hiyu* and *mitate* were a free use of metaphor and simile; *iikake* and *kochō* indicate use of double meaning and exaggeration. Such devices became part of Danrin style *renga* as well as *hokku,* seventeen-syllable independent verses. The seventeen and fourteen syllables of *renga* and *hokku* lines were cramped forms in which the spirit of the times somehow had to be accommodated. The importance of humor in *haikai* is one reflection of the energetic mood. Another is the speed composition contests called *yakazu haikai* (arrow-shot verses). With the speed contests in poetry considerations of taste were abandoned, a mess was made of poetic measure, and the whole ended not with creation but as exercise in demolition. The Danrin poetic movement may perhaps be considered as part of the birth trauma through which the superficial humor of the Teimon was left behind for the new poetic world of inner elegance created by Matsuo Bashō (1644–94). Yet even in his later years Bashō could speak in praise of the style: "If Sōin had not worked before me, then my *haikai* would still be licking after the drivel of old man Teitoku."

The extremes of the later Danrin writing caused some poets of the school to reconsider their position, and under the influence of poetry in Chinese some qualitative improvement began to be felt. Renascent Japanese poetry turned to the pursuit of meaning and spiritual depth, and one of the poets who contributed much to the change of mood, Kamijima Onitsura (1661–1738) struck the major chord, saying, "Outside of truth and sincerity there is no *haikai*." Onitsura's ideas were set out in full in a work of 1718 called *Hitorigoto* (*Soliloquies;* the same title was used by the poet Shinkei, 1406–75).

As a young man Matsuo Bashō composed *haikai* under Teimon direction, but at age twenty-eight he decided to make poetry his life's work and, moving to Edo, he devoted himself to the style of Sōin. As a Danrin poet Bashō quickly found that his sympathies were with the reform movement. In the 1683 anthology *Minashiguri* (*Hollow Chestnuts*), Bashō, along with Enomoto Kikaku (1661–1707) and other poets, attempted to reaffirm the poetic qualities of *haikai* through the study of Chinese poetry and by drawing on the style and spirit of ancient Japanese poets. In autumn of the following year, Bashō began the walking trip which produced *Nozarashi kikō* (*Weathering Journey*), visiting his home in Ueno of Iga province. While in the city of Nagoya with Yamamoto Kakei (1648–1716) and other poets, Bashō began a new direction in his own work. Poems of that meeting are collected in *Fuyu no hi* (*A Winter Day*) which was edited by Kakei and was the first of the *Haikai shichibushū* (*Seven Collections of Haikai*), the collected works of Bashō and his school. In Kyōto, Bashō was joined by his close friend Mukai Kyorai (1651–1704) and it is to Kyorai that we owe our knowledge of Bashō's teachings from the *Kyorai shō* (*Notes by Kyorai*) published in 1775. While living on the south shore of Lake Biwa, Bashō attracted students and disciples who remained in that place while Bashō himself returned to Edo. The collection *Kawazu awase* (*Frog Verses*), published in 1686, presents all the important poets of Bashō's circle: Kikaku and Kyorai, Sugiyama Sampū (1647–1732), Hattori Ransetsu (1654–1707), Iwanami Sora (1649–1710) and so forth. The theme of the poems was frogs and in the book Bashō's famous *haiku: Furuike ya/kawazu tobikomu/mizu no oto* (The old pond/frog jumps in/sound of water) first appeared. In the autumn of 1687 Bashō made another long trip through western Japan, collecting and writing the material which became *Oi no kobumi* (*Traveler's Notebook*).

His return to Edo in company with Kakei and Ochi Etsujin (1656–1739), one of his early disciples, took Bashō through Nagoya to Sarashina in Nagano Prefecture, a place famous as a site for moon-viewing, then to Zenkōji and Asama. That journey became the subject of Bashō's *Sarashina kikō* (*Sarashina Journey*). His most famous literary journey was begun in 1689, the second year of Genroku. In company with Iwanami Sora (1649–1710), Bashō toured the northern part of the island of Honshū, leaving his impressions in *Oku no hosomichi* (*The Narrow Road of Oku*). Altogether the travel writings occupy less than one hundred pages in printed texts. The trip to Oku also resulted in a book on poetry composition, *Yamanaka mondō* (*The Yamanaka Dialogue*), a collection of students' questions and Bashō's answers set down by Tachibana Hokushi (d. 1718). It is a basic text of Bashō's poetic theory. The trip ended in western Japan with a pilgrimage to Ise Shrine. While staying at that time in the Kyōto-Wakayama area Bashō visited Hattori Tohō (1657–1730) and other poets.

In 1690 the fourth volume of *Haikai shichibushū* was published. It was the anthology called *Hisago* (*Gourd*) and edited by Hamada Chinseki (d. 1737). The summer of 1690 found Bashō living on the south shore of Lake Biwa, at Mount Kokubu near Ōtsu, and there he wrote the essays of *Genjūan no ki* (*Notes From an Unreal Dwelling*). In his later years Bashō devoted his energies to the elegant form of mixed prose and poetry called *haibun* in which the prose serves as background and transition for the poems. The *haibun* of Bashō and his disciples was eventually collected in such works as *Honchō bunsen* (*Selections of Japanese Prose*), 1706, by Morikawa Kyoroku (1656–1715), one of Bashō's later disciples. Bashō was joined at that time by Kagami Shikō (1665–1731) and Naitō Jōsō (1662–1704), a Zen Buddhist monk who, after the poet's death, lived out his life in prayer near Bashō's memorial. The trip to Oku gave Bashō many new ideas which he planned to embody in a collection of poetry. He worked on it while living in Saga, on the western edge of Kyōto; the outcome, edited by Kyorai and Nozawa Bonchō (d. 1714) was *Sarumino* (*The Monkey's Straw Raincoat*), completed in 1691. It is the fifth collection of the Bashō school and was the most representative and influential—termed the *Shinkokinshū* of the *haikai* world. Bashō returned to Edo in 1692, accompanied at his Fukugawa cottage by several poets and his new disciple Kyoroku.

While Bashō condemned popular writing he nonetheless strove for the light spirit in poetry exemplified by the collection of his later work called *Sumidawara* (*Charcoal Bag*) which includes poems by Shida Yaha (1662–1740) and others. In 1694 Bashō made his last journey to the western regions. He died at an inn in the city of Ōsaka that November, surrounded by many of the disciples he had acquired in a lifetime dedicated to poetry.

Bashō's approach to poetry called for warmth as well as cool detachment, along with a profound self knowledge by the poet. What we know of the details of Bashō's theories comes not from Bashō himself but rather from notes taken by his disciples, since the master left no systematic treatise of his ideas. He seemed to regard the essence of *haikai* as refinement and truth. Bashō's concept of truth (*makoto*) rested on the abandonment of the self, the ego, one's personal sentiment and bias. Then, as regards the rest of humanity, it implied a realization of compassion and understanding. Concerning the world of nature and things, Bashō's ideal was to grasp the essential quality or essence of reality as understood in Zen Buddhism. The power to reach this goal of understanding lies within a child as it lies within the naive and receptive mind. The poet grows in awareness as he brings this way of looking at the natural world to his perception of humanity and discovers the deepest motives of human life. In the final analysis the truth that Bashō sought was humanistic and based on his commitment to humanity as the basic value of existence. This concept is, of course, a major theme in the literature of the Genroku period. Given such a spiritual outlook the consequence was affirmation of all human activity and all things of the natural world. The themes of poetry might then be found anywhere, even in those areas considered to be vulgar and therefore neglected in traditional literature. By refinement or elegance in poetry Bashō pointed to the quality that is also present in all classical literature, even while he was exceedingly critical of poetry masters and classical writers. In order to better understand the writing of the past, Bashō traveled all over Japan to the places famous in poetry, directly experiencing the sights mentioned in ancient poems and the inspiration of the poets. Clearly Bashō was concerned with the heart more than external things and he expressed also his concern for suggestiveness in writing with the words: "After everything is said there is still something that eludes words." This statement may be taken as rationalizing the extreme brevity of the *haikai* or *haiku,* but the transcendentalism implicit in Bashō's views also has strong roots going back to the early middle ages in Japan. Our interpretation of Bashō's writing must recognize the presence of the traditional spirit of Japanese literature along with the modernity of Genroku, for the two are quite mixed together. As though he himself felt a contradiction between the two forces, Bashō described a theory of immutability and popularity, or permanence and change, in literature. The immutable side embodied refinement or high poetic sensitivity and truth; together the two gave a work the permanence or durability to transcend any particular historical time. And yet, Bashō said: "Freshness, newness—these are the flower of *haikai.*" Perhaps this quality of novelty was really achieved through the discovery of "truth" which naturally led to popularity. Refinement and truth then, like durability and popularity, are seen as two aspects of the same thing. "There are no venerable and ancient poets in *haikai*," said Bashō, and this meant, of course, that modern poets could become the old masters of the new form.

In great part the beauty of *haikai* is intellectual, in its wit and in its critical stance—in contrast to the emotional and lyrical center of *renga*, linked verse. Certainly Teimon and Danrin poetry went too far in the intellectual direction, and Bashō's work substituted a spirit of natural grace and elegance for the critical, analytical stance of early *haikai*. At the same time his advice that the poet internalize his subject, structure it within his own mental framework, was a movement toward emotionalism and lyricism. With Bashō, *haikai* thus became lyrical poetry written with a perception for craft. Elements which contributed to this refinement were *sabi, shiori,* and *hosomi,* the same qualities recognized in *renga* and other poetry. *Sabi* may be described as an austere and elegant simplicity tinged with melancholy or loneliness; *shiori* is a feeling of pathetic charm; *hosomi* is a feeling for and expression of the delicacy and fragility of things. To incorporate this aesthetic into *haikai,* Bashō developed his theory of truth and symbolic rendering which stressed suggestiveness in the poem. The suggestiveness was described by such terms as *nioi* (fragrance), *hibiki* (echoing; emotional harmony and overtone), and *utsuri* (calculated transition in mood from verse to verse). Bashō seems to have achieved his mature aesthetic outlook about the time of *Sarumino* in 1691, but later he stressed two ideas in particular: return to the everyday world of life after a poet has achieved enlightenment or satori; a seeming naivete or lightness (*karumi*). The concept of lightness meant direct and lucid expression in *haikai,* avoiding the saccharine and contrived quality of the poetaster; it was a technique based on reason and design.

We can scarcely construct a complete poetics from the little in the way of theory that Bashō left to his disciples, but from what we have it is evident that Bashō himself was always conscious of the strength of Japanese poetic tradition, while at the same time being a great innovator. Perhaps for these reasons we find in him a major voice in the movement from medievalism to the emerging modern world.

Ihara Saikaku (1642–93) made his literary debut as a *haikai* poet of the Danrin school. His first work of fiction was *Kōshoku ichidai otoko* (*The Life of an Amorous Man*), published in 1682. Some aspects of the work are reminiscent of old *monogatari,* such as *Genji* and *Ise,* but its distinction lies in the daring with which it presents the erotic life of the age. Rather than the idealized characters of the *monogatari* world, Saikaku's figures are realistically and concretely drawn, as were the critiques of the gay quarters and their inhabitants that appeared earlier in the century. But Saikaku's work, going far beyond the colloquial sentence style which developed in the *kanazōshi,* achieved a high style in contemporary language with the added rhetorical flourishes of *haikai.* Characters in his stories have a new spirit, exuberant and urbane. The style, mood, and materials of Saikaku's writing combine features which developed separately in the *kanazōshi* and which Saikaku combined to produce the first approach to the novel in Japan's modern period. Following the popular success of *Kōshoku ichidai otoko,* Saikaku explored various aspects of eroticism in such works as *Kōshoku gonin onna (Five Amorous Women),* 1686; *Kōshoku ichidai onna (The Life of an Amorous Woman),* 1686; and *Danshoku ōkagami (The Great Mirror of Manly Love),* 1687. His early works were uncomplicated stories of love and lust, but he soon broadened his view to ethical and moral questions, and eventually examined the unhappiness which was a part of the rake's life. We find the next theme of Saikaku's writing anticipated in the early works as he turned to moral problems and produced a group of didactic stories and stories of military men, such as one might expect from the *kanazōshi* genre. In 1686 he published *Honchō nijū fukō (Twenty Breaches of Filial Piety)* in which he drew the lives and foibles of persons who had not honored their parents. The following year he produced *Budō denraiki (Traditions of the Samurai)* and in 1688 *Buke giri monogatari (Tales of Military Duty),* both were concerned with obligations entailed in vendettas and in the homosexual love affairs of the samurai. A third direction in Saikaku's prose, and one which was perhaps a natural outgrowth of his background as an Ōsaka townsman, is found in *Nihon eitaigura (The Eternal Storehouse of Japan),* the first of his "townsmen pieces" (*chōnin mono*), dated 1688. It was a collection of stories on ways of gaining and keeping money, but we should note that this theme had been explored earlier in the *kanazōshi.* His next works were *Honchō chōnin kagami (The Mirror of Townsmen of Japan)* and *Yo no hitogokoro (The Character of Modern People)* which are the first and second parts of *Saikaku oridome (The Last Scraps of Saikaku).* In these collections human character and motives were the central concern and remained so throughout the rest of his writing. In *Seken mune zanyō (This Scheming World),* published in 1692, close to the end of his life, Saikaku's perception of the variegated world of man is fully revealed, while in *Saikaku okimiyage (Saikaku's Parting Present),* published in 1693, we have perhaps the best of his work, depicting the range and complexities of emotion in men who ruined their lives in the gay quarter.

From the middle years of his writing onward Saikaku wrote in a variety of modes. Among his later works are: *Saikaku shokoku banashi (Saikaku's Tales of the Provinces),* 1685, a collection of stories about strange events; *Honchō ōin hiji (Cases in the Shade of the Cherry*

Tree), 1689, a collection of forty-four short stories based on a Chinese collection of the Sung Period and dealing with incidents of bribery and graft; *Shinkashōki* (*The New Laughable Tale*), 1688, the title of which derived from the *kanazōshi* by Joraishi but in content being twenty-six stories of the *setsuwa* type dealing with the life of the warrior. Besides those works either certainly or traditionally attributed to Saikaku we have collections of erotic stories (*kōshoku mono*) for which Saikaku wrote the introduction, with the stories themselves probably being the work of his disciples. A number of tales bearing the master's signature were published after Saikaku's death. Probably best regarded as the work of Saikaku's disciples, they were edited by Hōjō Dansui (1663–1711), a poet and disciple of Saikaku in the *ukiyōzōshi* genre. Among the posthumous works is *Yorozu no fumi hogo* (*Myriad Scraps of Old Letters*), 1696, which was sketches in epistolary form describing town life of the Genroku period; and *Saikaku nagori no tomo* (*Momentos of Saikaku*), a collection of anecdotes about *haikai* poets, published in 1699.

As we have indicated, Saikaku's writing offers a freshness that grew out of the vigor of Genroku, but the structure of his prose still owed much to *setsuwa* of the middle ages and did not abandon certain didactic qualities of *kanazōshi* literature—a quality which, along with gossip-as-entertainment, probably contributed to his popularity. A skilled writer of fiction and a master of realistic, vivid description and reporting, Saikaku could probe the mind of the society around him with an acuteness that surely made his didacticism palatable. Indeed, Saikaku's "entertainments" were close to high literary art. From the first, in *Kōshoku ichidai otoko,* Saikaku shows himself to be a writer conscious of traditional literature as well as the new direction which his own work was taking. He is critical of lives spent in the satisfaction of lusts, whether erotic or pecuniary, and he is obviously skeptical of religion and traditional ethics in their ability to influence behavior. He seems to have reached the belief that man's life is determined by the society in which he lives. As was befitting to a man of his time in Japan, Saikaku was also a humanist, believing that man's nature itself was adequate foundation for faith.

The mode which began with Saikaku is now known as *ukiyozōshi,* "stories of the floating world," (*ukiyo* being the Buddhist term meaning the present, transient existence which later became the epithet of the world of pleasure). The *ukiyōzōshi* genre thus begins with *Ichidai otoko* and, following the successes of Saikaku, many writers in the genre appeared among the *kana* book writers and *haikai* poets of the Kyōto-Ōsaka region. Erotic pieces close to the *kōshoku mono* of Saikaku appeared throughout the Genroku period, such books as *Kōshoku sandai otoko* (*The Life of an Amorous Man: Third Generation*), 1686, by the Kyōto writer Nishimura Ichirōemon, and *Kōshoku tabi nikki* (*Diary of an Amorous Journey*), 1687, presumed to be by the Ōsaka *haikai* poet Kataoka Shijo. Other excellent works in that mode were *Kōshoku mankintan* (*The Medicine of Love*) from 1694, and *Kōshoku ubuge* (*Downy Hair of Love*) published in Genroku. After Saikaku's death signed works by recognized authors—in contrast to the house writers of publishers like Hachimonjiya, the "Figure Eight Shop"—appeared more frequently. There were new works from writers, such as Dansui, who produced samurai stories, and Getsujindō, who wrote stories of the *chōnin* or townsmen, but while Saikaku's style affected all those who followed him, few exhibited his perception or skill.

The exuberance of Genroku touched all the arts of the capital and produced a new style of genre picture called *ukiyoe* or pictures of the floating world. The illustrations and designs of Hishikawa Moronobu (d. 1694) had long been popular, and *Ichidai otoko* quickly appeared in an Edo edition illustrated by Moronobu. The production of romantic, erotic stories continued, written and sometimes illustrated by such men as Ishikawa Tomonobu, Tateba Fukaku (1662–1753) and Tōrindō Chōmaro. Their work has the grace as well as the naivete of the *kanazōshi,* but the writing is overshadowed by the superb illustrations of those *ukiyoe* artists working in the tradition begun by Moronobu.

An interesting development of the early eighteenth century is the emergence of the long *ukiyozōshi,* in contrast to the short works of Saikaku which were close to *setsuwa* in size. The new writing took two forms: one, an imitation of the old *monogatari;* the other, long stories patterned on *kanazōshi.* Within the old form the Ōsaka writer Nishizawa Ippū (1665–1731) adapted the *Gikeiki* and *Heike monogatari* in works entitled *Fūryū gozen gikeiki* (*The Elegant Gikeiki*) in 1700 and *Fūryū ima heike* (*The Elegant Heike of Today*) in 1702. Both stories detailed lives of dissipation. Long stories on the other hand are related to the *kanazōshi* and the first example of that type is *Genroku soga monogatari* (*A Modern Tale of Soga*), published in 1702 by Miyako no Nishiki, a young, amateur writer who had earlier published erotic parodies of the *Kojiki* and *Genji monogatari.* The story was based on a vendetta slaying that had taken place barely three months earlier. Following that work there appeared such tales as *Karanashi daimon yashiki* (*The Great Portaled Mansion of the Chinese Quince*), published in 1705, a complicated story of wealth and intrigue extending over several generations from the time of Hideyoshi. Another in the style of *ukiyozōshi* which were based on incidents close to the time of writing was *Kyōnui kusari katabira* (*A Kyoto-Sewn Garment of Chain*), a story of a woman's vengeance, by Morimoto Tōchō. That work was published in 1706, the same year as another version of the Kyōto feud which provided material for the story called *Kumagaya onna amigasa* (*Lady of the Great Woven Hat*). However, neither the *monogatari* nor the extended *ukiyozōshi* developed further at that time, with the latter, as we have indicated, remaining tied closely to reportage.

The kabuki theater reached a high degree of development in the Genroku period and that achievement was closely related to the performance of linked *kyōgen* plays (*tsuzuki kyōgen*) dating from 1664 in both eastern and western Japan. The emergence of modern kabuki required some decades, but throughout the early years of Genroku the linking together of comic skits into long plays brought quite new qualities to the world of the theater. One innovation was the appearance of writers who specialized in the new-style plays (in contrast to the earlier *kyōgen* which were written as a side-line when they were recorded at all). Of the semi-specialists, one example is Ichikawa Danjūrō (1660–1704), an author and actor. The specialists begin with men like Tominaga Heibē (b. 1640), who was listed as the "*kyōgen* writer" on a theater program of 1676, and Chikamatsu Monzaemon (1653–1724), who gained fame writing for the puppet theater of Ōsaka. Another development in the new theater, especially in western Japan, was the intense realism of the staging. Further, since the live theater borrowed heavily from the puppet theater there was considerable competitive pressure for kabuki to create a distinctive and interesting style of its own—evidenced by the appearance of writers who specialized in one type of play, such as Danjūrō in martial plays, or Sakata Tōjūrō (1647–1709) in sentimental dramas. The quality of acting also improved as actors began to specialize in their roles. The physical theaters along with their orchestras improved considerably and many books were published on the subject of kabuki—a good indication of the degree of its popularity. The actor critique books (*yakusha hyōbanki*) now focused on the quality of the performances rather than the physical attractions of the actors. In 1699 the Hachimonjiya publishing house of Kyōto brought out *Yakusha kuchi samisen* (*The Versatile Actor*) by Ejima Kiseki. Through successive editions that work remained the standard of actor critiques for two centuries, devoting one volume to each of the three major cities—Kyōto, Ōsaka, and Edo —and under the names of the actors listed presenting comments on their work.

The kabuki theater customarily staged five plays in one day— after the pattern of Nō—with the principal offering being a period piece or historical play (*jidaimono*); realistic dramas of contemporary life (*sewamono*) were also staged, depicting scandals, vengeance, and love suicides, and offering those as "separate plays" (*hanare kyōgen*) in contrast to the "linked plays." The librettos were published as "illustrated *kyōgen*" and provide us with at least the general outlines of the Genroku theater if not the details of performance. In linked *kyōgen* many plays of the old *jōruri* tradition were retained: tales of strife and disturbances in the households of daimyo and persons of power; tales of miraculous happenings; and stories of Minamoto no Yoshitsune or the Soga brothers. The miracle plays were the standard opening in a day's presentation, and for all plays the invariable setting was one of the well known gay quarters presented in realistic staging. The later kabuki theater found fault with those performances for being fantastic and anachronistic, but obviously those qualities in some degree were vital to Genroku kabuki, and in all plays there was a liberal admixture of the manners and life of Genroku. The daimyo tales were quite popular and gave the actors a fine chance to show their skills. Among the popular productions were *Butsumo mayasan kaichō* (*The Sacred Relic of Mt. Maya*), first performed in Kyōto in 1693 and starring Sakata Tōjūrō; *Keisei hotoke no hara* (*A Courtesan's Field of Buddha*), first performed in Kyōto in 1699; and *Keisei mibu dainenbutsu* (*A Courtesan's Great Prayer at Mibu*), first staged in Kyōto in 1702. They were all by Chikamatsu Monzaemon and dealt with strife among the powerful families of the day. The plot or structure of those plays was not their strong point. Rather, their center of interest lay in the descriptions of emotion within the web of love, jealousy, and hardship. The performances of Tōjūrō and of Yoshizawa Ayame (d. 1729), a specialist in female roles, were an integral part of the realistic theater. In the Edo theater, Nakamura Shichisaburō became famous for his portrayal of delicate sentiment, and Danjūrō achieved renown for the martial roles which he both wrote and performed. Such plays, while deeply colored by the details of manners and everyday life of Genroku, were also often fantastic in their general outlines. Between eastern and western Japan differences in theatrical taste continued for some time, western Japan prefering the realistic genre pieces, while Edo gave its enthusiasm to the martial plays in which a bombastic "rough style" (*aragoto*) was featured.

Chikamatsu Monzaemon and Sakata Tōjūrō were the two playwrights who brought Genroku kabuki to maturity. Chikamatsu, in association with the chanter-reciter Takemoto Gidayū (1651–1714), completely changed the old *jōruri* into the puppet theater of modern times. Gidayū was once a member of the puppet theater of the chanter Uji Kaganojō, this being one of the last of the old *jōruri* troupes, but he set out as an independent after a disagreement with that company. His efforts to survive without backing failed, but in 1685 Gidayū began the Takemotoza ("za" meaning "company" or "theater") in the central district, called Dōtonbori, of Ōsaka. Gidayū was then thirty-three years old. The theater opened with a successful production of *Shusse soga* (*The Soga Victorious*) which Chikamatsu had written for Uji Kaganojō in 1683. Chikamatsu's association with Gidayū began in 1686 with the play that firmly established the Takemotoza: *Shusse kagekiyo* (*Kagekiyo Victorious*). Chikamatsu continued to write period pieces, but in 1703 composed the first of his genre plays, *Sonezaki shinjū* (*The Love Suicides at Sonezaki*). Two years later Gidayū turned over management of the theater to Takeda Izumo (1691–1756) and confined himself to performing only. Chikamatsu accepted the invitation to become writer for the Takemotoza and in 1705 moved from Kyōto to Ōsaka. After the death of Tōjūrō in 1709 Chikamatsu stopped writing for kabuki and specialized in the puppet theater, assisting the second Gidayū after the founder's death. Despite his youth, Takeda Izumo proved to be an able manager and, working with Chikamatsu, became an accomplished playwright as well, often collaborating with Chikamatsu. Chikamatsu continued writing up to his death at age seventy-two, leaving over one hundred plays, including the remarkable three-year hit *Kokusenya kassen* (*The Battles of Coxinga*), composed in 1715; *Soga kaikeizan* (*The Soga at Mount Kaikei*), 1718, a period piece; his masterpiece of domestic love tragedy, *Shinjū ten no amijima* (*The Love Suicides at Amijima*), produced in 1720; and the gripping tale of murder *Onna goroshi abura jigoku* (*The Woman-Killer and the Hell of Oil*), 1721. While Chikamatsu wrote for the reciters of the puppet theater, his work was quickly borrowed for performance on the kabuki stage so that he may truly be said to have reigned supreme in the theater of his time.

We may summarize the main features of Chikamatsu's *jōruri* in a few points. First and foremost, he gave the characters in his plays clearly theatrical quality and dimension. We may object, perhaps, that his people are stereotypes, but that quality was not ill-suited to the one-man puppets of the playwright's time. Further, although he drew his characters in the image of the Genroku era he knew so well, Chikamatsu succeeded in portraying universal human qualities. He set the pattern of the historical play (*jidaimono*) in five acts and the domestic play (*sewamono*) in three acts. Through such structuring *jōruri,* which had developed as a narrative performance or recitation, achieved a totally theatrical form. Another important creation was his aesthetic unification of the reciter, the puppet operator, and the text. In a work on *jōruri,* dated 1738, and called *Naniwa miyage* (*Naniwa Keepsake;* "Naniwa" being an old name for Ōsaka), apparently by the Confucian scholar and *jōruri* enthusiast Hozumi Ikan (1692–1769), we have a glimpse of Chikamatsu's attitudes and methods more or less in the playwright's own words. According to that source, Chikamatsu believed that theatrical effect was the first principle of *jōruri* and to that end he would allow the reciter liberties in presenting the text so that the reciter might make changes to accommodate the written lines to the actual unraveling of the story. The puppets' emotions were an exaggeration of normal emotions, and there was the necessity of descriptive explanations; all of which, in Chikamatsu's words, meant that "art is something that exists in that slender world between truth and falsehood." Chikamatsu was also aware of differences in talents of the various reciters and created separate works for Gidayū and Takemoto Masadayū, the latter having a great psychological sensitivity in his voice but lacking the force of Gidayū. This accommodation does not mean that the author was subordinate to the performers but rather that they worked in close cooperation. The texts of Chikamatsu's plays were popular as literature even in his own day. Clearly he brought the literature of the puppet theater to its highest point. Chikamatsu's view of his own work aimed for the highest aesthetic level; and while he saw the essence of his art in offering amusement to his audience, he constantly strived for literary perfection. Fundamental to that approach was his regard for the common bond in human feeling (*ninjō*) between his work and the audience, a relationship which he drew against the background of social obligation (*giri*). *Ninjō* is simply the emotional heritage common to all men, regardless of time or place, or the circumstances of their lives. Social obligation, in Chikamatsu's view, was something bound to the logic of the universe (feeling, viewed theoretically). If we may judge from that, it would seem that the general literary current of Genroku appears just as strongly in this poet of the theater as it does elsewhere. The traditional view of the complications of duty and feeling (*giri-ninjō*) suggest that *giri* is the whole set of ethics which externally pattern the lives of men in the feudal society, while *ninjō* arises out of pure emotion. However, in the works of Chikamatsu, *giri*, although still a pattern of ethics, is not external to the individual but a natural categorical imperative, something that might be called the public or social aspect of *ninjō*. Tragic situations in his plays show people who are bewildered by the collision of public and private affections. In Chikamatsu's later years, after 1716, the high tide of Genroku humanism declined before the increasing rigidness of the Tokugawa government. The change in society is reflected in literature which gradually came to stress the social ethics termed *giri,* but the works of Chikamatsu retain that abundance of human warmth that marks him as being essentially a poet of love.

In 1703, one of Gidayū's disciples, Toyotake Wakadayū (1681– 1764), working with a famous manipulator of female puppets, Tatsumatsu Hachirōbē (d. 1734), opened his own theater, called Toyotakeza, in Dōtonbori just east of the Takemotoza. Together the two competitors, the "east" and the "west" as they were known, made the most brilliant era of the puppet stage, the Toyotakeza having as its house writer the renowned Ki no Kaion (1663–1742). Among his many plays are *Kamakura sandaiki* (*Three Generations of Kamakura*) produced in 1718, and *Shinjū futatsu haraobi* (*The Severed Obi Love Suicides*). The latter play, based on an actual event, appeared shortly after Chikamatsu's play on the same incident, but Ki no Kaion's play was only a critical success and in general his work dwelt heavily on the social complexities of his characters' lives (the area of *giri*) at the expense of revealing their feelings. Like Chikamatsu, Ki no Kaion composed many works that are able to stand alone on their aesthetic merits and they have earned him due reputation as one of the significant authors of the age.

The Early Eighteenth Century

From about the middle of the Genroku era the remarkable prosperity of the townsmen began to diminish. Under the government of the shogun Yoshimune during the Kyōhō era, the decline in the fortunes of the *chōnin* class was conspicuous, and from that period Tokugawa society manifested its characteristic quality of stability, centered on and most favorable to the non-productive life of the military class, the samurai. Various new ideas which had emerged with the beginning of the *bakufu* or military government became formal elements of the social fabric. It was the age in which *bushidō*, the "way of the warrior," was systematized into Japanese life. In the *chōnin* world another characteristic of the times is seen in the popularity of such teachings as *shingaku* (taught by Ishida Baigan, 1685–1744) which offered a theoretical framework for daily life through unification of the three teachings (*sankyō itchi*): Shintō, Buddhism, and Confucianism.

In academic circles the free-wheeling critical spirit of Genroku gave way to more scientific study and observation, broader but more careful in approach. Empirical analysis and close reasoning were valued above emotional assertion. The many fields of learning hitherto merely appended to Confucian studies by the name *gakumon* (learning) became independent as humanistic and natural sciences, attracting many men who specialized in one area or another. There was a growing interest in the study of modern China and Korea, and indeed all foreign lands, but the taste for things Chinese was particularly active all through Japanese society. It was a time for the first budding of Dutch studies (*rangaku*) which paid particular attention to Western technology and medicine. Further, even among the Confucianists there was new interest in the study of ancient Japanese history, known as Japanese studies (*wagaku*). We might indeed term it the age of the encyclopedists, for its materialistic and practical inclinations, as well as for its concern for the realities of society. It was an age too for proliferation of theories of statecraft.

In the literary world of Kyōhō, Chinese poetry and prose, the traditional cultural adornment of Confucian intellectuals, became a more popular expressive form and many outstanding practitioners appeared, some even making a family tradition of writing in Chinese. One Shingaku book, the *Seikaron* (*Discussion of Household Management*) published in 1744, complained that "the academies of recent times are given to Chinese poetry, and the writings of the sages are neglected." Poetry teaching was no longer the special preserve of the aristocracy, and many strictly professional *haiku* masters appeared. The professionalization of writing for the theater had already taken place, and now there appeared specialists in fiction writing. Doubtless this was in part due to literature's important role in the formation of the modern world, but a more direct reason at that time was the recognition that literature had an independent social and economic existence.

The new place of literature in Japanese society also generated theories to explain the function of literature. Ogyū Sorai (1666–1728), the famous radical Confucianist, and those influenced by him proposed a utilitarian theory of literature. Sorai's general idea was that the *The Book of Songs* (*Shih ching*) and works deriving from it in the Chinese tradition, as well as similar works both ancient and modern composed in Japan, were pieces of literature that touch the most profound levels of human emotion, but the area of ethics, which teaches and explains human reason, belongs to an entirely separate realm. Literary works, through refinement of expression, inevitably embody the deepest, most significant human characteristics, and the reader through his own sympathetic aesthetic response is able to refine his own character. Excellent literature, therefore, offers refined sentiment, and in its expression or style must have truth and beauty. The archetype for this is found in poems of the *Kuo feng* and *Ya* sections of *The Book of Songs*. Sorai and his school took the ancient classics as their models and found in them a synthesis of truth and beauty. In contrast to the literary outlook of Genroku, which was humanistic and directed toward *ninjō* or human feeling, the Kyōhō period was interested in art for art's sake, an attitude noticeably touched with classicism. And in that regard for the classics rests, of course, the fundamental strength of Confucianism. As we look back over the course of literature since the beginning of the middle ages we see that it was subservient to intellectual ends. In the eighteenth century, however, literature achieved a recognized independent existence apart from intellectual pursuits with other than aesthetic goals. The separation was not im-

mediate or uniform and there were many reversals, but for the rest of
the Tokugawa period we may say that the general disposition vis a vis
literature recognized its aesthetic integrity. This attitude is found not
only among the Confucianists but also among the national studies
scholars (*kokugakusha*), men like Kamo Mabuchi (1697–1769) and
Motoori Norinaga (1730–1801), who took the classics as their models
and created a theory of literature based on elegance and refinement
in style—although their classicism recognized the primacy of Japanese
writing in Japan. With the exception of the last point, the outlook of the nationalist scholars was quite like that of Sorai and the
Confucianists.

In contrast to the refined elegance of traditional literature, the
new literature was regarded as vulgar. But during Kyōhō even the
"vulgar" popular writing became specialized, leaving to some works
didactic and reportorial qualities, while other writings aimed only to
serve the readers' entertainment and pleasure. A literature of amusement in fact came to be recognized as socially desirable. Erotic qualities
which were an element in the *ukiyozōshi,* the fiction of Genroku, were
now developed as the center of interest in erotic books known as
kōshokubon. Informative, didactic elements became the specialty of
works known as *yomihon* (reading books); and narrative fiction, the
pleasure reading of a sizable audience, was known as *fūryū yomihon*
(stylish reading books). In poetry *tentori haikai* (point-getting *haikai*)
in which a point system was used to judge the over-all merit of the
poem, and *zappai* (miscellaneous *haikai*), which was the generic name
for a variety of *haikai* games, were both popular and were the
inspiration for many books on *haikai.* As we have mentioned, in
writing for the theater Chikamatsu was aware of his art as one aiming
to amuse an audience, but after his time a new literary climate developed which was even more devoted to the goal of pure entertainment. Literature as diversion and amusement in fact continued to
dominate the popular scene for the rest of the Tokugawa period.

Earlier efforts in Chinese studies also began to bear fruit. There
was an active translation society at the school of Itō Jinsai, and studies
in Chinese phonology were pursued at the Mito school and by Sorai
and his followers. Itō Tōgai (1670–1736) and Asaka Tampaku (1656–
1737) were among the outstanding writers of Chinese who benefited
from those studies. From the school of Kinoshita Jun'an (1621–98),
which emphasized study of T'ang poetry, came a number of outstanding
scholars, among them Arai Hakuseki (1667–1727) and Gion Nankai
(1677–1751). Yanada Zeigan (1672–1757) was another worthy
poet in Chinese. The followers of Sorai studied the Chinese writers of
the Ming period particularly and were devoted to the archaic styles
of writers like Li P'an-lung and Wang Shih-chen. In poetry they

found a model in the *lu* and *chüeh* forms (of eight- and four-line
stanzas). Their model for prose was a pseudo-archaic style which
revived forms of the Chinese graph in use before the Han dynasty.
Sorai was interested in both prose and poetry. Hattori Nankaku (1683–
1759) was his outstanding disciple in poetry, and in prose Dazai Shundai
(1680–1747) was another of his talented students. Such scholars as
we have mentioned were the nucleus of the important rebirth of
writing in Chinese. The dominant figure, however, was Sorai, whose
style and advocacy of Confucian studies dominate his time. There was
a great popularity of writing in Chinese, stimulated particularly by two
books: *Shikasen (Four Master Writers)*, a critical collection edited by
Sorai, of the prose of Li P'an-lung, Wang Shih-chen, Han T'ui-chih,
and Liu Tsu-hou, published in 1761. The other work was *Tōshisen*
(*Selections from T'ang Verse*), edited by Nankaku and published in
1726. The disciples of Jun'an in poetry devoted themselves to Chinese
poetry of the T'ang dynasty (618–907) but their understanding of
verse of that period actually came from Ming dynasty (1368–1644)
studies and commentaries—to the extent that we should say that Ming
writing was the stronger influence in Tokugawa Japan. Beginning in
the Kyōhō years, young intellectuals in every province formed poetry
societies and the various styles and schools competed with one another.
There was no single dominant style, rather groups of poets centered
around individuals such as Tatsu Sōro (1714–92) and Emura Hokkai
(1713–88) in Kyōto, Katayama Hokkai (1723–90) in Ōsaka, and
Adachi Seika (1717–92) in Edo.

   In *haikai* the focus and inspiration provided by Bashō for his
disciples was not replaced after the master's death, and as the men
who had studied with Bashō gradually disappeared those who felt
themselves to be his followers could only hold their own within a
narrow sphere. In Edo a style heavily dependent on metaphor grew
up around Mizuma Tentoku (1661–1726), and the witty style of
Kikaku was carried on in the jocular poetry of Kishi Tenshū (1670–
1739). But the lyricism of the Bashō style disappeared, to be replaced
by writing that was merely an intellectual game, an exercise in technique. One consequence of the fad for writing *haikai* which were
judged on a point system was the independent status afforded to the
single verse (*ikkudachi*), rather than, as before, regarding it as a
link in a series of verses. Still there existed in the new writing an
urbanity and refinement which grew out of the free and light atmosphere
of the times. Tachiba Fukaku (1662–1735) was an influential poet
completely absorbed in the popular "point" writing. His was often an
eccentric style—but one easily imitated by the new wave of amateur
poets. It was known as the "chimera style" (*kechōfū*—referring to the
bird known as the *nue,* the ghost of Minamoto no Yorimasa). This

poetry was introduced from Edo to Ōsaka and western Japan by Matsuki Tantan (1674–1761), a man who considered himself in the Bashō school. However, he produced a succession of "point system" *haikai* collections and ended up writing in a style that blatantly curried favor with the lowest common taste. Iwata Ryōto (1661–1717) established an Ise branch of the Bashō school in which Nakagawa Otsuyū (1675–1739) participated, but it also went too far in seeking popularity through light and undisciplined writing. Kagami Shikō (1665–1731) was known as the Mino branch of the Bashō school and, rather presumptuously, he opened a school called the Lion Hermitage, Shishian, named himself "Bashō the Second," and sought to teach the Bashō approach to *haikai*. Branches of his school were established in some twenty provinces. The lofty style of Shikō's writing contrasts with the idea of such publications of his as *Haikai jūron* (*Ten Essays on Haikai*), 1719, and *Haikai kokonshō* (*Haikai Selections Ancient and Modern*), 1730. They were books on the theory and composition of *haikai* suitable for the widest audience. He argues that "eloquence and sensitivity can be brought within reach of everyone simply by using the language of ordinary conversation." Substance in *haikai* would be achieved through a mixture of irony and lyricism. In expressing truth, Shikō says, *haikai* is "skillful lying." Nonetheless his writings offered excellent advice on the grammar and vocabulary of *haikai;* and because of its great popularity among poetasters, the Shikō school later came to be called the "ogre of *haikai.*" Shikō himself was an innovator in *haibun* (the mixture of poetry and prose) and other forms, as we discover in his *Honchō bunkan* (*Mirror of Japanese Prose*), 1718, and *Wakan bunsō* (*Selected Essays of Japan and China*), 1727.

In addition to the men already noted, Morikawa Kyoroku (1656–1715) attracted disciples in Edo, and in western Japan a branch of the Bashō school was led by Shida Yaha (1662–1740). But among the various poetry masters there was often more concern for influence and disciples than for raising the quality of *haikai* poetry. Professional teachers flattered their disciples and in the process abandoned the high aesthetic qualities of Bashō's work. The result was that *haikai* became a bland and tasteless versifying. Intellectuals of the century tended to belittle *haikai* and a number of *haikai* poets also eventually had second thoughts about what the art had come to.

The decline in *haikai* poetry and its concessions to the taste of the general public were also reflected in the popularity of *haikai* amusements and competitions known as *zappai* (miscellaneous *haikai*). As a first step in learning *haikai* the approach known as *maekuzuke* (attaching a first verse) began to be used about 1660. In this the student composed a seventeen-syllable verse to accompany a verse of fourteen syllables which was given by the poetry master. Along with the widely practiced *maekuzuke,* competitive "point" composition, with prizes awarded, became popular and the whole movement drifted far from the serious spirit of *haikai.* By the Genroku period poems were being made on given topics ("fearsome things," for example) and seventeen-syllable verse more and more neglected the rules of linked-verse composition, growing into novel and surprising shapes and producing humorous verses on human affairs. The humorous poems became the seventeen-syllable *senryū* and were immensely popular. In Kyōto, with such men as Horiuchi Unko (1665–1727), new kinds of *zappai* were devised. It was truly popular *haikai,* the literary entertainment of the Kyōhō period, and it included a variety of devices: *kasazuke* (composing only the initial five syllables, the last twelve syllables already given), *ogura zuke* (composing the last twelve syllables, with the first five taken from a line in one of the *waka* in the *Ogura hyakunin isshū*), *dandan zuke* (taking the last five syllables of the preceding verse as the initial five syllables of the new verse), and *kutsu zuke* (composing the first twelve syllables to five last syllables already given). A great number of such poems were made into collections and piously offered to temples and shrines. There were also many publications offering selections of verses that had received high points in poetry competitions. Poetic novelties continued to appear: *oriku* (in *zappai* this meant that the referee gave the name of something as the opening five syllables; in older *waka* it meant being able to make the name of something through reading only the first syllables in each of the five lines), *kaibun* (a verse which said the same thing whether one began reading at the top or at the bottom). Such variations on the *haikai* idea found considerable popularity in the provinces down to the Meiji period, the end of the nineteenth century. In the cities, however, the movement away from traditional *haikai* was even more clearly defined with the emergence of *senryū,* humorous seventeen-syllable verse.

Kyōka, or humorous *waka,* were occasionally part of the poetry scene beginning in the late sixteenth century. We have collections of poems by individuals and anthologies, such as *Kokin ikyokushū* (*Collection of Ancient and Modern Humorous Verse*), 1665, *Gosen ikyokushū* (*Later Collection of Humorous Verse*), published in 1672, and *Gin'yō ikyokushū* (*Silver Leaf Collection of Humorous Verse*), published in 1678. All three were edited by the *kyōka* master known as Seihakudō Gyōfū. Nagata Teiryū (1654–1734), a student of Hōzōbō Shinkai (1626–88), formed a rather large *kyōka* poetry circle in Ōsaka and the group included many writers of somewhat keener sensitivities than the usual composers of *zappai.* Some time later the group divided into numerous branches, such as Kuriha and Maruha (names derived from the *gō* or pen names of their leading poets) and spread all over Japan. Teiryū himself closely followed and taught the style of Shinkai, who once said, "The *kyōka* style puts a rope belt on a gilded robe," meaning that the characteristic element of wit did not necessarily exclude depth and grace. Nonetheless, there were frequent lapses of taste in *kyōka,* much insipid writing passing itself off as high style, and a good deal of satire which presumably sharpened the insights of the poems. It is indicative of the place of *kyōka* in public life at that time that masters (such as Rikkatei Bokutan, d. 1773, in his *Kyōka tenare no kagami; The Mirror of Kyōka* were also advocates of the instructive utility of the verses.

Hachimonjiya of Kyōto was the leading publisher of entertainment reading from the beginning of Genroku through the Kyōhō period. The last works in the *ukiyozōshi* type were almost all from that house, and since the styles developed by the Hachimonjiya publishers covered nearly the whole field of fiction, the name of the shop has become synonymous with *ukiyozōshi* of the later period. Andō Hachizaemon (d. 1745), known as Jishō, son of the founder of the company, gained early success in publishing the texts of *jōruri* and kabuki. In 1701 he published the first of a new format which was to become quite popular. It was the story *Keisei irosamisen* (*The Courtesan's Amorous Samisen*) by Ejima Kiseki (1667–1735). That work was much indebted to Saikaku's erotic stories, but despite its clear and consistent story line and attention to the psychology and motivations of its characters, it lacks the depth of Saikaku's perception and the high style of his work. The elaborate plot reflected the fashion of the times, and its popularity led to sequels known as *samisen mono* or samisen stories. After nearly a decade of conflict between Jishō and Kiseki the latter returned to the Hachimonjiya and a publishing system which placed writers under contract to the publishers; this became characteristic of fiction publishing in the Kyōto region. During the first decade of the eighteenth century Kiseki devised two very popular styles: the *shibaimono,* or theatrical stories, and the *katagimono,* or character sketches. Under the pen name "Yatsushi" he also attempted fiction in the "true story" vein of late Genroku, but official censorship of that kind of writing forced him to stop. Instead, with a keen sense for theatrical prose, Kiseki found materials and techniques for long works of fiction in the literature of kabuki and *jōruri.* He specialized in period pieces and followed the five-part form of linked *kyōgen,* even to divisions in the stories like those of the scenes and acts on the stage. The result was stories that resemble nothing so much as theater; and, as in the theater of the time, there was little by way of didacticism or reportage and a good deal of fabrication and invention. In Kiseki's theatrical pieces, we have stories like *Daidairi ōtomo no matori* (*Imperial Eagle*), published in 1727, and *Otogi heike* (*The New Heike*) from 1729. The character sketches began with *Seken musuko katagi* (*Characters of Worldly Young Men*) and *Seken musume katagi* (*Characters of Worldly Young Women*), published in 1715 and 1716, respectively. They were collections of brief stories, in the vein of Saikaku's stories of townsmen or his miscellaneous tales, grouped by age of the chief characters, sex, social position, or occupation. The stories deal in a highly realistic way with manners and personalities of Kiseki's time, reflecting the general stability of Kyōhō society. In those works Kiseki avoided the fantasy and moralizing that tended to decorate fiction, creating his humor out of exaggeration of human ideosyncracies. His later sketches unfortunately descended to mere trivia. On the whole it seems likely that his readers were people of little education who delighted in this sort of theater-on-paper or the humorous recreation of the familiar material of their lives. Following Kiseki in the later publications of the Hachimonjiya were several memorable names: the Shintō scholar Ōta Nampo (1698–1750), who wrote fiction under various pen names; Nagaidō Kiyū (fl. ca. 1770), a later author of character sketches; and Ueda Akinari (1734–1809), who, writing under the name Wayaku Tarō, published two works: *Shodō chōji seken zaru* (*Various Worldly Monkeys*), 1766, and *Seken tekake katagi* (*Characters of Worldly Women*), 1767. They were the last interesting representatives of the character-sketch genre.

At the Takemoto and Toyotake theaters in Ōsaka, Sedayū and Wakadayū, renowned voices of the puppet theater, and the masters of the samisen who accompanied them, were at the height of prosperity. The puppeteers Yoshida Bunsaburō and Fujii Kosaburō (the latter known for his interpretation of female characters) brought the technique of the three-man puppet to perfection, with perfect coordination of all movements including the eyes, mouth, and nose. It was the golden age of the puppets, and works created during the Kyōhō period greatly influenced kabuki performances and even today continue in the repertory of the puppet theater. Among the famous plays of the time were: *Hōjō tokiyori ki* (*The Story of Hōjō Tokiyori*), 1716, by Nishizawa Ippū, Namiki Sōsuke, and others; *Dan no ura kabuto gunki* (*The Helmet of Dan no ura: A War Tale*), 1722; *Sugawara denju tenarai kagami* (*The Exemplary Mirror of the Sugawara*), 1746.

With all its accomplishments, however, a critical look at the puppet theater reveals various weaknesses. Compared with the era of Chikamatsu, the plots had become extremely complicated, and in order to manage them within the limits of the stage writers resorted to various unreasonable and tricky devices. Further, playwriting became a collaborative enterprise involving several writers and, as a result, acts and scenes were often disjointed and the story lacked real unity. The characters were not consistent; precipitous switches of good and evil personalities were not uncommon. Many plays, too, appropriated parts of older dramas, particularly sections of sure popularity, using the borrowed material in various degrees of revision and adaptation. In the opinion of a theatrical critique published in 1738, the overall quality of the writing declined from that time. The work we refer to is *Naniwa miyage* (*Naniwa Keepsake*) which says of the once carefully wrought journey or travel passage: "The prose of the *michiyuki* these days is something that merely falls from the lips like a ball-bouncing jingle or the lines in an illustrated *sōshi*—not even worth criticizing." Finally, in the style of the time, in historical plays the *giri* (obligation) relationship was treated ideologically, as an abstraction, and *ninjō* (human feeling or emotion) became more and more a superficial decoration. While faults such as these are generally attributable to the writers, it must also be noted that the writers took second place to the reciters and the puppeteers, a situation which surely did nothing to encourage their meeting the literary challenges of the theater. The puppet theater at last could only appeal to an audience through flattery of its lowest tastes. While the presentation of spectacle insured financial survival of the theater, it also led to abandonment of literary quality.

The *Jōrurifu* (*Jōruri Album*), a kind of critical chronology of the Takemoto and Toyotake theaters published in the late eighteenth century, mentions that "the puppet theater gradually became popular and kabuki all but disappeared." The age was one of economic recession and kabuki theater felt the effects of the difficult times. During one year in Ōsaka performances could not be financed and while the theaters were closed the companies split up and toured the provinces. The decline was also evident in the texts. One comment from the mid-century notes that "Plays by today's writers have nothing new in them at all since they merely pen variations on the old plays." Not only were there no playwrights of talent but the actor and his personality became the center of interest on the stage. The playwright Tsuuchi Jihē the Second (1679–1760) remarked that it was part of the writer's task to defer to the actor, to write specifically for the personality and talent of each performer. From the few remaining librettos and a number of illustrated *kyōgen* books we may judge what was being written. As was the case in the puppet theater, there were many complicated plots and structural novelties, as well as a tendency to fragmentize the plays into one-act scenes which were nearly independent plays in themselves. In Edo especially we find a mixture of the historical play and the genre piece in which the single act stood almost completely independent. The aim, of course, was to put on an entertaining show or spectacle, to attract an audience to kabuki. Thus, in contrast to the realistic kabuki of Ōsaka-Kyōto which had developed carefully structured plays of samurai heroes and historical events, the kabuki of

Edo created new music and dances and developed them as a theater of the spectacular, a tendency already strong in eastern Japan. The actor Ichikawa Danjūrō the Second (1688–1758) appeared in a number of plays (such as *Sukeroku, Yanone,* and *Kenuki,* works that are basically *kyōgen*) which are now counted in the repertory of the eighteen favorite kabuki plays (*kabuki jūhachiban*) of the Ichikawa tradition.

The Late Eighteenth Century

By the third quarter of the century Edo, the modern city of Tōkyō, had become the creative center of Japanese life and the active literary scene shifted from Kyōto to Edo. After 1767 the *ukiyozōshi,* long the mainstay of the Hachimonjiya, went into decline and the world of fiction came to be dominated by Edo publishers who brought out new lines of story books, such as *sharebon* (gay-quarter books), *kokkeibon* (humor books), and *yomihon* (reading books). *Kyōka* achieved great popularity in the new Temmei period style, and in *zappai* poetry there appeared a new style of *senryū* that became popular all over Japan. In place of the puppet theater, kabuki once again was the dominant theatrical medium as Edo both imported the Kyōto-Ōsaka theater and set about creating its own style of kabuki. The development was known as *tōzen,* the shift to the east, and was notable for bringing together the styles of Edo and Kyōto. *Haikai* poets, who had previously given allegiance to dozens of factions established all over Japan, now found common interests represented by the phrase "back to Bashō," and the idea verged on a new national movement. *Waka* poets, however, continued factional disputes between eastern and western Japan and various schools. Scholars of Chinese prose and poetry, like the *haikai* poets, lost their provincial loyalties and gradually the fad for traditional wine-and-poetry gatherings touched every corner of Japan. Such changes indicate that in great measure the literary scene in Japan was becoming national, engaging the whole country, but the new center of the literary world was Edo and the direction of cultural influence radiated outward from that city to the rest of Japan. One measure of that influence was commercial book publishing in which the voice of Edo publishers was important to the companies in other cities. The exclusive contract system of Kyōto-Ōsaka, whereby an author worked only for one publisher, was replaced in Edo by the modern system of the house selecting its authors and works one by one. The rest of Japan followed suit in that and in other ways so that the period clearly emerges one of the great transitions in modern Japanese literature.

Beginning in the Kyōhō period (1716–35) there appeared among progressive intellectuals literati known as *bunjin.* They were amateurs who, not finding sufficient exercise for their talents in everyday occupations, brought their energies to pursuits of the brush, including *sumie* painting, as an agreeable and tasteful avocation. One of the first of the *bunjin* was Yanagizawa Kien (1706–58) who produced a collection of twelve essays under the title *Hitorine (Sleeping Alone)*, and after him appeared the long line of men who dabbled in what is called the literary man's style of painting (*bunjinga*). Apart from their everyday occupations, the *bunjin* sought a life of taste and refinement that gave free reign to the spirit. That was another of the significantly modern qualities that appeared in the Kyōhō years: men found themselves tied to occupations which did not relate to their creative and spiritual interests, and yet they chose to embrace the situation despite the complexities it held for mind and spirit.

There was a growing narrowness and rigidity in Japanese society which stifled the free development of talent as a basic principle of life. The land was filled with able men for whom advancement in public life was closed. As a result many educated men as well as Confucian scholars turned to fiction writing. The phenomenon was noted by one writer of the time in these words: "After Kyōhō literary elegance reached down to the general populace." An interest in biography appeared in such publications as *Heian jimbutsu shi (Figures of the Heian Period)*. Underemployed and talented men turned to literary avocations to make a name for themselves. Further, from the viewpoint of the model scholars of the day, the Confucianists, such pursuits brought together traditional learning and the various arts, even though others might see them as frivolous and regard their lives as having fallen into dissipation. Of course such men also maintained their pride and self discipline; the society of that time was very stable and out of it they won praise for their accomplishments. Without any driving necessity to move in other directions, the number of men attracted to the life of the *bunjin* gradually increased and remained an important element in the cultural life of the century.

The *bunjin* literati naturally took traditional literature as their own, but their interest was far from a hindrance to working in new forms and styles as individual taste and talent indicated. They referred to the experimental area by names, such as *gesaku*, meaning light literature or entertainments. One distinction made was between belles lettres, literature as fine art, and popular literature, but the effect of *bunjin* involvement was that popular literature was raised in quality and set in a new direction. However, the writings of the *bunjin*, perhaps because they were men of leisure, tended to lack involvement and conviction. Their *gesaku* writing, while sensitive and technically interesting, lacked real affirmation of human values. In short, the literature of the late eighteenth century somehow seems to lack a vital center, and that was epitomized by the studied dilettantism known as *tsū*. The *bunjin* quality or outlook increasingly permeated aesthetic life and one common quality of the *gesaku* literature is seen in the growing interest in details, accompanied by a lack of spiritual depth or poetic vigor.

Kokugaku, national studies, initiated by Keichū, continued through the work of Kada no Azumamaro (1669–1736), Kamo no Mabuchi (1697–1769), and Motoori Norinaga (1730–1801). Mabuchi opened a private school called Agatai after the master's sobriquet and collected a considerable number of disciples. By Norinaga's time the nationalistic study of antiquity had taken on a rather scientific character. Hirata Atsutane (1776–1843) and scholars like him were among the important forces which moved Japan toward the Meiji Restoration of 1868. As we have noted, the *kokugaku* scholars were at once critical of the Japanese Confucianists and influenced by their rationalism.

Kamo no Mabuchi patterned his own work after Ogyū Sorai's studies in ancient texts and vocabulary, eventually maintaining that composing *waka* and prose in the old style was a discipline indispensable to the study of antiquity. Mabuchi's school enthusiastically followed his literary interests. During his early years of teaching in Edo Mabuchi chose as his model the poetry of the *Kokinshū* and the *Shinkokinshū*. That brought him close to men like Katō Chikage (1735–1808) and Murata Harumi (1746–1811), *kokugaku* scholars and poets of the mid-Tokugawa period. After Mabuchi's death those men became the nucleus of the Edo literary circle, writing in Japanese rather than in Chinese. In Edo, Mabuchi soon began to aim for the strength and directness which was characteristic of the *Man'yōshū,* having been inspired to this by the controversy aroused by *Kokka hachiron (Eight Essays on Japanese Poetry),* published in 1742 by Kada no Arimaro (1705–51). The details of Mabuchi's own poetic theory may be seen in such works as *Niimanabi (New Studies),* 1765, and *Ka'ikō (Thoughts on the Meaning of Poetry).* His disciples of that period included many poets who took up his *Man'yōshū* style: Tayasu Munetake (1715–71) and Katori Nahiko (1723–82), for example. The classic antique style of Mabuchi and his followers led, however, to a modern style of *waka* which, through attempting to write directly from the heart in a free poetic feeling, was able to overcome the Nijō style through the excellence of compositions rather than merely elaborate theoretical defense. In his views on poetry Motoori Norinaga looked to the *Shinkokinshū* as the supreme model of excellence. However, he was not a poet himself and is important as a critic and scholar. He is especially remembered for his theory that *mono no aware,* pathos or emotion, is the essence of the poem-tale—a view expressed in his *Genji monogatari tama no o-gushi (The Precious*

Comb to Unravel the Tale of Genji) from 1796, and *Iso no kami sasame goto* (*Dialogue on Poetry*), published 1816. Norinaga's interpretation of *mono no aware* as something expressed in the patina of ancient styles of speech owes a great deal to Ogyū Sorai as well as to Norinaga's Confucian teacher, Hori Keizan (1688–1757).

The *kokugaku* scholars with their antiquarian interests in such works as *Ise monogatari, Genji,* the *Man'yōshū* and the *Kokinshū* also looked to these works for their standards of composition. But the classic writings generally were too far removed from a wide audience and a truly vital role in the literary life of the day. In *waka* the poetry of the Nijō tradition was totally eclipsed. On the other hand, the *waka* of the *kokugaku* scholars, while striving to bring new life to poetry, suffered the enervating effects of an over-refined and pseudo-archaic style.

The period also saw renewed admiration for China. Beginning in Genroku there arose among Japanese literati a fervor for the study of Chinese language, the objectives being research into Ming dynasty writings and elimination of Japanese flavor from their own writings in Chinese. At the Edo school of Ogyū Sorai a study and translation group was formed and it invited the participation of Okajima Kanzan (1674–1728). The Confucian scholars of Kyōto worked on problems of ancient Chinese phonology through study of such men as Huang-nieh, a Zen Buddhist monk of the T'ang dynasty. Since Chinese colloquial fiction was chosen as the material of their studies, they called their work *haikan no gaku* (derived from the name of an official office, the *haikan,* or *pai kuan* in Chinese, which reported to the emperor on conditions among the citizenry) and termed themselves *shōsetsuka* (meaning a student of fiction or romances—in the modern sense a writer of novels). One activity of such scholars was translating and adapting Chinese fiction or novels into Japanese. Kanzan, Oka Hakku (1692–1767), Matsumuro Shōkyō (1692–1747), and Suyama Nantō (d. 1766) were prominent members of the group. Besides a number of books on Chinese language, Kanzan early produced a Japanese version of *Shui hu chuan* (*Water Margin* or *All Men Are Brothers*) up to chapter 24, the rest of this long undertaking being completed after Kanzan's death. Following Kanzan's lead there appeared in Japanese translation various Chinese story collections from the colloquial (*pai huah*) style, including excerpts from *Chin ku ch'i kuan* (*Marvelous Tales, Ancient and Modern*), a collection of forty stories from the late Ming period.

By that time Japanese classics such as *Genji monogatari* were quite difficult to read in the original, and the popular editions of the Hachimonjiya were vulgarized and confused. Furthermore, the classics of Japanese literature were not particularly in vogue even among discriminating readers of the time. The new popular literature rather followed the example of Chinese colloquial novels with carefully worked out structure, ample length, and exciting content. The style too was appealing to the intelligentsia, since in many ways the adaptations of Chinese stories had points of excellence as novels superior to Japanese writing of the time. Gradually the influence was felt in the publications of the Hachimonjiya. The world of fiction, which had been groping for a new direction through the realistic or historical novel and with collections of mystery stories, was inspired by the Chinese models to produce a new form of narrative fiction in the *yomihon,* which were an extension of the *gesaku* writings of the intellectuals.

The new *yomihon* style is first apparent in the three-part compositions modeled on Chinese collections of short stories. Early examples are *Hanabusa sōshi* (*Petal Tales*) of 1749, a work in the style of Chinese colloquial stories and reminiscent of the earlier Japanese *kana* books; *Shigeshigeyawa* (*Popular Evening Tales*), 1766; and *Hitsujigusa* (*Water Lilies*), 1785. These three books by the Ōsaka physician and Confucian scholar Tsuga Teishō (b. 1718) were far from polished fiction, but they succeeded in transposing some of the important novelistic qualities of their Chinese models into a background of Japanese history. Among the many writers influenced by the *jidaimono* or "period pieces" was Teishō's apprentice in medicine Ueda Akinari who produced, in 1858, the famous collection of nine ghost stories titled *Ugetsu monogatari* (*Tale of Moonlight and Rain*). As a student of Japanese antiquities, a *kokugaku* scholar, Akinari was quite familiar with the classical Japanese *monogatari.* He also held advanced views on the novel as a result of his extensive reading in Chinese fiction. Thus he was able to bring to his writing the symbolism and psychological subtlety of Chinese fiction. Further, his work in adapting Chinese writing to Japanese led him to structure his material in ways that also resemble the Nō drama, blending the polished rhetoric of Chinese and Japanese fine writing with effects far beyond mere display of poetic vocabulary. His themes and subjects have a wide range, touching on history, wealth, love, affection, women, art, and society. He was not concerned with shaping his material to prove a particular point, and consequently his work has the broad thematic interest of contemporary novels. In his middle years Akinari wrote two satirical novels, *Kakizome kigenkai* (*An Ocean of New Year Greetings*), in 1787, and *Kuse monogatari* (*A Tale of Folly*), of about 1790. From Akinari's last years we have the nine stories in *Harusame monogatari* (*Tales of the Spring Rains*). Not all of his writing has the polish of *Ugetsu monogatari,* and possibly his personal philosophy made inevitable the simplistic resolutions in his stories—popular as this surely was with his readers. However, *Chikatabira* (*A Bloody Summer Robe*) from his later years counts among his best pieces, and *Ugetsu,* of course, was a major influence on the writers of *yomihon* who followed him.

The compositions of both Teishō and Akinari were modest in length, for the equivalent of the long Chinese novel had not yet developed in the Tokugawa literary scene. But there appeared works modeled on *Water Margin,* such as *Shōchū hachiyūden* (*Eight Heroes of Hsiang*), thought to be by Nemoto Bui (1699–1764), and *Honchō suikoden* (*A Japanese Water Margin*), by Takebe Ayatari (1719–74). Ayatari's stories were set in Japan of the Nara period and offered a free and imaginative adaptation of the Chinese original. It became the model for succeeding long *yomihon* which, inspired by *Water Margin,* captured the popular audience held by the *shibaimono,* the theatrical stories of the Hachimonjiya.

During the early decades of the eighteenth century a fad arose for popular lectures given by learned men. The Buddhist clergy participated in the activity and there were also performers who delivered humorous parodies of the clerics' sermons. One of the lecturers and social critics was Masuho Zankō, a Shintoist and former Buddhist priest, who published, in 1714, the *Endō tsūgan* (*History of Love*), a critical collection of love stories going back to the Nara period. The first work in the genre known as *kokkeibon* (humor books) was a collection of humorous monologues by Seikenbō Kōa titled *Imayō heta dangi* (*Modern Bungled Lectures*), published in 1752. This work, based on the humorous lectures of performers in the Asakusa district of Edo, offered wry social critiques of an era which had nourished a variety of foibles and mannerisms. This kind of monologue book was the nucleus of the *kokkeibon* genre which eventually included a wide range of humorous writing. The descriptive passages, such as those in the *katagimono* or character sketches, were turned into dialogue and debate, and the didacticism of the writing lacked conviction or any positive view of human life. The result was a gradual accumulation of a great quantity of confused and formless writing which at best pointed out in a humorous way the weaknesses of human character. It was perhaps the inevitable posture of authors who found their basic stock in witticisms known as *ugachi.* This word originally meant a kind of sideways or backwards glance, and while at first the style may seem to be acute observation, it remained the irresponsible chatter of an observer rather than a participant. The technique began with the *kokkeibon* lecture books, but the method of developing a theme became a chacteristic of *sharebon, kibyōshi* and the other forms which developed in the eighteenth century. The quality of detachment characteristic of these writings was also notable in the works of the *bunjin* artists and writers. Hiraga Gennai (1720–79), a student of European science, or Dutch studies (*rangaku*), and a nationalist scholar brought the critical attitude of the lecture books to the device of a visit to Hades which was published as *Nenashigusa* (*Duckweed*) in ten volumes appearing between 1763 and 1769. The same device of stringing together critical comments inspired his *Fūryū shidō kenden* (*A Modern Search for the Way*), a foreign travel book published in 1763, and various short works collected in *Fūrai rokuroku bushū* (*Twelve Stories by Fūrai*)—"Fūrai Sanjin" being one of Gennai's pen names. Despite the harsh difficulties of Gennai's personal life, his work reflects only irony and a facility for witty chatter. Imitations of Gennai's style, dialogue books and other forms, flooded Edo and extended their influence to Kyōto-Ōsaka, especially in the character sketches of Nagaidō Kiyū, and in the works of Nishimura Teiga (1744–1826) and Tamiya Nakanobu. The humorous lectures and dialogues characteristic of the *kokkeibon* in the early years remained influential in later works, but in the *sharebon* wit developed into something like the *rakugo* or comic story performances of twentieth century Japan.

Literature of the gay quarters survived only in publications of the Hachimonjiya until late in the century when the genre was revived under the influence of Chinese stories of romance and the pleasure districts. The new descriptions of the brothel districts found an audience particularly among the youth of western Japan. The books were published in small format and were concerned with the quality of behavior called *sui* (chic) that had replaced the earlier term *tsū* (gallantry or savoir faire).

In Edo during the Meiwa Era (1764–71) the first book of the new *sharebon* (gay-quarter book) genre appeared. It was *Yūshi hōgen* (*Rake's Dialect*) by "Inakarōjin Tadanooyaji." The author's pen name is a complicated pun and the title of his work is a variation on a Chinese work on dialectology from the Han dynasty. The *sharebon*, as the librettos earlier and the more recent dialogue or lecture books, presented their stories primarily through conversation. Descriptive passages of great vividness are inserted, but rather like notes for stage settings. Another element in the *sharebon* which was reminiscent of the dialogue books is the use of debate on the topics of proper behavior in the gay quarters and the varieties of customers who appeared in the brothels. Those qualities earned the books a reputation of having been valued as guides or introductions to the districts, but in fact such was probably not the case. The essence of *sharebon* lies in the form of the books which was a display of wit in the context of a particular location or background. The books were written with a cool detachment in which it is difficult to discover any positive qualities which might be termed informative. The seemingly realistic descriptions are really quite formalized and do not go beyond the achievements of the older character sketches. While the subject matter was the gay quarters, the *sharebon* were also the writings of competent and educated men, which meant that their literary quality was quite exceptional. Following *Yūshi hōgen* at least 171 *sharebon* were mentioned in a critique of the genre called *Gesaku hyōban hana no origami* (*Paper Flowers, A Critique of Popular Fiction*), published in 1802. Among the outstanding titles were *Tatsumi no sono* (*Garden of the Southeast,* named for the location of the Edo gay quarter called Fukugawa), published in 1770, and *Nankei zatsuwa* (*Shinagawa Bedroom Chatter*), published in 1773. Some *sharebon* were set in the brothel districts of Ōsaka, and regional writers contributed to the genre with books on relatively obscure red-light districts of the provinces.

Santō Kyōden (1761–1816), one among the many talented *sharebon* authors, was a writer of first rank, a *chōnin* townsman, and master of a fine wit and sensitive spirit. His story collections, *Musukobeya* (*The Son's Room*), 1785, and *Tsūgen sōmagaki* (*Stars of the Brothel*), 1787, are among the best of the genre. *Sharebon* literature was proscribed by the government during the Kansei era, the last decade of the century, and Kyōden was punished for some of his writing during that period of reform—such works as *Shōgi kinuburui* (*The Harlot's Silken Net*) and *Nishiki no ura* (*Behind the Embroidery*), both from 1791. That legal difficulty marked a turning point in Kyōden's writing which until then had been devoted to the *sharebon* and *kibyōshi* (yellow-cover book) styles. In the two works just mentioned there was considerable depth of feeling for a *monogatari* or narrative approach which had not been achieved earlier in the genre. Following the Kansei Reform there was a marked improvement of psychological sensitivity and narrative technique in the *sharebon,* reflecting a change in both the authors and readers of the works.

The Kyōto-Ōsaka publishers had been turning out a type of picture book known as *kusazōshi,* which were collections of rather juvenile stories. In the wide sense of the word, *kusazōshi* is the general name for *akabon* (red-cover books), *kurobon* (black-cover books), *aobon* (green-cover books), *kibyōshi* (yellow-cover books), and *gōkan* (combined books). In the narrow definition it refers to *gōkan* only. The *kusazōshi* of western Japan were popular in the late seventeenth century, and a competing book was produced in Edo from the 1670s, while about 1720 red-cover books were produced in Edo with stories based on such old *setsuwa* material as *Shita kire susume* (*The Grateful Sparrow*). The texts of the stories were composed by the artists who did the illustrations, and while the illustrations were dominant in the books, gradually the artist-writers introduced a modern slant to the old stories. Between 1744 and 1770 the red-cover books were supplanted by black and then green covers, and the tendency to put new interpretations on traditional materials developed rapidly. In terms of subject matter the books gradually came to include history, military deeds, the theater, and so forth. The books thus offered a kind of basic cultural education for adults in an easy and often humorous form. Most of the illustrations for the later works were by artists of the Torii school, but particularly complicated stories required specialized talents, such as those of the designer and writer Tomikawa Ginsetsu. The physical form of the books became standardized at ten pages of about three by five inches.

Out of such simple materials was born the *kibyōshi,* the yellow-cover book, which achieved great success and remarkable quality as entertainment literature. The genre begins in 1775 with the appearance of the tale *Kinkin sensei eiga no yume* (*The Dream of Splendor of Master Gold*) by Aikawa Harumachi (1744–89). The story is based on the Nō play *Kantan*—the traveler's dream—but is adapted to the amusement world of Edo as the tale of a man who dreams of a profligate but finally tragic life, and gladly returns to his quiet village when he awakens. The story sparkles with the wit and savoir faire of the brothel districts of Edo, while the polished style and adult content reflect a mature taste for character, even though the appearance of the work was still that of the earlier juvenile picture books. Until the later arrival of the *gōkan,* the *kibyōshi* title for the works remained current. Nearly every intellectual who wrote *kyōka* or *gesaku* also tried his hand at writing *kibyōshi,* and the best of the *ukiyoe* artists lent their talents to them. While it is true that the books were comic in intent, the illustrations were scarcely cartoons. The humor needed a foundation in sincerity, if it was to have real flavor; thus the . . . descriptions, punning (*jiguchi*) conversations (kakiire), . . . and illustrations are finely matched to each other. All of the story materials in use since the red-cover books were employed in the *kibyōshi,* with variations or earlier stories doubtless contributing to the readers' amusement. The dialogues were a dense forest of puns and double meanings, initiating elaborate games between the writer and the reader who shared his tastes. The following men were among the popular authors: Hōseidō Kisanji (1735–1813), creator of *Nagaiki mitaiki* (*A Search for Long Life*), published in 1783; Shiba Zenkō (1750–93), author of *Daihi no senrokuhon* (*The Thousand-and-Six Radish-Handed Buddha of Mercy*), published in 1785; Ichiba Tsūshō (1739–1812), who continued the earlier style of juvenile writing; and Harumachi, mentioned earlier. None, however, surpassed Santō Kyōden. His *Edo umare uwaki no kabayaki* (*A Wanton Edo Born*), 1785, and *Kōshi jima toki ni aizome* (*Confucius a la mode*), 1789, are real masterpieces of creativity, humor, and the writer's craft.

The world of *haikai* achieved a renaissance in the late eighteenth

century due, in part, to a new consciousness of *haikai's* real literary
dimensions—as opposed to being merely a poetry of the colloquial.
The critical writings of Miyake Shōzan (1718–1801), for example his
Haikai kosen (Old Haikai), 1763, a selection of the best of Bashō
and his followers with commentary in Chinese, made the case for a
return to elegance and dignity in poetry. Another force was the *haikai*
poet Shaku Chōmu (1732–95) who was a devoted exponent of
Bashō's ideals. The movement launched by those two men reached
haikai circles all over Japan at about the same time. Hori Bakusui
(1718–83) in his *Shōmon ichiya kōju (An Evening's Lecture on
Bashō and His School)*, published in 1773, expressed his dissatisfaction
with the Mino school of colloquial *haikai* and called for refinement in
poetry and a return to the standards of the *Minashiguri* collection.
Kumura Kyōtai (1731–92) was another Mino poet who worked to
raise the quality of *haikai*. In 1772 he published *Aki no hi (Autumn
Day)*, a collection in the footsteps of *Fuyu no hi* and itself an important model of the elegant classical style in *haikai*. Yosa Buson
(1716–83) began his *haikai* study in Edo with Uchida Senzan. In
the Kyōto area he established a school known as Yahantei (after one
of his pen names: Old Man Yahan, "Old Man Midnight") and acquired various outstanding disciples in poetry who accepted his motto
of "return to Bashō." Among his followers were Kuroyanagi Shōha
(1727–71), Yoshiwake Tairo (d. 1778), and Takai Kitō (1741–89).
Buson was also an important painter in the style called *bunjinga* or
"painting in the literary style." His theory of *haikai* emerged from his
ideas on painting—that the artist should make use of ordinary materials
as a means to transcend the mundane. Buson was also concerned that
his pupils be well acquainted with classical poetry and writers. His
poetry, as shown in the major collections of his work *Buson shichibushū (Buson's Seven Anthologies)*, published in 1808, and *Buson
kushū (Collected Verse of Buson)*, published in 1784, reveals a
master of style and structure. He wrote a great number of poems that
are remarkable for their sensual, graphic beauty and a romantic
inclination based directly on classical poetry. Among the many *haikai*
poets of the new movement were Miura Chora (1729–80), Takakuwa
Rankō (1726–98), and Kaya Shirao (1738–91). Rankō, in his *Ari no
mama (As It Is)* of 1769, and Shirao, in *Kazarinashi (Unadorned)*
of 1771, rejected overly intellectualized and formalized poetry in favor
of direct and emotional writing. They worked in what Bashō termed
the "plain style." Ōshima Ryōta (1718–87), who wrote in the Edo
tradition of Ransetsu as expressed in the *Goshikizumi (Five-Colored
Ink)*, edited by Sōtan (d. 1744) and published in 1731, published
a number of instructional books, such as *Tsukiawase kokagami (The
Little Mirror of Composition)* of 1775, and by those works and glosses

on Bashō's writing helped promote a new poetry in the style of Bashō. Those men by their pursuit of a single ideal in the *haikai* restoration—namely, the return to Bashō—earned the comment that they were promoting "one style for all Japan."

The *bunjin* style or quality in art attempted to combine ordinariness and elegance. The result peculiarly but accurately reflected the mood of the time and is seen at its best in the work of Takebe Ayatari, the promoter of the *katauta* (an old word equivalent to *hokku*) movement in *haikai,* and in the work of Yokoi Yayū (1702–83), especially his remarkable collection of *haibun,* the combination of prose and poetry, titled *Uzura goromo* (*Patched Clothes*), published from 1777 to 1823. Tan Taigi (1709–71), another noteworthy poet in the revival of *haikai,* remained independent of the various schools and wrote about the Shimabara brothel district.

Collections of "high point" *maekuzuke* verses were frequently published in the Kyōto-Ōsaka region and that activity was soon taken up by the poetry masters of Edo. One representative work is *Haikai mutamagawa* (*Haikai of Mutama River*) published during the period 1750 to 1761. It was a collection of urbane and polished light verse in the colloquial *maekuzuke* style, edited by Kei Kiitsu (1695–1762). Competitive poetry composition was quite popular at that time and is reflected in the quantity of publishing. In 1765 a series began with the title *Haifū yanagidaru* (*Yanagida's Light Verse Collection*). It contained *maeku*—the first seventeen syllables of a *tanka*—which were judged to be complete and interesting in themselves. The editor was Karai Senryū (1718–90), poetry master of the "ten-thousand verse" competitions held in the Asakusa district of Edo. His collection encouraged a new appreciation of the art of adding on lines, *tsukeku,* and with it a new and independent *hokku* form was born. The verses were known then as *senryūten no maekuzuke;* today the short humorous poems are known as *senryū*. It seems likely that among the masters of *senryū* poetry were people of considerable education. The form used expressive devices from the *sharebon* and the *kibyōshi*.

Senryū deals with contemporary society, the world of man, through images and stereotypes used in a light and skillful way. The poems do not constitute a literature of irony, but they do offer the good-natured challenge of humorous comments on man's affairs. Among the important collections of *senryū* from that period are *Kawazoiyanagi* (*River Willows*), published from 1780 to 1783 by Karai Senryū, and *Kokin maekuzuke* (*New and Old Verses*), a collection from a ten-thousand verse competition involving Karai Senryū and other poetry masters.

In Edo about the year 1765 the young disciples of Uchiyama Gatei (1723–88) began to hold meetings for the composition of the humorous thirty-one syllable poems known as *kyōka*. The group included Karakoromo Kisshū (1743–1802), Yomo no Akara (1749–1823), Akaraku Kankō (1740–1800), and Heishū Tōsaku (1726–89), men whose urbanity and literary awareness brought new freshness to *kyōka* writing. Gradually the group attracted other outstanding poets, such as Taiya Teiryū (1734–1810) and Motono Mokuami (1724–1811). That was the beginning of a *kyōka* group in Edo and the style of those men, called the Temmei style after the era name for 1781–88, was of one piece with the literary mood reflected in *senryū* and *gesaku* writing. Kisshū was perhaps the most accomplished among the writers, known for his classical and correct style and his supple wit. He edited the *Kyōka wakabashū* (*The Fresh Leaves of Kyōka*), published in 1783. The writer known as Akara may be taken as representative of the cultivated man of his time. He brought his talent to a variety of *gesaku* writing under the name Ōta Nampo, and with Kankō edited two collections: *Manzai kyōkashū* (*The Kyōka Omnibus*), 1783, and a continuation called *Tokuwaka gomanzaishū* (*The Perennial Kyōka Omnibus*) in 1785. Both collections are representative of the Tenmei style. Akara was noted for the light and rhythmical quality of his *kyōka*. He was sociable and more popular than Kisshū, becoming rather the leader in Tenmei *kyōka* circles and the doyen of the *gesaku* literary world. Writing under the pen name of Neboke Sensei, Professor Drowsy, Akara emerges also as an accomplished writer of *hyōshi* (comic poems in Chinese) and along with Hatanaka Kansai was praised as a master of the art.

The kabuki theater, earlier regarded as second best to the puppet theater, found new prosperity and success in the 1770s and 1780s, the period of Tanuma Okitsugu's influence on the shogunate. In the theaters of western Japan, fine actors appeared, such as Nakamura Utaemon the First (1714–91) and Arashi Sūjo (1741–94). In Edo the talented new faces were Ichikawa Danjūrō the Fifth (1741–1806), a man also known as a playwright; Nakamura Nakazō the Fourth (1738–90); Matsumoto Kōshirō (1737–1802); Nakamura Tomijūrō the First (1719–86), a remarkable female impersonator; and Segawa Kikunojō (1750–1810). The city also boasted three outstanding theaters: the Nakamuraza, Ichimuraza, and Moritaza.

Kabuki was still an actors' theater, but the playwrights became aware that "the actor is the soldier, the author is the strategist; if the strategist lacks authority then the soldier will not follow his command" (*Gezairoku*). The final maturation of kabuki during the so-called "period of completion" was in great part due to the skill of the new writers for the theater. The direction was now realism. In the theaters of Kyōto and Ōsaka, Namiki Shōzō (1730–73) left writing for the puppet theater and moved to kabuki, bringing the best qualities of *jōruri* to the theater of live actors. Shōzō was the originator of the revolving stage and use of large-size stage properties. Such plays as his *Sanjikkoku yofune no hajimari* (*Night Boat of the Yodo River*), 1758, were imaginative works that raised the curtain on the new age. Namiki Gohei (1747–1808) began in western Japan, writing such plays as *Kimmon gosan no kiri* (*Paulownia of the Five Mountain Gate of Gold*) in 1778, but in later years he moved to Edo, bringing with him the rational and realistic style of kabuki drama. Through Gohei the long-standing Edo custom of mixing *jidaimono* and *sewamono* in one play was broken, each kind of play and subject matter becoming independent. In Edo, Gohei produced such famous *sewa kyō-gen,* domestic plays, as *Godairiki koi no fūjime* (*The Love Letter*) in 1795, and *Sumidaharu geisha katagi* (*Sumida Spring—The Character of Geisha*) in 1796. Another Edo writer, Sakurada Jisuke (1734–1806), followed Gohei's methods and drew on his experience in the theater world of Ōsaka. His realistic plays brought new quality to kabuki, as in his *Datekurabe okuni kabuki* (*The Date Family*) of 1778. He also composed a number of dance pieces using the music called *tokiwazu-bushi* and *tomimoto-bushi* from the puppet theater.

In his *Gezairoku* (*Mine of Wit*), a commentary on the theaters of the three major cities written in 1801, Gohei notes that even though the several great cities retained their local flavor, improvements in the theater of the time also brought a blending of the styles of Edo, Ōsaka, and Kyōto. Our later view confirms this as the general case for the late eighteenth-century theater world in Japan.

Development of the Edo puppet theater began during the Kyōhō era with the opening of two theaters connected with the Toyotakeza: the Bizenza and the Gekiza. Among the plays performed were: *Shinreiyaguchi no watashi* (*Yaguchi Crossing*), 1770, based on events in the *Taiheiki,* by Fukuchi Kigai (pen name of Hiraga Gennai, 1726–79); and *Gotaiheiki shiraishi banashi* (*White Stones of the Taiheiki*) by Ki no Jōtarō and others, first performed in 1780. In western Japan, Chikamatsu Hanji (1724–83), writing for the Take-motoza, produced in his later years such plays as *Honchō nijūshikō* (*Twenty-four Filial Sons of Japan*), 1766, and *Igagoe dōchū sugoroku* (*Vengeance on the Iga Road*), 1783. Hanji's work was heavily influenced by kabuki and one finds in it, as in all the later *jōruri,* a certain fading vitality. The puppet theater survived, but without the brilliance and invention of its earlier years.

The humorous stories which were prominent in the literature of early Tokugawa became popular with the general public through the wayside storytellers who added pantomime and gestures. Among those monologue performers of *rakugo,* as this was called, were several who achieved considerable fame: Shikano Buzaemon (1649–99) of Edo,

Tsuyu no Gorōbei (1642–1703) in Kyōto and Yonezawa Hikohachi (fl. ca. 1700) in Ōsaka. Books of humorous stories were published under their names. In the Kyōto-Ōsaka area the art of *rakugo*, rather like that of verse composition, grew in popularity to the point where regular meetings of amateur performers were held. Chinese humorous stories also were imported and students of the genre, in order to perfect their own work, composed humorous stories in Chinese or *kambun*, and in the style of the Chinese originals. Those too eventually found their way into print. The stories in Chinese stimulated publication of small, one-volume books, each with ten short humorous stories. The books were popular among the intelligentsia of Edo and were known as *kobanashibon* (little story books) or *hanashibon*. The genre begins with works, such as *Kanoko mochi* (*Dappled Dumplings*), 1772, by Kimuro Dōun (1708–83), and *Kikijōzu* (*The Ideal Listener*), 1772, by Komatsuya Hyakuki (1730–93), and includes collections by Akara, Hōseidō Kisanji (Tegura no Okamochi, 1735–1813), and Santō Kyōden (1761–1816). Most of the stories were skillfully developed and had witty endings. The *hanashibon* were a minor current in Tokugawa literature, but their excellence in the *gesaku* tradition should not be missed.

The Last Century of Edo

The reforms of the Kansei era (1789–1800) under Matsudaira Sadanobu (1758–1829) attempted to halt the declining strength of the Tokugawa government, but the political events were also occasion for great changes in the world of literature. Intellectuals, long active in the field of popular literature, were henceforth attracted to scholarly areas: Dutch studies (*rangaku*), which connoted the whole field of European learning, but particularly medicine, astronomy, ballistics and the like; national studies (*kokugaku*), which focused on Japanese history and literature; economics and government. The appointment system initiated in Kansei provided a way for the emergence of a number of talented men into public life as officials and administrators. In popular literature, however, numerous men appeared who gave themselves the title of *gesaku* writers but who lacked the education of their predecessors. They acquired certain techniques of writing and some were able to earn their livelihood as fiction writers. The audience for *gesaku* writing changed too. The high quality of the earlier works doubtless attracted readers of some intellectual discernment, perhaps with educations comparable to the level of that of the writers, but after the beginning of Kansei there was a considerable broadening of the class of readers for those works, possibly one result of the success of public education in central Japan. The relationship between author and reader was changing. Writers sought, and their readers awarded them, the kind of respect achieved by the writers of the previous period, but as writing became more and more a commercial enterprise there was a decline in quality among writers whose only claim was that of writing for entertainment. Publishers too came to treat work simply as commercial property. Indeed those and later *gesaku* writers, it was said, made a boast of their vulgarity. The situation was not much different in poetry where the function of *haikai* master or teacher grew as a business as it declined as an art. Works of popular literature aimed at appealing to the widest audience; consequently, structure and technical skills suffered and there was a general decline in artistic quality. The position of writers at the time was rather anomalous and in fact not unlike that of the intellectual writers of the earlier years of the eighteenth century. Popular literature did not engender any new insights as literature, being frankly bourgeois and pleasure seeking, but the overall literary scene was taking on new dimensions due to the rapid growth of literacy and the tendency toward specialization among writers.

In fine writing, particularly poetry and prose in Chinese, there emerges in the Kansei years a new awareness of realism and individualism, an intimation of the modern attitude in literature.

In a time of enthusiasm for the study of old literature, pseudo-archaism, and concern for ancient styles and rhetoric, writers in western Japan found cause to criticize the restraints such literature made on individual thought and feeling. Theorists praised the poetry styles of T'ang China. In their actual compositions they heeded the Sung style which emphasized the content of poetry, and with the appearance of Kan Sazan (1748–1827) and others, poetry in Chinese underwent a complete change in the work of the Kyōto-Ōsaka writers. In Edo too the view of Chinese writing changed. One representative of the new outlook was Yamamoto Hokuzan (1752–1812) who wrote two critical works: *Sakubun shikō* (*The Aims of Prose*) in 1779 and *Sakushi shikō* (*The Aims of Poetry*) in 1783. Hokuzan turned away from the work of Li Po and Wang Wei, the two great T'ang poets, and followed the approach of the Ming dynasty poet Yuan Hung-tao (En Kōdō in Japanese) who argued for the primary importance of the human spirit in poetry. Hokuzan was insistent that only through expression of the poet's own voice and inner feelings was new poetry possible. People had unique natures, the times in which men lived differed, and only through individual poetry could we approach our true inner selves. He viewed Sung poetry as the embodiment of this truth. The spread of the Sung style in Edo produced several outstanding poets, particularly from the school of Ichikawa Kansai (1749–1820): Kashiwagi Jotei (1763–1819) and Kikuchi Gozan (1772–1855),

among others. Thus for a while Sung poetry rather than poetry of the
Ming dynasty was most influential in Japan. But later, in the words of
Hokuzan, the feeling was that "the poetry of today sufficed for today,"
(*Kōkyōrō shiwa: Hokuzan's Talks on Poetry*) and models of composition were taken from whatever source the poet's taste found appealing, from late T'ang to the contemporary period. Yanagawa Seigan
(1789–1858) of the Yamamoto Hokuzan school, and Rai San'yō
(1780–1833), who was close to Sazan, were noted for their writing
in Chinese. Other men of importance in this area were Nomura Kōen
(1775–1842) and Tomono Kashū (1791–1849). Matsuzaki Kōdō
(1771–1844), one of the Confucianists of the Shōheikō, the *bakufu*
school begun by Hayashi Razan in 1630, pointed out that it was
natural for Chinese writing in Japan to have a Japanese flavor—an
intimation, even in the conservative world of Chinese letters, of the
respect for true individuality and the realities of the world which was
to become manifest in the social revolution of the later nineteenth
century and the Meiji Era.

The most notable areas of writing in Chinese during the
Tokugawa period were development of expository prose and the revival of the long poem, the latter having all but disappeared in Japan
with the beginning of the Heian period. Among the outstanding works
were Arai Hakuseki's autobiography *Oritakushiba no ki* (*Brushwood*)
of 1716, the *Kagetsu sōshi* (*Moon and Flower Book*), essays by
Matsudaira Sadanobu from about 1800, and Buson's *Shumpū batei
kyoku* (*Spring Breeze on the Kema Embankment*), a collection of
long poems in *Yahanraku* (*Midnight Music*), published in 1777.
Previously there was a good deal of writing in Chinese which suffered
through an overdose of Confucianism and through too close an imitation of Chinese styles. Now, however, even Confucianists in Japan
preferred to write as men of letters concerned with the realities of
life around them. Their style cannot be measured by some more or
less close approximation to the Chinese model but must rather be
seen in its own terms as an attempt to deal more freely with the
ideas and feelings then current in Japan. The results of this concern
may be seen in the historical writing of Rai San'yō, the travel pieces
of Saitō Setsudō (1797–1865), and the sketches of Terakado Seiken
(1796–1868), whose work appeared in *Edo hanjōki* (*Flourishing
Edo*), published between 1832 and 1836.

Ozawa Roan (1723–1801) was the first to examine critically the
conflict in poetic outlook between archaic expression which turned to
the classics for models and the free-spirited approach which emphasized the natural expression of human feelings, the idea behind Kamo
Mabuchi's theory of poetry. Roan maintained that the value of the
Man'yōshū, for example, lay in expressing the feeling of its time

precisely in its own language, in the language of the people of antiquity. He thought that archaism in language was anathema to poetry, saying: "Poetry is speaking of the present, following our own reason, saying what we think in our own words." His affirmation of the present, of the contemporary world, led him also to affirm the necessity of individualism. "Nothing precedes my own heart," he said. The expression of his own transient and changing feelings leads to awareness and perception of what is unchanging in human emotion. Thus, he thought, poetry, *waka,* held a special significance for the time of its composition. The Edo poet and *kokugaku* scholar Murata Harumi (1746–1811) and his group further developed the argument in favor of contemporary language. Indeed, there were many outside of the *kokugaku* school who approved of Roan's thesis. It would seem, however, that Roan was ahead of his time in his theories more than in actual poetry composition, for he looked to the *Kokinshū* as a model for his own poetry. Kagawa Kageki (1768–1843), a follower of Roan, went a step further in his book *Shingaku iken (Comments on the New School of Poetry)* of 1813, insisting that Mabuchi's devotion to the *Kokinshū* and the ensuing archaism of his style failed in not being true to human feeling. "The poetry of today's world must be in the language of today and in the rhythm of today," he wrote. Kageki's *waka* put his theory into practice, creating a wholly new poetry. Through his disciples his views acquired considerable prestige and became the vehicle for examining some of the current abuses of poetry. For one thing, it was deplorable to those men that *waka* had turned into little more than a polite bourgeois accomplishment, no longer an outpouring of poetic feeling but totally imitative and contrived. Further, they detested the mannered style of *waka* which aimed at elegance through use of the old vocabulary in a resigned and passive way—defending contemporary language by saying that to reject it was rather like despising oneself for the odor of the human body. In this world one must use the language of the world; *waka* was one's own mind expressed in one's own words. Essentially they were suggesting that literature must somehow correspond to one's present real life, that it derive from life rather than other literature. They felt too that *waka* was a "divine melody" with its vitality rooted in one's time and one's true self; they called it kinship with the immortals. One of those men, Uchiyama Mayumi (1784–1852), wrote that one must totally discard devices in poetry; that all naturalness was lost when the poet made contrivance and submission to standards of the past his main guides. Kageki himself said that "poetry is not reasoning but rather an inquiry," developing that idea to a reproach of the concept of *giri,* obligation, in literature on grounds that it was repressive to the creative spirit, and that the devices of poetry are merely artful structurings which have degraded poetry. Besides offering those quite advanced views on poetry, clear anticipations of the modern world, Kageki was himself an accomplished poet who brought new vitality to the art of *waka*. His school of poetry, known as the Keien, or "Cinnamon Garden," filled the position left vacant by the retreat of the Nijō school and occupied the center of the poetry world. Kageki's collected poetry, under the title of *Keien isshi* (*A Branch from the Cinnamon Garden*), published in 1830, nonetheless reflects a considerable debt to the *Kokinshū*, a point which we must acknowledge as a typical limitation of the Tokugawa period.

Although their influence was slight, we may note in passing the work of Fujitani Nariakira (1738–79) and Mitsue (1768–1823), father and son, who brought considerable psychological subtlety to an attempt to synthesize ancient and modern poetic theories.

The first part of Santō Kyōden's *Chūshin suikoden* (*Water Margin of the Loyal Retainers*) appeared in 1799; the second part appeared in 1801. Following this there began the device of combining the *Water Margin* stories with elements from the world of Japanese theater, notably by Takizawa Bakin (1767–1848) and Shin Rotei (d. 1815). There were, of course, some elements carried over from the theatrical stories, *shibaimono*, published by the Hachimonjiya, but the new books, through careful and practical adoption of techniques from the Chinese novel as well as through a new sentence style which combined Chinese with colloquial Japanese, represented a truly new form of the long story or novel in Japanese. Those were the books known as *yomihon*, reading books. The form was perfected in the competition among the three Edo writers just mentioned, all of whom profited from the earlier work of Tsuga Teishō and Ueda Akinari. Santō Kyōden made wide use of Chinese colloquial novels—studying the Japanese adaptations, since he was unable to read the originals. Shin Rotei too made use of translations of Chinese novels. The *yomihon* drew on the many Buddhist *setsuwa* which had been published during the Tokugawa period, putting into the form of the long novel the highly condensed *setsuwa* literature from Buddhist and also from historical sources. Examples of this kind of adaptation are Bakin's *Sayonakayama sekigen'ikyō* (*Echoes of the Rocks of Sayonakayama*), published in 1804, which drew on the *setsuwa* called *Sayonakayama reishōki* (*The Spirit Bells of Sayonakayama*), and Kyōden's work of 1765, *Sakurahime zenden akebono no sōshi* (*The Tale of Princess Cherry Blossom*) from the *setsuwa* titled *Kanzen sakurahimeden* (*The Enlightening Story of Princess Cherry Blossom*). Bakin's adaptations of Chinese novels rested on his limited knowledge of colloquial Chinese, but his writing took in most of the essentials of the originals. He introduced to Japan a new literary device, that of the ruffian hero, as in his

Shitennō sōtō iroku (*The Secret Story of Yorimitsu and His Men*). Bakin also urged writers to abandon the libretto-like story books published by the Hachimonjiya. His masterpiece was modeled on the Chinese *Water Margin,* drawing on the Japanese war tales and on Japanese history to produce *Chinsetsu yumiharitsuki* (*A Camellia Tale of the Waxing Moon*) published between 1807 and 1811. Kyōden, on the other hand, avoided the area of adaptation and devoted most of his attention to popular novels in a graceful, flowing style. In this he stands apart from the main development in *yomihon,* more and more of which found their stories in vendettas and in the lives of the nobles set against the panorama of Japanese history. Their plots were driven by the principles of karma, spiritual cause and effect, a feature common to both Buddhist *setsuwa* and Chinese novels. The result was the truly romantic novel in which strange and marvelous events surrounded a variegated cast of characters—beautiful women, villains, renowned monks, and superhuman heroes in the roles of idealized warriors. That was a new development in Japanese novels and the authors devoted great care to the structure of those long works. The emergence of the later *yomihon* and their subsequent dramatization on the kabuki stage was a reversal of the interplay between fiction and the theater during the height of the Hachimonjiya. At the beginning of the nineteenth century it was instead the novel, in the form of the *yomihon,* which held the central role in the world of literature.

A kind of true-story novel had survived in western Japan, circulated in hand-copied form. It too was turned into *yomihon* material and printed under the name of *ehon-yomihon,* illustrated reading books, with pictures by such artists as Hayami Shungyōsai (d. 1823) and Okada Gyokuzan (d. 1812). *Ehon taikōki* (*The Story of Hideyoshi Illustrated*), from 1797, and *Ehon chūshingura* (*The Loyal Ronin Illustrated*), published in 1807–8, are examples of the illustrated *yomihon.*

The period from 1804 to 1817, the Bunka era, represents the creative years of the *yomihon.* Signs of decline gradually appeared in the following decade with the publication of older compositions to which illustrations were added, works known as *zuai,* which attempted to make up for the lack of *yomihon* writing. Only Takizawa Bakin continued to produce new work, such long novels as *Nansō satomi hakkenden* (*The Eight Retainers of Satomi*), published serially between 1814 and 1841, and *Asahina juntōki,* or *Asahina shimameguri no ki* (*The Travels of Asahina Yoshihide*), published from 1815 to 1826. Bakin's devotion to his writing was remarkable, especially when we consider that he was afflicted with blindness in his later years. He prided himself that his own work was more meticulous and better structured than the corresponding Chinese novels, and indeed his prose style was a fine blend of Japanese and Chinese, making frequent use of rhythmical alternation of five- and seven-syllable phrases— the basic meter of Japanese poetry. The moralism of Bakin's work is famous but perhaps also generally misunderstood, since the author himself left his theories in this area incompletely explained. "If a writer is ignorant," he said, "then his moral decisions cannot be just." Of course, Bakin himself was well read in literature and history, but he nonetheless placed aesthetic and entertainment values foremost in his own writing. He explains in his fiction that an author articulates the principles of human existence through Buddhist and Confucian value systems and his own particular view of man. For its time, that was a rather liberal outlook, but the tolerant relativism and good sense of Bakin's ideas about fiction are clearly manifested in his writing. Not surprisingly, Bakin was adverse to being classified with the usual run of *gesaku* novelists and was frequently at odds with and critical of his fellow writers.

In the humor-books known as *kokkeibon* a turning point was reached with the publication of *Inaka shibai* (*Country Theater*) by Manzōtei (1754–1808) in 1787. That work made use of the dialect and the village theater of Niigata district, but as stories of the gay quarters they were a reaction against the limitations of *sharebon*. *Inaka shibai*, with its republication in 1801, began to draw serious regard from such writers as Jippensha Ikku (1765–1831) and Shikitei Sanba (1776–1822). With his skill at adaptation, Ikku turned the earlier work into a comic picaresque tale, his *Tōkaidōchū hizakurige* (*A Shank's Mare Tour of the Eastern Sea Road*), which was produced serially between 1802 and 1822. The artless and slapstick humor of that work was exceedingly popular and Ikku continued that story and mode for the rest of his life. With the appearance of numerous imitations of *Hizakurige* by other authors the pattern was set for the later style of the humor-books. Kawatei Onitake (1760–1818) varied the device with the rustic tourist sightseeing in Edo and produced *Kyūkanchō* (*The Tourist's Notebook*) in the years from 1805 to 1809. There is a resemblance to the earliest cinema in those works, with characters appearing within a fixed scene: for example, the compositions of Shikitei Samba who placed his characters on a simple stage where vocal wit, Samba's specialty, held reign. Among his works in that framework were such popular collections as *Ukiyoburo* (*Bath House of the Floating World*), published from 1809 to 1813; *Ukiyodoko* (*Barber Shop of the Floating World*), published from 1811 through 1815; and *Kyakusha hyōbanki* (*Guests at the Brothel, A Critique*) of 1811—the last identical in title to a famous 1780 work by Utei Enba (1743–1822), a *gesaku* writer and *kyōka* poet. Perhaps Sanba's greatest work is his *Kokon hyakubaka* (*A Collection of One*

Hundred Fools, Ancient and Modern) from 1814, in which the colloquial language of his time is meticulously preserved. Sanba saw his own work as being in the true tradition of the earlier *gesaku* writers. He maintained his witty posture and was ever on the lookout for the humorous situation, even if slightly forced. His success was due in no small part to his craftsman-like attention to detail.

Imitators of the various devices in *kokkeibon* appeared, being slight variations on the originals. The humor-books were totally devoted to entertainment and the demands they made on the reader were far less than the more literary *yomihon*. Increasingly, however, authors made use of old material without any visible regard for their own repetitiousness. One event in the field of *kokkeibon* which is of particular interest was the emergence of the first full-time commercial writer in Japan; that was Jippensha Ikku, mentioned above. Though of limited talents, he remained a popular author into the Meija era. Despite their shortcomings, the various genres remain important legacies from the fiction of the late Tokugawa period: the *sharebon* and *kokkeibon* for their realistic observation as well as their skill in dialogue and the competence in structuring fiction developed in the *yomihon*.

By the time of the Kansei era, the last decade of the eighteenth century, scholars and intellectuals had all but disappeared from the ranks of *kibyōshi* writers. In their place appeared specialists like Kyōden, Ikku, and Sanba. The writing turned commercial to suit the bourgeois townsmen audience, flavored with a taste of erudition as suited the times, yet filled with goblins and bombast. The decade did see the creation of a new kind of story, however, in exceedingly popular tales of revenge or vendetta called *katakiuchi mono*. They began in 1795 with the publication of *Katakiuchi gijo no hanabusa* (*Fair Petals of Vengeance*) by Nansenshōso Mabito (1749–1807). The style was that of the true-story novel in condensed form. In such works success depended on the patronage of readers with slight discrimination. Consequently a fast-paced story with lots of action took precedence over a carefully worked out plot and subtle development. The *kibyōshi*, which until then had been complete in two or three volumes, each with five pages, were gradually lengthened. At the same time there appeared in the bookstalls illustrated war stories in one volume with several tens of pages, by such authors as Kitao Masayoshi (1760–1824) and Kitao Shigemasa (1739–1820). Those stories were most popular with young readers and the books may have raised the idea of combining two or three volumes of *kibyōshi* into one volume, for at that time such books appeared, under the name of *gōkan* or combined volumes. The *kusazōshi* or "grass books" published after 1807 were totally in the *gōkan* format. Between 1815 and 1820 there was a revival of *kokkeibon* and republication of *kibyōshi,* but the predominant type was fiction of the *yomihon* kind which, in its true-story variety, influenced the kabuki stage. *Ukiyoe* artists frequently used the faces of popular actors in the lavish illustrations which were part of those books and it is probably well to regard the later *gōkan* simply as illustrated *yomihon,* a kind of kabuki on paper. Many *gōkan* were highly erotic in their illustrations as well as in their texts—to an extent which frequently brought government censorship.

Ryūtei Tanehiko (1783–1842) is a representative *gōkan* writer. His *Shōhon jitate (Kabuki Stories),* published between 1815 and 1831, was a libretto-style work which borrowed kabuki stories and illustrations directly from the stage—the illustrations designed by Utagawa Kunisada.

The *gōkan* of the period during which Kyōden and Sanba were active were published in great quantity. Each year seemed to produce a new attempt at adapting *Water Margin* or *The Tale of Genji;* for example, Bakin's *Keisei suikoden (Courtesan's Water Margin),* 1825–34, and *Nisemurasaki inaka genji (A Rustic Genji)* published from 1829 through 1842. The latter work by Tanehiko placed Genji in a setting from the Muromachi period, but the work is thought to have been a parody of the shogun Tokugawa Ienari and his harem. *Gōkan* adaptations of Japanese and Chinese stories, as well as condensed versions of *yomihon,* were very popular. Serial publication of stories became the rule, and writers like Santō Kyōden (1769–1858) came to write long stories exclusively. Some of the *gōkan* stretched out their narratives into the Meiji period. The readers seem to have been women and young people or persons generally of little education; further, the books came to be regarded as appropriate souvenirs of Edo and were sent to the provinces and distributed at New Year as famous products of the capital.

In *haikai* poetry there was a great increase in the number of poets as a consequence of the dominance of one school all over Japan. There was a corresponding growth too in the ranks of *haikai* teachers, professional poets who made direction and instruction of amateurs their daily business. However, as the quantity of poetry grew, the quality declined. *Haikai* turned into a social activity, a genteel and cultured pastime for the common people, and the professional poets who depended for their livelihoods on bourgeois patronage could not maintain any literary spirit. Poets became poetry teachers and the quality of their writing declined. *Haikai* flowed like a smooth stream from the brushes of the new writers, without the slightest individuality and totally uninspired. That was the era when regularly held meetings for *haikai* composition were most popular, and the name for those monthly or twice-a-month gatherings, *tsukinami,* became synonymous with mediocrity. Even the work of the *sōshō,* the poetry masters, was devoid of seriousness and vitality.

Some poetry masters of the Edo school and of the various branches of the Mino school maintained their scope and energies where the tradition of the leaders of the *haikai* revival was still vital. In Edo Suzuki Michihiko (1757–1819) of the Kaya Shirao (1738–91) line held his ground by reason of his political skill; in central Japan Inoue Shirō (1742–1812) from the school of Katō Gyōdai (1732–92) gained popularity for his warm character; in Kyōto Emori Gekkyo (1756–1824) of the Buson school was influential. Those three men were the outstanding poets of the Kansei era. Kobayashi Issa (1763–1827) was an individualist who followed a highly subjective path, making free use of the colloquial language and in general opposing the traditional refinement of classical *haikai.* The poet known as Otsuni (1756–1823) is representative of those writers whose work is heavy with local color—a phenomenon which appeared after the diffusion of *haikai* all over Japan. Besides those men there was a scattering of poets who continued the *bunjin* style of the 1780s, their work surviving in several collections. Representatives of that group are Natsume Seibi (1749–1816) of Edo, Ōtomo Ōemaru (1722–1805) of Ōsaka, and Sakai Hōitsu (1761–1827), but there was little creativeness in their work. From the fourth decade of the nineteenth century, roughly the Tempō era (1830–44), three poets of some note remain: Tagawa Hōrō (1762–1845), a native of Kumamoto who took up residence in Edo; Narita Sōgyū (1761–1842), a member of the Rankō (1726–98) poetry group in Kyōto; and Sakurai Baishitsu (1769–1852). But for the most part, outside of the work of a few men, *haikai* remained immersed in the mediocre conventional style.

In *kyōka* and *senryū* during the 1780s the style of Teiryū spread throughout the country. Teiryū's disciples dominated the era. Shikatsube Magao (1753–1829) succeeded to the leadership of Ōta Nampo's followers; another of Nampo's disciples, the man called Yadoya no Meshimori (1753–1830), that being the pen name of Ishikawa Masamochi, achieved some prominence and various groups were formed, such as the Suichiku (which published the work of its members under the title of *Suichikushū: Imbibers' Collection*), and the Motomachi group. Magao and Meshimori were the most influential of the poetry masters and there was considerable competition between the two. Magao, a worldly wit, became quite skilled in his style and had a large following; Meshimori adhered to the tradition of humor known as *rakusho,* which was satirical and critical. *Kyōka,* comic 31-syllable poems, were produced in great quantity, but the quality of the writing severely declined and in fact that literary form ended in the Tokugawa period.

Yanagidaru continued publication through the 167th edition, which appeared in 1838. As ever it was the weather vane of *senryū* poetry and reflected the changing styles. As a short poetry form, *senryū* was a literature of meaning and exposition in contrast to *haikai,* a literature of feeling and suggestion. *Senryū,* of course, provided a fine medium for men of sensitivity and keen powers of observation, but with the rising tide of popular competitions in *senryū* writing, the subtleties turned to conventions, with too many poets depending on devices and rules. Half of the interest in such writing was purely formal and conventional, with concept and meaning being rather devoid of literary qualities. The result was little more than a riddle and the poets' efforts at expression generated only facile word games. After about 1810 leaders of that verse style were known as *kyōku,* as were the verses themselves; thus the fourth generation Senryū, Hitomi Mintei (1778–1844), styled himself *haifū kyōku genso* or "Founder of the Light Verse Style."

Senryū composition flourished in the provinces as well as in the cities. In Yamagata, in northern Japan, a collection was published in 1780; in Matsumoto, in central Japan, a *senryū* collection was published about 1810. The list could be extended, but the styles of the provincial writers reflected without change the Edo style and serve mostly to indicate the diffusion of the Edo mode. *Zappai* was also popular and occasionally some truly regional qualities appeared, such as the *kyōkai* or *kammurizuke* which was adding the final twelve syllables to a given opening line of five syllables, an activity popular around Nagoya and elsewhere along the Tōkaidō, the highway between Kyōto and Edo.

The impending changes in Japanese society produced various symptoms as the period of Tokugawa rule came to a close. Writers and intellectuals turned away from the study of literature and gave their energies to the various social movements which preceded the Meiji Restoration. Many of those educated people were active in national affairs and when they took up the brush to write it was often to compose poems with critical social overtones or to set out their ideas on government. The average man, however, took little notice of the dangerous condition of the country, having grown complacent over the years and unable to conceive of change or to imagine a way of life other than the one to which he had grown accustomed. But great changes indeed were taking place in Japan. The ethics of neo-Confucianism, which had been society's foundation in early Tokugawa, by now had all but vanished despite the oppressive reform efforts of the Tempō era under Mizuno Tadakuni (1794–1851). There was no way to reform the trend toward hedonism and corruption. In the lives of ordinary men there was no room for an unhurried appreciation of literature; and in the competition of the marketplace the literary and theatrical worlds aimed only to please their audience's lowest tastes.

However, the laxness which had spread through society during the long period of feudal government also allowed something new to emerge here and there in the arts: on the stage appeared the figure of the thief as hero, and in the fiction called *ninjōbon* appeared a kind of woman who, though fragile, was strongly set on living her own life. In the popular literary arts a tone of resistance was heard against the established order of things; there was a groping for a new way of life. The secluded poet, of course, reflected none of this movement, but the emergence of individuality in the literary image of man is as recognizable there as it is in its present form in the twentieth century.

In western Japan popular actors appeared, such as Nakamura Utaemon the Third (1778–1838), and, of course, there was no lack of writing talent for the stage, but by the last decades of Tokugawa the center of kabuki had shifted to Edo. As the leading entertainment medium of the day, Edo kabuki made great advances in offering spectacle and sensuous beauty. The theater provided a high level of technical achievement in acting and production, enhanced by a stage that was flexible and mechanically sophisticated. The quick change of costume came into use along with a style of recitation known as *Kiyomoto-bushi,* after the samisen artist Kiyomoto Enjūdayū (d. 1811). The repertory included excellent plays by such men as Bandō Mitsugorō the Third (1775–1831); Matsumoto Kōshirō the Fifth (1762–1838); Ichikawa Danjūrō the Seventh (1791–1849), who arranged the eighteen favorite plays of the standard repertory; Onoe Kikugorō the Third (1784–1849); Ichikawa Kodanji the Fourth (1812–66), who was a collaborator of Mokuami; and Iwai Hanshirō the Fifth (1766–1849), whose realistic acting greatly enhanced his texts. All those men worked in the ever-popular genre of *sewamono,* plays of contemporary life. Those plays took their characters from the lowest level of Edo society and portrayed in sometimes brutally realistic terms scenes of murder and bloodshed as well as situations involving blackmail, love, and the supernatural.

The first librettist who was able to control how the actors handled the play was Tsuruya Namboku the Fourth (1755–1829), the author of *Tōkaidō yotsuya kaidan* (*A Ghost Tale of Yotsuya*). Namboku initiated the device of offering main characters who were thoroughly evil, immersed in deeds of vengeance and wickedness. His plays were sharply perceptive and kept tight control of complicated plots. Another writer of talent was Segawa Jokō the Third (1806–81). The major playwright of late Tokugawa, however, was Furukawa Mokuami, generally known as Kawatake Mokuami (1816–93). Mokuami produced a great variety of plays, but his masterpieces were pure *sewamono,* such dramas as *Tsuta momiji utsu no ya tōge* (*Scarlet Ivy and the Pass of Tsuta*), 1856; *Nezumi komon haru no shingata* (*The Master Burglar*), 1857; *Sannin kichiza kuruwa no hatsugai* (*The Thieves*), 1860; and *Kanzen chōaku nozoki karakuri* (*A Villain's Fate*), 1862. While Mokuami's sensitivity to nuances of character was perhaps less than that of Namboku, he brought the full potential of kabuki to fruition and maintained compact dramatic structure. In his *shiranami* or "white-wave" plays, such as *Shiranami gonin otoko* (*Five Thieves*) of 1862, one indeed finds praise of criminals, but except for those *shiranami* plays in which thieves are the heroes, Mokuami generally took the orthodox approach, praising virtue and reproving vice. However one may feel about the content of his plays, in them kabuki found its finest exponent. Mokuami's career flourished into the early years of Meiji with new *sewamono,* called *zangirimono* after the new male hairstyle, and *katsurekigeki* (living-history drama) which dealt with the recent past in realistic terms.

Among the books published as *yomihon* there was an early type of intermediate length which had as its subject matter the everyday life of commoners. From about 1825 such medium size *yomihon* appeared more frequently. In this format Jippensha Ikku wove romantic elements into stories of the domestic affairs of the *chōnin* and tradesmen. Bizanjin (1790–1858), a disciple of Santō Kyōden, continued his mentor's style, and Umebori Kokuga (1750–1821) extended the length of the *sharebon* and evidenced some care with his plots. At some point in the early nineteenth century those variations on *yomihon* came to be known as *chūhon,* literally "medium-size books." Tamenaga Shunsui (1790–1843), working with other writers, became one of the first specialists in the genre which in the early decades of the nineteenth century combined elements from almost all the popular forms, and even made use of elements from the puppet theater. During the Tempō era a serial publication followed the success of *Shunshoku umegoyomi* (*Plum Calendar of Spring*) and was continued into the Meiji period. With that work and others, such as *Harutsugedori* (*Harbinger of Spring*) of 1837, the *ninjōbon,* books of sentiment, arrived as the latest development in fiction. There were a number of excellent works; for example, *Kanamajiri musume setsuyō* (*A Lexicon of Women*) by Kyokusanjin (d. ca 1840), published 1831–34. The writer Tamenaga Shunsui styled himself the "grandaddy of *ninjōbon.*" He assembled a group of young writers who called themselves the "Tamenaga Group," with whom he produced several new books each year, working also with Shōtei Kinsui (1794–1862) who revised and edited Shunsui's work. During the reforms of the Tempō era woodblocks of the *ninjōbon* were destroyed by the government, and Shunsui along with other writers was imprisoned under the charge of corrupting public morals. Nonetheless, the momentum and popularity of the *ninjōbon* continued into the Meiji era.

As *ninjōbon* matured they became involved with the joys and sorrows of love in realistic erotic detail. Shunsui remarked that the books held nothing back concerning the suffering and heartache between men and women, and that the writers really understood their characters and expressed their subtle feelings. Very likely there was considerable sharing between the lives of the young girl readers and the characters portrayed in the stories that dealt with ordinary people, their joys and sorrows. Through the *ninjōbon,* characters in fiction regained the broad human qualities which had been lost to cynicism or moralizing in earlier Tokugawa fiction. Authors of those works presented no profound interpretation of life; they pandered to their readers, inserted the lyrics of popular songs in their stories, explained customs, and slipped in advertising for cosmetic shops and so forth. Despite such adulteration, appealing to the unsophisticated feelings of ordinary readers, the books clearly brought the art of fiction back to its proper path, even to the point of portraying women in psychological depth, as real human beings.

Among the men who were writing the anecdotal stories called *kobanashibon*—such Edo writers as Utei Emba (1743–1822)—a group was formed to present original compositions in the form of dramatic readings. The members met privately for a number of years, the story-telling technique they used achieving a fine polish, until in 1798 the first public presentation was made of the vaudeville monologue by Sanshōtei Karaku (d. 1833). The performance was known either as *kobanashi,* "anecdotes," or *otoshibanashi* (the Chinese graphs now more commonly read as *rakugo*), "punch-line stories." Karaku is recognized as the founder of the Tōkyō *rakugo* theater and his successors have continued the art down to the present. Professionalization advanced the story-teller's art greatly and various new forms were invented. Karaku himself began the *sandai banashi* (three-topic story) which is a humorous tale woven together from three topics supplied by the audience during the performance. Asanebō Muraku ("Sleepy-Head Muraku," 1777–1831) developed the long story called *ninjō banashi,* "sentimental stories." Hayashiya Shōzō (1780–1842) specialized in ghost stories; San'yūtei Enshō (1768–1838) did *shibai banashi,* theatricals or stories acted out; and Sen'yūtei Senkyō (d. 1892) worked with musical accompaniment. By the end of the Tokugawa period renowned performers appeared in the various styles—Tachikawa, San'yū, Yanagi—and those men further extended the popularity of *rakugo* by drawing on fiction and the theater for material. Finally in that period there appeared the famous San'yūtei Enchō (1839–1900) whose popularity lasted into Meiji.

In the Kyōto-Ōsaka area amateur story-telling groups had existed from the Kan'ei era (1772–80). Such groups became particularly numerous during the last decade of the eighteenth century when Katsura Bunji (1773–1815) appeared. He is known as the founder of *rakugo* theater in western Japan.

Story-telling during Tokugawa was an art of significant quality. In Edo during the late eighteenth century, there were popular narrators, such as Baba Bunkō (1715–58) and Morikawa Bakoku (1714–91), who gave performances that were popular with the townsmen. Even after Bunkō's execution for writings critical of the government—he was known as a *gesaku* writer—Bakoku and other story-tellers were invited to perform for the upper classes, the nobles and daimyo. Tōrintei Tōgyoku (1787–1850) was probably the strongest force in creating a durable narrative style for popular audiences. Others of note were Nankaku, founder of the Tanabe line of performers; Enshin (1761–1840), founder of the Itō school of story-tellers; Hakuen the Second; Hakuzan (d. 1873), famous for his thieves tales; Enryō; and Ishikawa Ichimu (d. 1854) who specialized in military tales and biography. Some performers specialized in the kind of domestic tale called *sewamono* in the theater, while Hakuen and Hokuzan are said to have influenced the kabuki playwright Mokuami. The performer Kenkonbō Ryōsai (1769–1860) was particularly influential in broadening the scope of *rakugo* and was an inspiration for the late Edo *gesaku* writer Tamenaga Shunsui. From about 1775 in Ōsaka, Yoshida Ippo and Shibaya Katsusuke (also called Ozaki Katsusuke, a *jōruri* and *kyōgen* writer) performed long stories taken from Chinese novels, but by the end of Tokugawa it was commonplace that story-tellers from Edo dominated the field in western Japan as well as in the east.

Kabuki was still the leading theater, but for most people it had already become rather inaccessible. The plebeian art of the time was story-vaudeville. Considering the influence of that art on the written literature of the period, we might even propose it as one of the truly representative literary arts of late Tokugawa.

The decline in prose literature during late Tokugawa was complemented by the rise of vaudeville as the popular literary art. However, the most excellent and most progressive literature of the time was the product of recluses who had withdrawn from the social chaos. Those writers were almost totally divorced from the various literary cliques. Ōnuma Chinzan (1818–91) and Nakajima Sōin (1780–1856) were such men, both writers of Chinese poetry, who, as urban recluses, rejected their society. We might also point to some of the poets writing in Japanese: Kumagai Naoyoshi (1782–1862) and Hatta Tomonori (1799–1873). Tomonori was invited into the Meiji government where he advised on matters of poetry. His reputation grew from the honesty and sincerity with which he expressed his inner life, a quality that made him a remarkably individualistic poet. Yamamoto Ryōkan (1758–1831), from Niigata on the Japan Sea, was an ardent admirer of the *Man'yōshū* and sought to express pure emotion in his work, rejecting the conventions of poetry. Another man who took the *Man'yōshū* as an ideal was Hiraga Motoyoshi (1800–65). He produced fine love poems without the archaisms of the Gikoha, the Antiquity School, which grew up during mid-Meiji. Ōkuma Kotomichi (1795–1868)—under the influence of Kageki and Hirose Tansō (1782–1856), both writers of Chinese verse—completed a book of criticism called *Hitorigochi* (*Musings*) in 1857, in which he made a case for individualism and modernity, asserting that poetry was for a particular time and society, and need not follow the poetry of another day. Even though his own work was close to the *Kokinshū,* his style was his own and his poetry vibrated with a strong and fresh spirit. Tachibana Akemi (1812–88), an ardent nationalist and supporter of the emperor, ended his life as an impoverished recluse; his *waka* were in a free style and intimately reflected the poet's real life. *Waka* poetry had a difficult and uneven existence during the Tokugawa period, but with such poets as those just mentioned, the form gives a clear feeling of having stepped into the Japanese world which began with the Meiji Restoration.

Contemporary Period

A.D. 1868 TO 1945

by

HASEGAWA IZUMI AND SAEGUSA YASUTAKA

The Meiji, Taishō, and Shōwa Periods

Tokugawa was called "Modern" p. [105]

THE BEGINNING of the Meiji period is generally considered to be the beginning of modern literature in Japan. Through the restoration of the Emperor and the reorganization of government, Japan abandoned feudalism and moved quickly into the modern age. The country opened itself to the world after two centuries of official seclusion and began to adapt to the new currents of life. Foreign cultural influences, particularly from Europe, began to transform Japan's outlook and society. The extent of this change was greater than any previous transition in the life of the nation.

Modern literature takes modern society for its background and it is frequently concerned with the problem of how men can or should live in the new world, a world which was motivated by capitalism and inspired by the democratic ideals that grew out of liberalism and individualism. In the new setting modern man, freed of the constraints of a feudal society, became liberated and politically the equal of all other men. The modern ego or concept of self which emerged in Japan took humanism as its intellectual foundation, but along with the growth of modern capitalism structural contradictions within the society appeared. In reaction to that socialism soon found adherents, and the struggle between the two views of society became explicit. The fabric of modern society was complicated further by the great strides made in natural sciences at the beginning of the space age. The thought and emotions of man living in this century became ever more complex and variegated. With such a background there appeared in literature an intensification of both self-consciousness, or individuality, and the search for new meaning in the life of man.

Traditional Japanese literature, developing in isolation during Tokugawa, was given a tremendous stimulus through the efforts of the enlightened men who introduced European literature during the first decades of the Meiji era. Foreign literature in translation and new literary ideals brought a completely new atmosphere to the scene once

173

dominated by *gesaku* writers. Popular fiction writers quickly followed
the current of foreign styles, but some time passed before they even
began to catch up with western developments. Realism, romanticism,
and naturalism made headway under the tutelage of European writing,
but a time lag remained between the maturing of those styles in the
West and their assimilation in Japan. Only after the end of World War
I did the Japanese literary world become truly contemporary with the
literary activity of Europe and America.

In naturalism modern literature reached a decisive turning point
in both subject matter and technique; and through naturalism the
foundations of modern Japanese literature were established. Of course,
the theory had its opponents, and there emerged an anti-naturalistic
movement critical of naturalism's faults, but the *fūzoku shōsetsu*
(novel of manners) and the first-person, "I" novel, *shishōsetsu,* of
modern Japan were rooted in and have continued to grow from the
naturalistic tradition.

The democratic movement in Japan which arose after World
War I was also reflected in a considerable proletarian literature.
Modernism too, through its background in avant-garde art, had a
revolutionizing effect on the old forms. Thus modernism, proletarian
or social literature, and naturalism were the three legs of the literary
kettle. Under pressure from the military government and the war-time
conditions beginning in the 1930s, proletarian literature disintegrated
and modernism also lost its creativeness, though for a brief period
Japanese literature enjoyed a creative revival before it completely
succumbed to government control. A three-part division of literature
re-emerged after the end of World War II: the traditional literature
which had grown up in Meiji; socially oriented liberal literature; and
various styles that developed after 1945. Within the varied scenes of
greatly enlarged mass media many new readers joined the writers'
audience.

If we consider the various genres in the period from 1868 to the
post-war years, we find that the novel occupies the dominant position.
While *waka* and *haikai* also underwent great changes, their formal
limitations and their brevity kept either from assuming an important
role. Poetry in new forms and styles arose together with new theater—
both looking to foreign models in their successful challenge to tradition.
Critical writing too came to be recognized as a separate discipline,
another of the noteworthy developments of the century.

The Meiji Enlightenment and New Literary Forms from the West

The *gesaku* themes which were rooted in the tradition of Tokugawa literature gradually faded during the early years of Meiji and the

pioneer efforts of literary men were directed to matters of immediate practical value: translating and producing new works on science, economics, and politics, all of which bore directly on the social revolution of the time. The *gesaku* writers still produced works which were chiefly intended as pastimes for the reader, but their content was heavy with satirical comments on the new age. Among the few writers of old-style pulp-fiction remaining then—such men as Kanagaki Robun (1829–94), Ryūtei Tanehiko the Third (1838–85), and Tamenaga Shunsui the Second (1823–86)—Kanagaki Robun produced the most sensitive response to the changes about him, particularly in his *Bankoku kōkai: seiyō dōchū hizakurige* (*Voyage to Myriad Countries: A Hiking-Tour in the West*), published 1870–76, and *Aguranabe* (*Idle Talks in the Sukiyaki House*), published 1871–72, both of which brought information about the world to readers with little education.

Fukuzawa Yukichi (1834–1901) and Nishi Amane (1829–97) were among the many men who studied abroad and absorbed the new knowledge which made the Meiji "enlightenment." Both men considerably influenced literature, adopting rather utilitarian and materialistic outlooks, and both were intent on introducing Western culture to Japan. Fukuzawa left such works as *Seiyō jijō* (*Institutions of the West*), 1866 to 1869, *Gakumon no susume* (*Encouragement of Learning*), 1872 to 1876, and a sarcastic allegory titled *Katawa musume* (*The Maimed Maiden*), published in 1872. Nishi Amane acquired a breadth of learning that reached from natural science through the humanities. He was an intellectual of very broad interests and his books reflect that quality. His work is represented by the collection of his lectures called *Hyakugaku renkan* (*Chain of a Hundred Studies*), begun in 1870, and he is credited with introducing basic concepts of Western literature to Japan.

During this revolutionary period in Japanese literature, literary theories advocating change were much in evidence, but actual writing fell short of the theoretical goals. There soon appeared, however, a number of adaptations and translations of popular works from Western literature. Among the first to reach the Japanese audience were *Robinson Crusoe* (*Robinson zenden*), translated by Saitō Ryōan in 1872, and *The Arabian Nights* (*Arabiya monogatari*) in abridged translation by Nagamine Hideki in 1875. Jules Verne's *Around the World in Eighty Days* (*Hachijūnichi-kan sekai isshū*) appeared in 1878, translated by Kawashima Tadanosuke, and *A Voyage to the Moon* (*Gessekai ryokō*) in 1880, the Japanese version by Inoue Tsutomu. Lytton's *Ernest Maltravers* (*Karyū shunwa*), a work much admired at the time in Japan, was translated in 1878 by Niwa Jun'ichirō. Such works were enthusiastically received by Japanese readers and by comparison pointed up the crudeness of *gesaku* writing. Following Nishi Amane's introduction of literary criticism, Nakae

Chōmin (1847–1901) published a translation of Eugene Veron's *L'Esthetique* in 1883–84 under the title *Ishi bigaku.* That was just five years after the book appeared in France and its ideas brought not only an empirical and systematic view of fiction writing but also the new currents of romanticism and naturalism.

Another popular area, one linked to the rise of democratic ideals and the movement toward a new society, was that of political novels which joined new political movements with personal political concepts. Representative books of that kind are *Keikoku bidan* (*Noble Tales of Statesmanship*), published in 1884 by Yano Ryūkei (1850–1931); *Kajin no kigū* (*A Chance Meeting with Two Beauties*) by Tōkai Sanshi (1852–1922), published from 1885 to 1897; and *Setchūbai* (*Plum Blossoms in the Snow*) by Suehiro Tettchō (1859–96), published in 1886. Such novels were primarily propaganda pieces and it is difficult to find great literary value in them. Nonetheless they are clear reflections of the thought of their day and went far toward relating literature to the society at large. Those works along with translations brought elements to literature which had been absent in the past.

In the theater as late as the second decade of Meiji, the 1880s, kabuki had the general support of the public, as it had had through most of the Tokugawa period. The dramatist Kawatake Mokuami, famous for his genre plays, continued in popularity; his best work of the last period in his career being *Shima-chidori tsuki no shiranami* (*Island Plovers Over the Moonlit Waves*), produced in 1881. This was one of the new *zangirimono,* plays which replaced *sewamono* as the genre pieces of the new age—*zangiri* being the popular name for men's cropped-hair style, and a symbol of the times.

To better express the feelings of the new Japan in poetry, there was a movement to create poems different from the old *waka, haikai,* and Chinese forms which had come to seem inadequate. In 1882 Inoue Tetsujirō (1855–1944), Yatabe Ryōkichi (1852–99), and Toyama Masakazu (known as Chūzan, 1848–1900), all rising young scholars at Tōkyō Imperial University, published a collection called *Shintai shishō* (*A Collection of New Style Poetry*). It was basically an instruction book based on long poems from Western poetry. It employed the classic alternation of five- and seven-syllable lines and was far from satisfactory in many respects, but it set a spark to the new poetry styles of Meiji and thus stands as one of the important books of its time. From that collection the opening lines of Tennyson's "The Charge of the Light Brigade," as rendered by Toyama Masakazu, are as follows:

Ichiri-han nari ichiri-han   Half a league, half a league,
narabite susumu ichiri-han   Half a league onward,

shichi ni noriiru roppyakki	All in the valley of Death
shō wa kakare no mei kudasu	Rode the six hundred.
shisotsu taru mi no mi o motte	'Forward the Light Brigade!
wake o tadasu wa bun narazu	Charge for the guns!' he said.
kotae o nasu mo bun narazu	Into the valley of Death
kore mei kore ni shitagaite	Rode the six hundred.
shinuru no hoka wa arazaran	
shichi ni noriiru roppyakki	

The long-poem style of the *Shintai shishō* was widely admired, and soon refinements were made in the form and content of original works. *Kōjo shiragiku no uta* (*The Song of the Filial Daughter Shiragiku*), written in 1888 by Ochiai Naobumi (1861–1903), and long poems translated from the Chinese by Inoue Tetsujirō were highly praised.

The New Realism

In the literary ideas of Tokugawa there were two strong currents: that literature existed merely to amuse, the *gesaku* ideal; and that literature existed as a means of "advancing virtue and reproving vice," the pragmatic, didactic view. The dominant literary theory of the new age, which was a denial of the past and a statement of the autonomous nature of the art, was realism, the straightforward representation of everyday life. The foundation of this new movement in Japan was built on the study of foreign literature, rather than a purely internal, self-generating condition. Realism, as the keystone, did not remain simply a theory, as did some later ideas on literature, but was advocated by men who actually wrote fiction and who turned to realistic methods in their own work.

Shōsetsu shinzui (*The Essence of the Novel*) by Tsubouchi Shōyō (1859–1935), published in 1886, became the theoretical guidepost for the new writing. Shōyō's thesis was that the novel should present a faithful copy of human feelings and reflect contemporary life in society; it advocated as a method not simply reporting externals but real penetration to the heart of the novel's subject. Moralizing, didacticism, and the strictly-for-amusement attitude of *gesaku* writing were rejected; in place of those old attitudes, *Shōsetsu shinzui* proposed the techniques of realism as the essence of literature. Based on his knowledge of English literature, Shōyō attempted to demonstrate his views in the novel *Tōsei shosei katagi* (*Character of Modern Students*), published in 1885–86. The result was a vivid portrait of student life, but the work failed as a rigorous application of the realistic method advocated in *Shōsetsu shinzui*. The novel retained too much of the flavor of Tokugawa fiction, or the "character sketch" as the title indicates.

A more thorough examination of realism and the approach advocated in *Shōsetsu shinzui* was made by Futabatei Shimei (1864–1909)
in his *Shōsetsu sōron* (*A General Discussion of the Novel*), published
in 1886. Based on his knowledge of Russian literature, Futabatei
was able to criticize *Tōsei shosei katagi,* particularly with the help of
the ideas of the Russian critic Belinsky. Futabatei, as had Shōyō,
put the theory of realism to the test in a novel, but this time with
consummate success. The result was *Ukigumo* (*Floating Cloud*), published in 1887 to 1889, a novel which also successfully brought
together the colloquial and the written languages. The hero of
Ukigumo is Utsumi Bunzō, a man who discovers himself caught in a
modern situation: an intellectual fighting against the meanness of
bureaucracy and slavish subservience to power which typified the old
feudalism. The portrait of Bunzō and the pain he feels in his struggle
is quite vivid, and the language of the work (a compromise between
literary and colloquial called *gembun itchi*) emerges as a fine and
free medium. Indeed, between realism and the new style of expression, Futabatei created a new character type in Japanese writing,
and his achievement is recognized as the beginning of contemporary
Japanese literature. Futabatei's fine colloquial translations from
Turgenev—*Rendezvous* (*Aibiki*) and *A Chance Meeting* (*Meguriai*),
both published in 1888—created a considerable stir for their freshness in description. The influence of those works was considerable.
Another writer of note, one who tried to combine the written and
spoken languages, was Yamada Bimyō (1868–1910), who produced
a collection of short stories called *Natsu kodachi* (*Summer Grove*)
in 1888.

In the theater world the spirit of realism was cultivated in historical dramas which rejected escapist or trivial entertainment. While
such attempts opened a new direction, they were doubtless weakened
by too close adherence to the facts of history, often with sacrifice of
dramatic tension. The type may be seen in such plays as *Yoshinoshūi
meika no homare* (*In Praise of an Excellent Poem in the Supplement
to the Yoshino Anthology*), by Yoda Gakkai (1823–1909) in 1886,
and *Kasuga no tsubone kennyo no kagami* (*Lady Kasuga, Model of a
Wise Woman*), from 1888 by Fukuchi Ōchi (1841–1906). However,
real advances in historical drama were made by Tsubouchi Shōyō
who insisted on the need for clear character portrayal and attention
to a motivational or internal interpretation of history. Shōyō worked
toward the creation of a new theater in various ways: offering a
translation of Shakespeare's *Julius Ceasar* (titled *Jiyū no tachi nagori
no kireaji:* "The Sword of Freedom and Farewell") and various original plays such as *Kiri hitoha* (*One Leaf of Paulownia*) in 1894,
Maki no kata (*Lady Maki*) in 1896, and *Hototogisu kojō no rakugetsu*

(*The Cuckoo and the Setting Moon over the Solitary Castle*) in 1897, all of which were leading plays in the new theater movement.

Neo-Classicism

The Westernization of Japan during the Meiji period was exceedingly rapid. Perhaps inevitably there was also a reaction away from change, against the imported literature and ways of thinking—feelings which led to critical expression and personal resistance to the current of the times. The tide from Europe continued until about 1887, then began a turnabout which took a highly nationalistic direction. In the literary world there appeared a back-to-the-classics movement and a reappraisal of the writing of the Genroku period—of Chikamatsu and especially Saikaku. This archaizing movement was organized as the Ken'yūsha or "Friends of the Inkstone Society" and was centered around Ozaki Kōyō (1867–1903) and the magazine *Garakuta bunko* (*Library of Miscellany*). The magazine was started in 1885 and was the first literary magazine of Meiji as well as the first coterie magazine in Japan.

Kōyō made his literary debut in 1889 with *Ninin bikuni irozange* (*Confessions of Two Nuns*), followed by *Kyara makura* (*The Perfumed Pillow*), 1890, *Ninin nyōbō* (*Two Ladies*), 1891, and *Sannin zuma* (*Three Wives*), 1892. In these stories the influence of Saikaku is very evident. His *Tajō takon* (*Tears and Regrets*), 1896, and *Konjiki yasha* (*The Gold Demon*), published serially from 1897 to 1902, reflect a keen interest in contemporary manners and a step forward in psychological description. Among his disciples were Izumi Kyōka (1873–1939), Oguri Fūyō (1875–1926), and Tokuda Shūsei (1871–1943).

Kōda Rohan (1867–1947), a writer popular for his crisp pseudo-archaic style modeled on Saikaku, was as influential as Kōyō, sharing with him leadership of the Japanese literary world during the third decade of Meiji, from about 1887 to 1897. Kōyō's forte was in drawing female characters and he brought this talent to numerous *fūzoku shōsetsu* or "genre novels." Rohan himself excelled in male characters and the idealistic novel, making wide use of Chinese and Buddhist vocabulary. Representative of his work are the following, all published in 1889: *Tsuyu dandan* (*Immaculate Dewdrops*), *Issetsuna* (*A Moment in Time*), and *Fūryūbutsu* (*The Stylish Buddha*), his first big success. Rohan wrote about ideal and religious love involving characters devoted to the arts. *Ikkōken* (*One Sword*), 1890, and *Gojū no tō* (*Five Storied Pagoda*), 1891, are typical of his stories using idealized male heroes who are caught up in a particular art. Among his other notable works are *Taidokuro* (*Facing the Skull*), which was

first published as *Engai en* (Without Ties) in 1890; *Fūryū mijinzō*
(*The Stylish Small Idol*), 1893–95; and *Sora utsu nami* (*Waves
Against the Sky*), published in 1903 to 1905. Besides his work in
fiction, Rohan left excellent work in essays, history, biography, and
scholarship. Especially valued is his *Hyōshaku bashō shichibushū*
(*The Annotated Bashō*), published between 1937 and 1949. The
breadth of his writing defines the well-educated man of letters in the
Far Eastern tradition.

Higuchi Ichiyō (1872–96) was a close follower of Rohan. She
wrote first in a *gesaku* vein under the influence of Nakarai Tōsui
(1860–1926) but soon found her way to a more personal expression.
Takekurabe (*Growing Up*) from 1896, *Nigorie* (*The Muddied
Stream*) of 1895, and *Jūsan'ya* (*Two Nights Before Full Moon*) from
1895 are typical of her work. *Takekurabe* is especially interesting
for its background of the Daion Temple near the Yoshiwara brothel
district and its examination of the delicate psychological changes in
a young boy and a young girl approaching puberty. The story is
poetic and romantic, and uses to good effect the colloquial-literary
compromise style employed by Saikaku. In her novels, Ichiyō dealt
primarily with the tragedy of women constrained within a feudal
society. Her diary too ranks among the best in the long tradition of
women's diaries in Japan. Regretably, Ichiyō died very young, in her
twenty-fifth year.

Haikai poetry of the early Meiji did not progress beyond the
rote-poetry, *tsukinami haikai*, of Sōgi and others of the earlier period,
but with the appearance of Masaoka Shiki (1867–1902) the form
began a comeback. First, Shiki brought new interpretations to the
writings of outstanding *haikai* poets through various critical studies:
Dassai shooku haiwa (*The Haiku Talks of Dassai Shooku*—"Dassai
Shooku," a humorous pen name meaning "Master of the Otter's Festival Room"), published in 1893; *Bashō zōdan* (*Talks on Bashō*),
published 1893–94; and *Haijin buson* (*The Poet Buson*), 1899.
Shiki was primarily concerned with the literary and descriptive qualities of verse and regarded *tsukinami haikai* as being valueless. He
was involved with the "return to the *Man'yōshū*" movement and
adopted the term *shasei*, copying life, from the technical vocabulary
of Western painting to express his theory of realism in verse. For
Shiki this was a very concrete approach to description of nature,
opposed to the idealistic tendency of traditional *haikai*. The term he
used for the new kind of seventeen-syllable poetry was *haiku*, his
name for the initial verse of *renku* (linked verse) which had previously been called *hokku*. Within the restricted and traditional form
he sought new poetic beauty through realistic description. He looked
to the *haikai* styles of Genroku and Temmei, the late seventeenth

and the late eighteenth centuries, for appropriate models and out of his reappraisal of Buson especially justified his own impressionistic and pictorial taste. Along with Naitō Meisetsu (1847–1926), Natsume Sōseki (1867–1916), Takahama Kyoshi (1874–1959), Kawahigashi Hekigodō (1873–1937) and Sakamoto Shihōda (1873–1917), he organized—and was very active in—the group known as the Nihonha, the Japan School. In 1898 Shiki began publishing *Hototogisu* (*The Cuckoo*), the leading *haikai* magazine of the time and an influential medium of *shasei*-writing, the attempt to view nature objectively.

The reform movements in *haikai* did not reach to *waka* which remained heavily traditional, clinging to the style of the Keien school (the chief influence in the Court Bureau of Music, Ōutadokoro) and Kagawa Kageki even after the beginning of Meiji. Slowly but surely the antiquated style began to move toward new words and rhythms to express the new thoughts and feelings. The reform in *tanka* was chiefly inspired by Ochiai Naobumi (1861–1903) who organized the Asakasha, The Faint Perfume Society, in 1893 with such men as Yosano Tekkan (1873–1935), Kaneko Kun'en (1876–1951), Hattori Motoharu (1875–1925) and Onoe Saishū (1876–1957). More significant changes were later brought about by Tekkan and others, while Naobumi's work remained mild and classical.

Romanticism

Mori Ōgai (1862–1922) was the leading force in romanticism, a movement which made a place for itself in Japanese literature during the last decade of the nineteenth century. As a young army physician, Ōgai studied in Germany and after his return to Japan in 1888 he was very active in introducing the broad spectrum of aesthetic, philosophical, and literary ideas which he had gained in Europe. His interests were remarkably wide and in several areas his learning was profound. In *Shigaramizōshi* (*Tangled Tales*), published in 1889, he expanded his critical ideas, based principally on the aesthetics of the German philosopher Karl Hartman (d. 1906). Due largely to Ōgai's work, modern literary criticism became a recognized form in Japanese letters. The discussions precipitated by Ōgai, Ishibashi Ningetsu (1865–1926), and Tsubouchi Shōyō (with whom Ōgai argued over the realistic approach) brought new seriousness and acuteness to the debates in Japanese aesthetics. Through the magazine *Waseda bungaku,* Shōyō defended realism and its manifestations since the publication of *Shōsetsu shinzui.* Opposed to this, Ōgai presented the aesthetics of idealism derived from Hartman, notably in three novels based on his experiences in Germany: *Maihime* (*The*

Dancing Girl), published in 1890; *Utakata no ki* (*A Transient Life*), 1890; and *Fumizukai* (*The Messenger*), 1891. They were all stories of tragic love, heavy with romantic mood and the melancholy of adolescence, and written in a particularly elaborate style. Ōgai's translation of Hans Christian Andersen's novel *Improvisatoren* (*Sokkyō shijin*) was particularly praised (as being better than the original) and with his other writings, such as the long story *Gan* (*Wild Geese*), he led the Romantic literary movement. *Omokage* (*Vestiges*), published in 1889, brought the new poetic style to a high level. It was a collection of poems translated from Western languages and published by the Shinseisha, New Voice Group, around Ōgai. The collection was built on the foundation laid by *Shintai shishō* and it accelerated the blossoming of new poetry in the Romantic mode.

The magazine *Bungakkai* (*Literary World*) was begun in 1893, and its pages offered well developed statement of Romanticism. Kitamura Tōkoku (1868–94), one of the founders of the magazine along with Shimazaki Tōson and others, wrote under the influence of Byron and Emerson and produced critical writings for the Romantic cause, such as *Jinsei ni aiwataru to wa nan no īzo* (*Human Relations: What Do They Mean?*) and *Naibu seimeiron* (*A Study of the Interior Life*), both dated 1893. In 1891 Tōkoku wrote an impassioned and dramatic poem titled *Hōraikyoku* (*Song of Fairyland*) and Shimazaki Tōson published a number of youthful but vigorous poems in *Bungakkai*. Tōson's first collection, *Wakanashū* (*Young Greens*), appeared in 1897 and was followed by *Hitohabune* (*The Leaf Boat*) in 1898, *Natsugusa* (*Summer Grasses*), also 1898, and *Rakubaishū* (*Fallen Plum Blossoms*) in 1901. There are many fine love poems and poems on the emotions of traveling. The collections just mentioned were combined into the *Tōson shishū* (*Collected Poetry of Tōson*) in 1904, with two particularly famous verses: *Koromo naru kojō no hotori* (*At The Ruins of Koromo Castle*) and *Chikumagawa ryojō no uta* (*Song of a Traveler on the Chikuma River*).

In contrast to Tōson's tender and melancholy poems on the sadness of modern times and youthful love, Doi Bansui (also known as Tsuchii Bansui, 1871–1952) dealt with the aspirations of the common people in heroic *kambun* style which was narrative and masculine as opposed to Tōson's lyrical and feminine works. Bansui's representative collections are *Tenchi ujō* (*Sentient World*), 1899, and *Gyōshō* (*Morning Bell*), 1901. The former collection contains his famous historical poem *Hoshi otsu shūfū gojōgen* (*Stars Fall and the Autumn Wind Blows on the Field of Gojō*), based on the Chinese novel *San kuo chih yen i* (*Romance of the Three Kingdoms*) and the famous military leader Chu-ko Liang. After Tōson and Bansui the leadership of Romantic poetry passed to Susukida Kyūkin

(1877–1945), a man who greatly admired Keats and who made free use of the classical language in poetry. His work tended to an art-for-art's-sake aestheticism and is represented by the collections *Nijū-gogen* (*Twenty-Five Strings*), published in 1905, and *Hakuyōkyū* (*White Sheep Palace*), published in 1906.

The magazine *Bunko* (*Literary Storehouse*) grew out of *Shōnen bunko* (*Youth's Literary Storehouse*) in 1895 and presented the work of a number of poets, including Kawai Suimei (1874–1965) and Irako Seihaku (1877–1946). Seihaku's collection, *Kujakubune* (*Peacock Boat*) of 1906, exemplifies the *Bunko* style, a seven-five-syllable alternation, simple and direct in sentiment, which was much admired in the Meiji era.

French symbolist poetry was introduced by Ueda Bin (1874–1916) through translations which greatly influenced modern poets in Japan. His *Kaichōon* (*Sound of the Tide*), a collection of poems in translation from 1905, exhibited excellence of a degree that not only placed the poems on the level of original work but also was of considerable technical interest to Japanese translators of western poetry. Kambara Ariake (1876–1952) was equally important in the symbolist poetry movement. Bin's translations and Ariake's original poems were no less than epoch-making contributions to modern Japanese poetry. Ariake's work is dark in feeling and in a minor key but also graceful in rhythm. Among collections of his poems are *Shunchōshū* (*Spring Bird Anthology*), 1905, and *Yūmeishū* (*Ariake Anthology*), published in 1908.

Yosano Tekkan was a romantic *waka* poet and a writer of modern poetry. He was an important figure in the publication of *Myōjō* (*Morning Star*), a magazine which was begun in 1900 and became a key factor in the brilliant era of Japanese poetry during the early years of the century. Tekkan worked in a very masculine and heroic vein and through such collections as *Tōzai namboku* (*East, West, North, South*) of 1896, *Tenchigenkō* (*Black Heaven, Yellow Earth*) in 1897 and *Murasaki* (*Purple*) in 1901, he became leader of the reform movement. *Myōjō* became the vehicle for the romantic movement at the height of its prosperity and was a great influence on *waka* poetry.

Yosano Akiko (1878–1942) was a disciple of Tekkan and later became his wife. She wrote impassioned and highly imaginative verse. Akiko's work established *waka* as a poetic voice of the modern spirit. She was the most talented of the excellent poets who were the backbone of Tekkan's reform movement. Her first collection of poetry, *Midaregami* (*Disheveled Hair*) of 1901, was an affirmation of human nature and liberation of the self, fiery and passionate in its sentiments of love. Her writing, while aesthetic in its approach, offered a direct challenge to the constraints of feudalism and the old morality. Akiko's poetry, graceful and charming as it was, often startled readers by its emancipated quality, and along with *Myōjō,* held a leading position for a whole generation. Among the many talented writers associated with the journal *Myōjō* were Hirano Banri (1885–1947), Takamura Kōtaro (1883–1956), Kubota Utsubo (1887–1967), Yoshii Isamu (1886–1960), Nagata Hideo (1885–1949), Ishikawa Takuboku (1886–1912), Kinoshita Mokutarō (1885–1945), and Kitahara Hakushū (1885–1942).

Sasaki Nobutsuna (1872–1963) appeared shortly after Ochiai Naobumi and sought reform in *waka* through the aid of classical poetry from the *Man'yōshū*—a collection he knew well. He began the magazine *Kokoro no hana* (*Flower of the Heart*) in 1898 as the organ of the Chikuhakukai, the Bamboo and Oak Society, of which he was the leader. His style was gentle and eclectic and he was known as a scholar as well as a poet. Nobutsuna's associates included Kinoshita Rigen (1886–1925), Ishikure Chimata (1869–1942), Kawada Jun (1882–1966) and Kujō Takeko (1887–1928).

Onoe Saishū and Kaneko Kun'en, like Tekkan, came from the Asakasha and were known for refined, dignified drawings of the natural scene, following a road independent of the *Myōjō* school. Wakayama Bokusui (1885–1928), Maeda Yūgure (1883–1951) and Toki Aika (Zemmaro, b. 1885) were disciples of Saishū and Kun'en.

The *Myōjō* school of poets found a competitor in Masaoka Shiki. Shiki rejected the old styles of *waka* and advocated his own kind of reform with the publication of *Uta yomi ni atauru sho* (*An Open Letter to Waka Poets*) in 1898. The following year he organized Negishi Tankakai, The Negishi Tanka Society. His interest was in description which he supported through examples from the *Man'yōshū*. He tried to extend the reforms made in *haiku* to *waka* poetry. Indeed, his school produced work which was fresh in its description and excelled in compressed expression, qualities that grew out of an insistence on objective observation. Shiki's disciples included Itō Sachio (1865–1913), Nagatsuka Takashi (1879–1915), Katori Hozuma (1874–1954), and Oka Fumoto (1877–1951). After Shiki's death, Itō Sachio became the center of the group which published the magazines *Ashibi* in 1903 and *Araragi* in 1908. *Araragi* became the dominant publication in *waka* poetry during the Taishō Era, having moved away from the *Man'yōshū* oriented classicism of Sachio and into a more naturalistic mode which was symbolic, descriptive, and bucolic in mood—as opposed to the "urban" mood of the *waka* classicists.

Sachio offered a theory of *waka* centered on the idea of *sakebi,* a cry or exclamation. For him the essence of *waka* was in direct expression of a selfless and momentary impression, and his own poetry tended to be serious and intense. In contrast to Sachio's strongly passionate verse, Nagatsuku Takashi worked in a bright but still insightful mood, recording sharp emotions with an exceptionally delicate and sensitive power of observation that he summed up in the term *sae,* meaning clarity.

Takayama Chogyū (1871–1902) completed a romantic historical novel called *Takiguchi nyūdō* (*The Lay Priest Takiguchi*) which was published in 1904, but after that devoted himself, as did Mori Ōgai, to critical writing based on his study of the philosophy of aesthetics. His writing appeared in *Taiyō* (*The Sun*), a general-interest magazine dating from 1895. Chogyū began as an ardent nationalist, then abandoned his Japan-first ideals to take up a philosophic position of extreme individualism influenced by Nietzsche; after a period of aestheticism, he eventually found his way to Nichiren Buddhism. In all of these allegiances Chogyū's romantic nature encountered contradictions between his hopes and reality, leaving him always in search of the ideal faith.

Izumi Kyōka was a disciple of Kōyō from the Ken'yūsha and began his writing with such novels as *Yakō junsa* (*Night Patrolman*) and *Gekashitsu* (*The Surgery*), both published in 1895. These were *kannen shōsetsu,* ideological novels, that explored the contradictions of existence, but from them he shifted to romantic and gothic themes in fiction. Of this kind we have such novels as *Teriha kyōgen* (*Teriha: A Comedy*), published in 1896; *Kōya hijiri* (*The Sage of Mt. Kōya*), 1900; *Onna keizu* (*A Woman's Destiny*), 1907; and *Uta andon* (*Song and Lamp*), 1910. While those works show a fondness for mysterious and strange situations, Kyōka also had marvelous skill in describing feminine beauty and he dealt expertly with the conflict between pure love and the coarseness of human society— all in a lapidary style that defied imitation.

Tokutomi Roka (1868–1927) was a liberal and a Christian who attacked the faults of the Japanese family system in an 1898 novel titled *Hototogisu* (*The Cuckoo*), a work which the youth of the day found profoundly moving. In 1900 he produced *Omoide no ki* (*Memories*), a story of personal struggle, but his reputation was made by another work in the same year, *Shizen to jinsei* (*Man and Nature*), which was especially attractive for its fresh, new use of the literary language. It offered a romantic view of natural beauty and, while close to *Aibiki* (Futabatei's translation of *Rendezvous*) was itself an impressive rediscovery of the natural world.

Kunikida Doppo (1871–1908) also dwelt on the quiet beauty of nature in his 1901 novel *Musashino* (*Musashino Province*). His outlook was nurtured by Turgenev and Wordsworth and he brought a poet's skill to many outstanding short works, among which are *Gen oji* (*Uncle Gen*), 1897, and *Bajō no tomo* (*Friend on Horse-*

back), 1903. Doppo wrote of daily life with richly humanistic sympathy and in his later writing came close to Naturalism.

Naturalism

The interest of Japanese writers in the approach of Naturalism was awakened by the French writer Emile Zola. The first knowledge of Zola's work was provided by Nakae Chōmin's translation of *L'Esthetique,* after which the technique itself was practiced by such Japanese writers as Mori Ōgai, Kosugi Tengai (1865–1952), and Nagai Kafū (1876–1959). In the view of Naturalism, the writer needed to bring the attitude of scientific observation to literature, to observe and record reality just as it was. This attempt at objectivity gained force in literary circles and is clearly demonstrated in Tengai's *Hatsusugata* (*The New Year Dress*) of 1900 and Kafū's *Jigoku no hana* (*Flower of Hell*) published in 1902.

Shimazaki Tōson first appeared on the literary scene with his poetry, published in the magazine *Bungakkai,* but switched to fiction writing and at his own expense published *Hakai* (*Broken Commandment*) in 1906. This novel portrayed the suffering of a modern man who challenges the feudal role of *burakumin,* then an outcaste group in Japan. The story is remarkable both for its subject and for the vividness of its descriptive passages. Along with Tayama Katai's *Futon* (*The Quilt*) of 1907, it stands as a pioneer novel of Japanese Naturalism. *Futon* was drawn from the author's own life and described his attraction for a girl who was one of his students. The novel created a sensation in literary circles of the time with its sensual frankness. Naturalistic literature in Japan developed on the tone set by *Futon* rather than *Hakai,* tending toward description of ordinary life rather than special social problems. Tōson himself set out in a new direction after *Hakai,* and with such novels as *Haru* (*Spring*), 1908, *Ie* (*A Family*), 1910, and *Shinsei* (*New Life*), 1918, he produced a long series of stories with strong autobiographical elements. His basic theme throughout is human love and he never loses a poetic feeling of wonder and surprise. Among his excellent short pieces are the stories *Nobi shitaku* (*To Grow Up*), 1925, and *Arashi* (*Storm*), 1926. Tayama Katai (1871–1930), with works like *Futon* and *Inaka kyōshi* (*The Country Teacher*), the latter published in 1909, became the leading writer in Japanese Naturalism and as a theoretician he advocated straightforward external description. Other writers and partisans of the technique were: Hasegawa Tenkei (1876–1940), author of *Shizenshugi* (*Naturalism*), published in 1908; Shimamura Hōgetsu (1873–1918), author of *Kindai bungei no kenkyū* (*A Study of Modern Literature*), published in 1909; and

Iwano Hōmei (1873–1920), who wrote *Shimpiteki hanjūshugi*
(*Mystic Pseudo-Animalism*) in 1906.

Naturalism had other represēntatives in Japan. Two who worked
even more rigorously within the technique were Masamune Hakuchō
(1879–1962) and Tokuda Shūsei (1871–1943). Hakuchō dealt with
nihilism in novels such as *Doko e* (*Wither*), 1908; *Doro ningyō* *Whither?*
(*The Clay Doll*), 1911; and *Irie no hotori* (*By the Inlet*), 1915.
Shūsei was a disciple of Kōyō but was regarded as a naturalistic
writer with such novels as *Arajotai* (*The New Household*), 1910;
Ashiato (*Footprints*), 1910; *Tadare* (*Corruption*), 1913; and *Ara-
kure* (*Indulgence*), 1915. His writing was devoid of sentiment and
drew, sometimes shockingly, the dark side of existence. The naturalistic method, thoroughly realistic and focusing on daily life, was
used by Mayama Seika (1878–1948) in his novel *Minami koizumi-
mura* (*South Koizumi Village*), 1907, and by Iwano Hōmei in
Tandeki (*Addiction*), 1909, and *Hōrō* (*Wandering*), 1910.
Both men were outstanding naturalistic writers and from their work
grew the *shishōsetsu* or first person novel of the Taishō period, beginning
about 1920.

The *shishōsetsu* and *shinkyō shōsetsu,* mental-state novels (the
terms are nearly synonymous), of the late Taishō years were produced
under the influence of Naturalism. Writers, such as Uno Kōji (1891–
1961), Kasai Zenzō (1887–1928), and Hirotsu Kazuo (b. 1891)
drew from their own lives and the lives of persons close to them and
produced works of acute sensitivity. Representative novels of the
genre include *Kura no naka* (*In the Storage Room*), 1919; *Ku no
sekai* (*World of Suffering*), 1919; *Ko o kashiya* (*The Child Shop*),
1922, by Uno Kōji; Kasai's *Kanashiki chichi* (*Sad Father*), 1912,
and *Ko 'o tsurete* (*Together With Children*), 1918; and Hirotsu's
Shinkeibyō jidai (*Neurotic Age*), 1917. Since these works the first-
person novel has remained an important type in modern Japanese
literature, close in feeling to the *fūzoku shōsetsu* or genre novel.

Modernization in *waka* was achieved principally through the
efforts of three men: Tekkan, Nobutsuna, and Shiki. The *Myōjō-ha,*
or Morning Star Group, under Tekkan, was deeply immersed in the
current of Romanticism and was the leading group in poetry circles.
From about 1907 the influence of Naturalism began to be felt in
poetry as it had already appeared in fiction. The naturalistic movement in poetry was a reaction to the romantic mannerisms of the
Myōjō group and attempted to write a direct expression of the self,
to compose poetry directly from life, as Naturalism tried to draw
from life. The movement attracted such men as Saishū, Kun'en,
Sachio, and Takashi, but of more importance were Wakayama
Bokusui, Maeda Yūgure, Ishikawa Takuboku, and Toki Aika who

were in the center of naturalistic writing and who attempted to compose directly from life with the materials of man's weariness and fatigue. Bokusui found in nature consolation for human suffering and opened a window on a personal, lyrical verse style, though still centered on life's griefs as subject. His poetic voice was clear and sonorous, with a fine sense of rhythm. Maeda Yūgure, in an anguish less intense than Bokusui's, took up fragments of daily life about which he wrote in a straightforward and unaffected style. He later shifted to a sensuous mood which was rich in his own personality and outlook.

Takuboku, once part of the *Myōjō* school, was strongly concerned with social problems and wrote in a language close to that of daily speech, focusing on the emotions of suffering. He aimed to join poetry and everyday life, and to that end employed a prose-like form, very direct, called *sangyōgaki,* three-line writing. He attracted many readers and, without losing a natural, lyrical flavor pioneered the Seikatsuha, Life School, of *tanka,* which included Maeda Yūgure and Toki Aika. Takuboku is the representative poet of Naturalism in Japan. His poems are collected in *Ichiaku no suna (Handful of Sand)* and *Kanashiki gangu (Sad Toys),* both from 1910. The following is an example of Takuboku's *sangyōgaki* verse.

Inochi naki suna no kanashisa yo	We grasp it, and it slips
sara sara to	through our fingers with a hush.
nigireba yubi no aida yori otsu	What a sad thing, this lifeless sand.

Toki Aika, a poet equal to Takuboku, wrote in a naturalistic style that was close to prose. In his first collection he made a new departure in the *sangyōgaki* style by writing in *romaji,* roman script, rather than in the usual mixture of Chinese graphs and the *kana* syllabary. The following was originally written in romanized form.

Waga gotoki yonotsunebito wa,	A common man,
Modae sezu,	Without knowing I
Metorite, umite, oite, shinubeshi!	Wed, beget, age, and die.
	(from *Nakiwarai: Tearful Laughter,* 1910)

Like Takuboku, Kubota Utsubo was a poet from the *Myōjō* group. He wrote on human life and experience in a free vocabulary, much indebted to Naturalism, and in fact close to Takuboku and others of the new movement in *waka.*

After the death of Shiki the world of *haiku* split into two groups around Shiki's disciples Hekigodō and Kyoshi. Hekigodō sought to bring a new spiritual depth to Shiki's descriptivism and to that end emphasized individuality in observation of nature. He rejected the traditional interest in seasonal association for *haiku* and recommended realistic verse based on personal emotion. He experimented with variations on the short form, outside of the traditional 5–7–5 syllable lines, and we find in his writing influences from Naturalism.

The new style of Hekigodō was given a theoretical base by Ōsuga Otsuji (1881–1920). It was a symbolic interpretation which he felt was appropriate to seasonal topics and direct experience; out of that view he created a new direction for *haiku*, separate from the extreme position of Hekigodō. Otsuji eventually came back to a neo-classical, reactionary position, but other poets such as Nakatsuka Ippekirō (1887–1946) and Ogiwara Seisensui (b. 1884) completely eliminated the seasonal orientation of *haiku* as well as the 5–7–5 pattern, moving into free rhythm which left *haiku* as a short-verse form, only approximating seventeen syllables in length. Such *haiku*, lacking fixed form, placed the base of composition in direct expression of the emotions and impressions of a moment, aiming for a brief poem close to colloquial expression. This revolution in poetry was perhaps too rapid; the approach did not become generally popular and the movement lost its force.

Naturalism was an important influence in poetry circles where it encouraged a spirit of free verse, unrestricted by traditional rules of composition. The free-verse movement used colloquial language and developed rhythms outside of the traditional five- and seven-syllable phrases. Kawaji Ryūkō (1888–1959) and Sōma Gyofū (1883–1950) were the first of the new poets to attempt verse in the colloquial language, but aesthetically their work remained experimental. Using the literary style of written Japanese the Taitōha, Decadent School, achieved notable success through such poets as Kitahara Hakushū, Kinoshita Mokutarō, and Miki Rofū (1889–1964). The work that followed those men became the mainstream of poetry outside of the areas of *waka* and *haiku*.

The New Wave Theater (*shimpageki*) took the new age and the new configuration of Japanese society as its starting point, in contrast to the traditional or historical theater which grew out of the *kabuki* tradition and found its materials in the past. The earliest manifestation of new work in the theater came with *sōshi shibai*, political plays, and *shosei shibai*, student plays, beginning about 1887, the third decade of Meiji. The New Wave Theater Group was composed of such men as Kawakami Otojirō (1864–1911), Ii Yōhō (1871–1932), Kawai Takeo (1877–1942), and Kitamura Rokurō (1871–1961). The new wave, in the fourth decade of Meiji, challenged the traditional theater with such productions as *Hototogisu* (*Cuckoo*); *Konjiki yasha* (*The Gold Demon*), adapted from Kōyō's story; Izumi Kyōka's (1873–1939) *Onna keizu* (*A Woman's Destiny*) and *Taki no shiraito* (*The Waterfall's White Thread*) which was adapted from *Giketsu kyōketsu* (*Blood of Honor*), a novel co-authored by Izumi Kyōka and Ozaki Kōyō. Kabuki, which had long exhibited symptoms of decline, was eventually overwhelmed by the new style and the new plays.

Mori Ōgai too was important in introducing the literature of Western theater to Japan. He translated a variety of works in a wide range of forms and himself wrote epics like *Tamakushige futari urashima* (*The Two Urashimas*) in 1902 and *Nichiren shōnin tsuji seppō* (*The Wayside Preaching of Nichiren*) in 1904. Both Ōgai and Shōyō were extremely important to the creation of a modern theater in Japan. As leader of the Shingeki movement, New Theater, which portrayed contemporary life (in contrast to the New Wave Theater and kabuki which then dealt in historical plays), Tsubouchi Shōyō organized the very influential Bungei Kyōkai, Association for Literature and Art in 1906. From Shōyō's tutelage came Shimamura Hōgetsu, a leading theorist of Naturalism. An important milestone was the production of Ibsen's *A Doll's House* with Matsui Sumako, the leading actress of Shingeki in the starring role. The company of actors known as the Geijutsuza, The Fine Arts Theater, the leading group of Taishō period New Theater, was the creation of Hōgetsu and Sumako. Finally, the transition from traditional to modern theater was capped by the work of Osanai Kaoru (1881–1928). In 1908 he organized Jiyūgekijō, The Liberty Theater, together with Ichikawa Sadanji the Second (1880–1940) and produced a succession of modern plays by such writers as Ibsen, Chekhov, and Hauptmann. Mori Ōgai actively supported this group. Because there were still too few plays in the new or Western style being written in Japan, fine plays were imported from Europe to the Japanese stage where they became the foundation of contemporary theater.

Anti-Naturalism

Naturalistic literature enriched modern writing through methods of realism, which meant directly confronting the subject and attempting to describe it faithfully. However, there were failures and abuses in Naturalism too. Writers seemed to dwell on the ugly side of reality, dramatizing almost exclusively the dark and mean qualities in man's nature. A reaction to that arose in an art-for-art's sake movement in literature which took a broad view of life, pursued high ideals, and tried to bring some intellectual clarity to interpreting the conditions of the modern world. Reactions in opposition to Naturalism took various forms: writings of the Tambiha, the Aesthetic School, and the Shirakabaha, White Birch School; the novels of Ōgai and Sōseki; and the highly intellectual approach of Akutagawa Ryūnosuke (1892–1927).

In the Aesthetic School, Nagai Kafū, who began as a Naturalistic writer, produced *Amerika monogatari* (*Tale of America*) in 1908, and *Furansu monogatari* (*Tale of France*) in 1909. They were written after a period of study and travel in Europe and America. Disillusionment with Japan of the time led Kafū to a nostalgic tone heavy with the flavor of old Edo and he found his themes in the demi-monde society of the previous age which he presented in such novels as *Sumidagawa* (*The River Sumida*), 1909, *Udekurabe* (*Competition*), 1916–17, and *Okamezasa* (*Bamboo*), 1918. Kafū's response to Japan of the early century was to retreat into a feeling of oppression of the self, of being, as a writer, somehow inferior within Japanese society. This attitude of withdrawal or sulking did not alter even in his later years and in fact it was this very personal outlook that produced genre novels of great sensitivity, especially in dealing with erotic materials. In 1913 Kafū published a collection of modern French verse in Japanese translation called *Sangoshū* (*The Coral Anthology*) which was well received and quite influential.

Tanizaki Jun'ichirō (1886–1965) worked somewhat in the same epicurean mode as Kafū, but Tanizaki inclined to morbidity in dealing with sensuality and feminine beauty. His *Irezumi* (*The Tattoo*) of 1910 portrayed the mental state of a man infatuated with the sensual beauty of women. *Chijin no ai* (*Fool's Love*), 1924, is representative of the mode which continued through his later works, such as *Kagi* (*The Key*) in 1961. In contrast to Kafū's nihilism, Tanizaki, however, offers a positive view of human existence.

Satō Haruo (1892–1964), in such works as *Den'en no yūutsu* (*Country Melancholy*), 1917, and *Tokai no yūutsu* (*City Melancholy*), 1922, wrote in the Aesthetic School vein with a tone of intellectual world-weariness. His novels are of fine poetic quality in an end-of-the-century mood. A collection of his verse from 1921 called *Junjō shishū* (*Resigned to Die*) uses the elegant style of fixed classical rhythms.

From the last years of Meiji to the beginning of Taishō, roughly the years 1905 to 1915, Kitahara Hakushū was the leading figure in symbolic poetry. The magazine *Subaru* (*Pleiades*), successor to *Myōjō*, begun in 1909, was the chief medium for his verse. His mood as a poet is summed up in his first collection, entitled *Jashūmon* (*An Evil Faith*) and published in 1909. The verses bring out his epicurean and morbid sensitivity and interest in exotic mood. Hakushū was certainly the first genius of modern poetry and with Yoshii Isamu (1886–1960) was the leading representative of the Aesthetic School. His collections include *Omoide* (*Recollections*), 1911, and *Tōkyō keibutsushi oyobi sono hoka* (*The Sights of Tōkyō and Other Poems*), published in 1913. From the same year his collection *Kiri no hana* (*Paulownia Flowers*) secured his fame and brought a clearly modern style to Japanese symbolist poetry. Hakushū also worked in *tanka* and in his later years adopted the calm, profoundly suggestive tone of the classical poets of the Far East.

In contrast to the exoticism of Hakushū, Yoshii Isamu brought to his collections *Gion kashū* (*Poems of the Gion District*), 1915, and *Gion sōshi* (*The Gion Book*), 1917, a decadent mood but one colored with the ardor and sweet emotions of adolescence. His best known collection is *Sake hogai* (*In Praise of Wine*), 1910. Another poet interested in exoticism was Kinoshita Mokutarō, a poet close to Hakushū but more intellectual in his approach. His work is collected in *Shokugo no uta* (*After-Meal Poems*), 1920. Miki Rofū was another symbolist of note, but one who worked in a quiet, simple style very different from Hakushū's. His work is collected in *Haien* (*A Ruined Garden*), 1909, and *Shiroki te no karyūdo* (*White-Handed Hunter*), 1913.

Mori Ōgai and Natsume Sōseki were the two great figures in the anti-Naturalistic schools of modern writing. Both men were well acquainted with foreign literature and were able to take an exceptionally broad critical view of the art. They rejected literary methods which were content to produce a flat copy of reality, and the work of both is illuminated by a logical and critical spirit appropriate to their humanistic education. They examined their subjects with leisurely eyes and we detect, from time to time, a degree of aloofness, but modern Japanese literature long felt the influence of both of these men.

Among the works of Ōgai, who was the inspiration for the young writers associated with *Subaru*, were *Vita sekusuarisu* (*Vita Sexualis*), published in 1909, *Seinen* (*Youth*), 1910–11, and *Gan* (*Wild Geese*), 1911–13. Ōgai's interest in historical fiction produced *Abe ichizoku* (*The Abe Family*) in 1913, *Kanzan jittoku* (*The Priests Han Shan and Shih Te*) in 1916, *Takasebune* (*Takase River Boat*), 1916, and other works. He made use of historical materials to which he brought a fine interpretive sense, creating a model for the historical novel. His later writing included pure historical writing, such as *Shibue chūsai* (*Biography of Shibue Chūsai,* Confucian scholar and physician, d. 1858), published in 1916. Ōgai's prose style was exceptionally precise and refined and his work initiated an important current in modern letters.

Natsume Sōseki has been identified with various labels: Yoyūha, Leisure School; Haikaiha, Haikai School; Kōtōha, Transcendental School, and so forth. He was a friend of Masaoka Shiki and while a skilled writer of realistic prose, he viewed life with a quiet detachment reminiscent of the *haikai* poets. Sōseki first achieved recognition through the sarcastic wit of *Wagahai wa neko de aru* (*I Am a Cat*), published in 1905–06, and *Botchan* (*Sonny*) in 1906. His *Kusamakura* (*The Grass Pillow*), also 1906, established a personal style of writing which was calm and other-worldly. Sōseki's other representative works are: *Sanshirō* (the title is a personal name), 1908; *Sorekara* (*And Then*), 1909; *Mon* (*The Gate*), 1910; *Kōjin* (*The Wayfarer*), 1912–13; *Kokoro* (*Mind*), 1914; *Michigusa* (*Loitering*), 1915; and *Meian* (*Light and Darkness*), which was incomplete at Sōseki's death in 1916. Sōseki is noted for his lofty moral outlook, and in his later years he developed a philosophical position which he summed up in the phrase *sokuten kyoshi* ("conform to heaven and forsake the self"), an attitude that influenced his disciples and several generations of readers. Two of his disciples—Abe Jirō (1883–1959) and Abe Yoshishige (1883–1966)—were prolific writers of critiques opposed to Naturalism. Such men as Takahama Kyoshi, Yoshimura Fuyuhiko (known as Terada Torahiko, 1878–1935), and Nagatsuka Takashi were novelists working in the same style as Sōseki. The essays of Fuyuhiko and Takashi's long novel *Tsuchi* (*The Soil*), published in 1910, are famous.

In *haikai* after Shiki's death in 1902, Takahama Kyoshi continued the magazine *Hototogisu* and, with his traditional approach to poetry, continued the rivalry with Hekigodō. Kyoshi first devoted himself to the prose style called *shaseibun*, a kind of writing which tried to sketch directly from life. But because of the success of Hekigodō's new *haiku*, Kyoshi turned his attention to seventeen-syllable verse beginning in the early years of the Taishō period, about 1915. He attempted to preserve the 5–7–5 form as well as the traditional seasonal association in *haiku*, calling himself the "Shukyūha," School to Preserve Antiquity. He was an active critic of new directions in *haiku* and strove to extend the influence of the *Hototogisu* group. There was a strong emotional tone in his work until the early 1920s, after which he wrote more descriptively or objectively. By the early Shōwa period, about 1930, realistic and objective imagery completely disappeared from the work of Kyoshi and his followers, all of whom returned to strong traditionalism. Among his disciples in the early years were Murakami Kijō (1865–1938), Iida Dakotsu (1885–1962), and Watanabe Suiha (1882–1946). In the later years his disciples included Mizuhara Shūōshi, (b. 1892), Yamaguchi Seishi (b. 1901), Hino Sōjō (1901–65), Tomiyasu Fūsei (b. 1885), Nakamura Kusatao (b. 1901), Kawabata Bōsha (1900–41), and Hara Sekitei (1886–1951).

The most talented of Sōseki's disciples was Akutagawa Ryūnosuke. Akutagawa entered the literary world through Sōseki's encouragement of his satirical novel *Hana* (*The Nose*), written in 1916. Akutagawa's principal contribution was the reinterpretation of historical materials in the formation of witty and vital subject matter. He is noted too for the fineness of his style and the new interpretations he brought to such literature as the medieval *setsuwa*. His works include *Rashōmon* (*Rashō Gate*), 1917, *Gesaku zammai* (*Fiction Writing Mania*), 1917, and *Karenoshō* (*Death of Bashō*), 1918. He was one of the outstanding intellects of his time, and, appropriately, his writing is sometimes termed the Richiha, Intellectual School, or Shingenjitsuha, New Reality School. His later works include *Kappa* (*River Elf*) and *Haguruma* (*The Cogwheel*), both in 1927. These two stories clearly reveal the skepticism and pain which grew from a spirit unable to accommodate the changes and contradictions of Japan at that time.

Kikuchi Kan (1888–1948), Kume Masao (1891–1952) and Yamamoto Yūzō (b. 1887) were among the writers publishing in the same coterie magazines as Akutagawa. Kikuchi, while not as discerning an intellect as Akutagawa, wrote lucid thematic novels, such as *Tadanao-kyō gyōjōki* (*The Affairs of Lord Tadanao*) in 1916, *Onshū no kanata ni* (*Land Beyond Love and Hate*) in 1919, and *Rangaku kotohajime* (*The Beginning of European Studies in Japan*) in 1921. He later produced many works of popular fiction and was active in education. Kume Masao also became a popular novelist, but his early writings were marvelously lyrical. *Hasen* (*Shipwreck*), 1922, was based on his experience of unrequited love and is one of his best works. Yamamoto Yūzō first worked as a dramatist but is best known for his long novels which include *Nami* (*Waves*), 1928, *Kaze* (*Wind*), 1930, and *Onna no isshō* (*A Woman's Life*), 1933. All were critical examinations of the human conditions based on Yūzō's humanistic philosophy.

The Shirakabaha, White Birch School, expressed another reaction against the pessimistic view of life which had overtaken Naturalism. The Shirakaba group represented humanism, respect for individuality, and an attempt to reassert human dignity. The name of the group came from the magazine *Shirakaba,* founded in 1910. Its representative authors were Mushanokōji Saneatsu (b. 1885), Shiga Naoya (1883–1972), Arishima Takeo (1878–1923), Nagayo Yoshirō (1888–1961), and Satomi Ton (b. 1888). Their outlook brought a change of air to the literary world of Japan, producing an atmosphere of idealism quite different from the outlook of Naturalism. Saneatsu was the leading theoretician of the Shirakabaha and, to offer a living and personal demonstration of his faith, he established a community called Atarashiki-mura, New Village, in Miyazaki Prefecture. His representative works are *Omedetaki hito* (*God's Fool*), 1911, and *Kōfukusha* (*The Happy One*), 1919. The influence of Tolstoi is strong in Saneatsu, who wrote in a simple style which was given great cohesive-

ness by his own ideals and affirmation of life. He is especially noted
for maintaining in his writing a fine and uncontrived humor.

Shiga Naoya was also a strong voice against injustice and dis-
honesty. He wrote out of a humanistic philosophy, but he was master
of a cool, penetrating view of man. The conciseness of his descriptions
reveals a personal clarity and the influence of realism. His work was
short in form, among the best being *Kozō no kamisama* (*A Young
Man's God*), 1920, *Kinosaki nite* (*At Cape Ki*) and *Wakai* (*Reconcil-
liation*), both 1917. His only long work, *An'ya kōro* (*Road Through
the Dark Night*), written between 1921 and 1937, remains one of the
outstanding pieces of modern Japanese fiction. The struggle in his
personal life is revealed by the autobiographical elements in *An'ya
kōro* and indeed his writing evolved into a history of the development
and purification of the spirit.

Arishima Takeo, the most political writer of the Shirakaba group,
was involved in the tide of socialistic thought which reached
Japan after World War I. Takeo was greatly concerned with the duties
of the intellectual in society, an interest expressed in his *Sengen
hitotsu* (*A Declaration*) written in 1922. He turned over to private
cultivators the farm land he owned in Hokkaido. His novels include
Kain no matsuei (*Cain's Descendants*), 1918; *Aru onna* (*A Certain
Woman*), 1919; and *Umareizuru nayami* (*Birth Pains*), 1918.

Satomi Ton, younger brother of Arishima Takeo and another
Shirakaba writer, explored the theme of human sincerity in such
novels as *Zenshin akushin* (*Virtue and Malice*) in 1916 and *Tajō
busshin* (*Passionate Heart, Pious Heart*) in 1922–23. A representative
work of Nagayo Yoshirō is *Takezawa sensei to iu hito* (*A Man Called
Takezawa*), 1924.

The poet Takamura Kōtarō (1883–1956) worked first in a
delicate, epicurean style. Later, under the influence of the Shirakabaha,
his work moved in an idealistic and humanistic direction. In literary
terms he shifted from verse in the literary style to colloquial free verse
in which he perfected a simple and powerful poetic voice. His *Dōtei*
(*Journeys*) is one of the best collections of poetry from the Taishō
period, and his *Chieko shō* (*For Chieko*) of 1941, verses dedicated
to his deceased wife, is an outstanding collection. Yamamura Bochō
(1884–1924) and Murō Saisei (1889–1962) were poets, like Kōtarō,
strongly idealistic in their work. The following, from *Dōtei,* is the title
poem of the collection.

Dōtei
Boku no mae ni michi wa nai
Boku no ushiro ni michi wa dekiru
Aa, shizen yo
Chichi yo

Boku o hitori dachi ni sasetai kodai na chichi yo
Boku kara me o hanasanai de mamoru koto o seyo
Tsune ni chichi no kihaku o boku ni mitaseyo
Kono tōi dōtei no tame
Kono tōi dōtei no tame

Journeys
Ahead of me there is no road
The road behind me is done
Nature, my fathers!
Awesome fathers who have made me so alone
Their eyes fixed on me, caring for me.
Fill me always with the spirit of my fathers
For this long journey
For this long journey.

Takamura Kōtarō

The colloquial free verse style was given a clear course for future development by Kōtarō. With the poetry of Kawaji Ryūkō (1888–1959) this movement reached maturity. Poets of the liberal and democratic poetry groups naturally began with colloquial free verse. Such men included: Senke Motomaro (1888–1948), Fukushi Kōjirō (1889–1946), Fukuda Masao (1893–1952), Momota Sōji (1893–1955), Tomita Saika (b. 1890), and Shiratori Shōgo (b. 1890), all writers of the Shirakabaha.

The acknowledged master of colloquial free verse, however, was Hagiwara Sakutarō (1886–1942). Sakutarō was greatly concerned with originality in free verse and is famous also for his symbolistic style, a blend of fantasy and the near-macabre, which seemed to offer a perfect expression for his inner life. Among his collections of verse are *Tsuki ni hoeru* (*Barking at the Moon*), 1917; *Aoneko* (*The Blue Cat*), 1923; and *Hyōtō* (*Ice Island*) which appeared in 1934. Since the Taishō period he has been a major influence in Japanese poetry. The following poem is from his collection *Tsuki ni hoeru*.

Take
Hikaru jimen ni take ga hae,
Aodake ga hae,
Chika ni wa take no ne ga hae,
Ne ga shidai ni hosorami,
Ne no saki yori watage ga hae,
Kasuka ni keburu watage ga hae,
Kasuka ni furue.
Kataki jimen ni take ga hae,
Chijō ni surudoku take ga hae,
Masshigura ni take ga hae,
Kōreru fushibushi rinrin to,
Aodake no moto ni take ga hae,
Take, take, take ga hae.

Bamboo
On the sparkling earth the bamboos grow,
The green bamboos grow,
Beneath the earth the bamboo roots,
The roots gradually growing, slender,
From their tips cotton thread roots,
Smoky haze of cotton thread roots grow,
Trembling faintly.
On the hard earth the bamboos grow,
Above the earth the sharp bamboos grow,
Straight up the bamboos grow,
Vigorously out of frozen joints,
At the foot of the green bamboo the bamboos grow,
Bamboos, bamboos, bamboos grow.
                                        Hagiwara Sakutarō

The Symbolist School (*shōchōha*) included Hinatsu Kōnosuke
(b. 1890) and Saijō Yaso (b. 1892), both of whom achieved considerable originality of style. Noguchi Yonejirō (1875–1941) wrote in
English as well as in Japanese and produced intellectual verse of
highly exotic quality.

From about the year 1917 the central force in traditional Japanese poetry circles was the realistic poetry of the Araragiha, Araragi
School, which found its inspiration in the spirit of the *Man'yōshū*. The
Araragi group counted among its outstanding poets Saitō Mokichi
(1882–1953), Shimaki Akahiko (1876–1926), Nakamura Kenkichi
(1889–1934), Koizumi Chikashi (1886–1927), Tsuchiya Bummei
(b. 1891), Shaku Chōkū (1887–1953), Ishihara Jun (1881–1947)
and Imai Kuniko (1890–1948). All of these men published in the
group's magazine, *Araragi,* which began in October, 1908. The tone
of their work derived from the *Man'yōshū* style and imagistic methods
praised by Masaoka Shiki. This approach, especially in the hands of
Akahiko and Mokichi, achieved real psychological depth. The Araragi
group was diametrically opposed to the Myōjō poets in avoiding sub-
jectivism, and tried to view its subjects directly. Through an unswerving
and fixed gaze they meant to discover and portray a deeper reality.
To an audience which had learned the aesthetic views of Naturalism,
this style was familiar and welcome. Saitō Mokichi brought a romantic
tone to the *Man'yōshū* style and with his formidable poetic sensitivity
created an idea of a "life-force." This vitalism, influential far beyond
poetry circles, is expressed in Mokichi's verse collection *Shakkō*
(*Crimson Light*), published in 1913, which offered sensual expression
and outstanding modern lyricism. He carried Shiki's *shasei* theory,
descriptivism, somewhat further and set as his own ideal a unity of
self and nature. His *shasei* approach seems to have advanced to the
plane of symbolism. Mokichi's best known collection is *Aratama*

(*Uncut Gems*), published in 1921. His *Kakinomoto hitomaro,* a study of the *Man'yōshū* poet, published 1920–26, is also a major work.

Shimaki Akahiko, with a taste for seriousness and pathos, sought to infuse the idea of vitalism into the *tanka* form through themes focused on the loneliness of human life. He too was concerned with extending the *shasei* theory and in his work produced a style of graphic realism.

Kinoshita Rigen (1886–1925), a poet of the Shirakaba group, was a humanist in *tanka,* his verses filled with the warmth of colloquial expression, sometimes irregular in rhythm, but fresh and very personal. Ōta Mizuho (1876–1955), another vocal opponent of the Araragi school's view of *shasei,* took a symbolistic direction inspired by the *haikai* of Matsuo Bashō. By the end of Taishō the various groups which were opposed to the leading Araragi school formed a clique themselves and began publishing the magazine *Nikkō* (*Sunlight*) as a medium for their work.

The success of New Theater was achieved through translated plays and soon produced a succession of Japanese dramatists, as well as novelists who occasionally wrote for the theater. The new plays included *Shūzenji monogatari* (*The Story of Shūzen Temple*), 1911, by Okamoto Kidō (1872–1939); *Ii tairō no shi* (*The Death of Lord Ii, Chief Minister of the Shōgun*), 1920, by Nakamura Kichizō (1877–1940); *Shukke to sono deshi* (*The Priest and His Disciples*), by Kurata Hyakuzō (1891–1943); *Gemboku to chōei* (*Hsuan-p'o and Chang-in*), 1924, *Taira no masakado* (*Taira no Masakado;* Heian period warrior, d. 940), and *Genroku chūshingura* (*The Loyal Samurai of the Genroku Period*), 1941, by Mayama Seika (1878–1948). In the same style Tsubouchi Shōyō wrote the historical play *Nagori no hoshizukiyo* (*Starry Night of Parting*) in 1917. The Taishō period saw many plays by literary men. Among them the following are outstanding: *Izumiya somemonoten* (*The Izumiya Dyer*), 1911, and *Nambanji monzen* (*In Front of the Church*), 1914, by Kinoshita Mokutarō; *Sono imōto* (*The Little Sister*), 1915, and *Aiyoku* (*Passion*), 1926, by Mushanokōji Saneatsu; *Eiji goroshi* (*The Infant Killer*), 1920, and *Seimei no kammuri* (*Crown of Fate*), 1920, by Yamamoto Yūzō; *Chichi kaeru* (*Father Returns*), 1917, by Kikuchi Kan; *Gyūnyūya no kyōdai* (*The Dairy Shop Brothers*), 1914, by Kume Masao; and *Amazora* (*Rainy Sky*), 1920, by Kubota Mantarō (1889–1963). Led by such works, new plays soon came to dominate the theater.

Impressionism

The Impressionist writing of Europe was introduced to Japan in 1924 through translation of Paul Morand's *Ouvert la nuit* (*Yoru hiraku*), the first new work of significance to appear in France after World War I. Only a short while earlier the avant-garde work of European artists—Futurism, Expressionism, Constructivism, Dada, and so forth—had become known in Japan. The Japanese response to such stimuli was the formation of the Shinkankakuha, Neo-Impressionist School, which aimed at a total revision of literary techniques and expression. The group itself reflected the fragmented intellectual state of Japan in the late Taishō and early Shōwa years. The writers central to the movement came from those men associated with the magazine *Bungei shunjū* (*Literature Spring and Autumn*) which Kikuchi Kan had begun in 1923. The new group began its own journal called *Bungei jidai* (*Literary Age*) in 1924. Their aesthetic background was made up of the various avant-garde schools of Europe, and in literature their expressionistic technique gave their work a sharpness of observation quite in contrast to the mood of Naturalism, which they criticized for being pedestrian or conventional appreciation of beauty.

Yokomitsu Riichi (1898–1947) became the first theoretician of the Neo-Impressionists and his own novels are a full demonstration of the method. *Nichirin* (*The Sun*) of 1923, a close predecessor of Neo-Impressionism, was his first great success. Then appeared *Naporeon to tamushi* (*Ringworm and Napoleon*) in 1925, *Shanhai* (*Shanghai*) in 1928, *Kikai* (*The Machine*) in 1930, *Monshō* (*Family Crest*) in 1934, and *Ryoshū* (*Lonely Journey*) between 1937 and 1946.

Kawabata Yasunari (1899–1972) is known for his numerous short novels, "palm of the hand" novellas. More lyrical than Yokomitsu, he is master of a cool and rather nihilistic tone which gives a singular edge to his portraits of women. Among his representative works are *Izu no odoriko* (*Dancing-Girl of Izu*), 1926, *Asakusa kurenaidan* (*The Crimson Gang of Asakusa*), 1929, and *Kinjū* (*Birds and Beasts*), 1933. His *Yukiguni* (*Snow Country*), written between 1934 and 1947, has received high praise in Japan and is the recipient of a Nobel Prize in Literature.

Other writers in the Neo-Impressionist movement were: Nakagawa Yoichi (b. 1897), author of *Keishikishugi geijutsuron* (*A Treatise on Formalism in Art*), 1930; Kataoka Teppei (1894–1944); Sasaki Mosaku (b. 1894); Jūichiya Gisaburō (1897–1937); Iketani Shinzaburō (1900–33); Kon Tōkō (b. 1898); and Kishida Kunio (1890–1954), who was particularly active as a dramatist and was much influenced by French literature.

Proletarian Literature

Proletarian or socialistic literature reached its high point during the early Shōwa years, around 1930. Yokomitsu Riichi, whose own views were directly opposed to those of the political-social writers, described the force of this movement vividly as "ruling a generation so far, it seems, that for the sake of sunlight they would turn the world to darkness." The roots of this literary movement can be traced back to the political and socialistic novels of the Meiji period, especially such works as *Hi no hashira* (*Pillar of Fire*) in 1904 and *Otto no jiyū* (*A Husband's Freedom*) in 1906, by Kinoshita Naoe (1896–1937). In the Meiji period, however, with its strong ties to the feudalistic past, the laborer himself was shunted from rural areas to the cities or mines, or else he was set down as simply an urban commoner who had failed to make something of his life. A view of the worker as an element in the political scene had to await the tide of democratic ideals and the influence of the Soviet Union during the Taishō period. The real beginning of proletarian literature in Japan can be seen by about 1918 when novels and a "theory of people's art" (*minshū geijutsuron*) first appeared.

The first Japanese works to take up in significant degree the matter of a people's art were *Minshū geijutsu no igi oyobi kachi* (*The Meaning and Value of a People's Art*) by Homma Hisao (b. 1886) in 1916, and *Minshū geijutsuron* (*A Treatise on People's Art*) by Ōsugi Sakae (1885–1923), translated from Romain Rolland's *A Theater of the People*. Katō Kazuo (1887–1951) was also highly interested in the idea but meant by it something more like humanism. The first writer to take up the problem of social class as a literary problem was Nakano Hideo in an article in 1920 titled *Daiyonkaikyū no bungaku* ("Literature of the Working Class"). He maintained that the relationship should be studied in a broad context and without special pleading. By 1922 the writings of Hirabayashi Hatsunosuke (1892–1931) and Miyajima Sukeo (1886–1951) had given a firm root to the new endeavor. In this period too the worker-authors Miyajima Sukeo and Miyaji Karoku (b. 1884) first achieved fame. They were followed by Yoshida Kaneshige (b. 1892), Naitō Tatsuo (b. 1893), Arai Kiichi (b. 1890), and Maedakō Hiroichirō (1888–1957) who for the most part in their writings drew from their own experience as workingmen. Particularly in Miyajima's novels, *Kōfu* (*The Miner*), 1916, and *Yama no kajiya* (*Mountain Blacksmith*), 1919, there is a powerful spirit of the defiant worker. The freshness and strength of the new genre is clear in Miyaji's *Aru shokkō no shuki* (*A Worker's Notebook*), 1919, and Maedakō's *Santō senkyaku* (*Third Class Passage*), 1920, and *Madorosu no mure* (*Forecastle Gang*).

The first May Day celebration in Japan was held in Tōkyō's Ueno Park in 1920 and following that event socialist and labor union leaders planned the formation of the Japan Socialist Alliance for which an inaugural congress was held in December of 1922. The

Alliance was officially banned six months later, but by July of 1922 the Japanese Communist Party came into being.

In February of 1921 the magazine *Tanemakuhito* (*The Sowers*) began publication in Tozaki City, Akita Prefecture. Among those associated with it were Komaki Ōmi (b. 1894), Kaneko Yōbun (b. 1894), Imano Kenzō (b. 1893), and Yamakawa Ryō (1887–1957). This small publication—barely eighteen pages, with a first edition of two hundred copies—achieved great significance in the history of proletarian literature. The first publication of *Tanemakuhito* was inspired by the message of the Clarté movement begun by Henri Barbusse and Anatole France which was introduced to Japan by Komaki Ōmi. The magazine suspended publication after the third issue, having, however, introduced the program of the Third International to Japan. In October of 1921 preparations were completed for the second series of *Tanemakuhito* and publication was resumed with a format extended to fifty-six pages and the edition running to 3,000 copies. The famous proclamation which appeared in it began with the words "Once man created God. Now man has killed God. We must understand the fate of things created." The statement ended with, "It is for life itself that we hold dear the truths of the revolution. We sowers arise—with our comrades of the world!" In addition to the names already mentioned, others who became part of the movement were: Muramatsu Masatoshi, Yanase Masayume, Matsumoto Kōji, Aono Suekichi, Ueno Torao, Nakanishi Inosuke, Sano Kasami, Mutō Naoji, and Yamada Seizaburō. The first number made an "appeal to thinking men" to aid in relief of the famine in Russia; the third issue, in 1921, proclaimed its "*anchi miritarisuto no tachiba*" (anti-militaristic position) and total opposition to imperialistic wars; the fourth issue carried an article titled "Militarism and Anti-Militarism" by Karl Liebknecht, the German socialist leader, which finally brought down government censorship of the publication. The Tanemakisha, Sowers Society, was not simply a literary movement but a group that strongly advocated internationalism, anti-imperialism, and anti-war causes and that tried to involve the youth and the women of Japan.

The primary orientation of the magazine *Tanemakuhito* was theoretical. Hirabayashi Hatsunosuke, a leading figure in the group, stated in 1921 that the recent movement of a class art must find its place as part of the class struggle. This commitment was renewed by Aono Suekichi. However, in terms of actual composition that escaped emotionalism or primitive anger, we find only Kaneko's *Jigoku* (*Hell*) of 1923 and Nakanishi's *Shado ni megumu mono* (*Raised in Red Soil*) of 1922. Under the influence of these works appeared such novels as *Jokō aishi* (*The Sad Lives of Factory Girls*), 1925, and *Kōba* (*The Factory*), 1924, by Hosoi Wakizō (1897–1925). The great earthquake in the Tōkyō area on September 1, 1923, brought a temporary halt to publication of *Tanemakuhito* until January of the following year. Next, a special supplement called *Tanemaki zakki* (*The Sowers Miscellany*), published accounts of the Kamedo incident in which Hirazawa Keishichi (1885–1923) and eight members of the Nankatsu Labor Union were shot to death at the Kamedo police station following the catastrophe of the earthquake and fire. About that time too, under cover of the security laws, more than 3,000 Koreans resident in Japan were slain at the hands of vigilantes and others. Ōsugi Sakae, along with his wife and nephew, were shot to death by the military police. Such right-wing terrorism led the Japanese Communist Party, which had prompted the social unrest, to conclude that the formation of a party was premature. At the instigation of Yamakawa Hitoshi, who stressed the necessity of creating a popular base for the revolutionary movement, the Party was dissolved in March of 1924. Yamakawa did not long remain silent. In June of that year he began publishing the magazine *Bungei sensen* (*The Literary Front*) which stood "on the united battle-front of art," and had as its motto "Freedom is the thought and action of every individual." His co-founders in the publication were Imano, Kaneko, Nakanishi, Aono, Hirabayashi, Maedakō Hiroichirō, Muramatsu, Yanase, Mutō Naoji, and Sasaki Takamaru. Two months later Yamada Seizaburō joined the group. In June, 1925, the Nihon Puroretaria Bungei Remmei, Japan League for Proletarian Literature, was formed to include members of the *Bungei sensen* and other groups, and with this the proletarian literary movement entered the "second phase of the struggle."

In the second period Aono became leader of the movement and was particularly influential with his articles *Shirabeta geijustu* ("An Examined Art") published in July, 1925, and *Shizen seichō to mokuteki ishiki* ("Natural Development and Consciousness of Purpose"). The former showed Aono's distrust of the first-person novel, advocating rigorous circumscription of subject matter and arguing that the writer should analyze and describe the world of the proletariat which bears the burden of production. In the second article he proposed that the literary movement be socialistically organized and he criticized the ideology of proletarian literature, saying that "the proletarian literary movement, as opposed to proletarian literature which arose naturally, cultivates a consciousness of purpose." This "consciousness of purpose" idea was adopted from Lenin's article "What Must Be Done" and further introduced a theory of "fragmentation before unification" proposed by Fukumoto Kazuo, a proposal which shifted the Anarchist-Marxist movement closer to pure Marxism. One consequence of this new emphasis was the withdrawal of Nakanishi, Muramatsu, and Matsumoto, who were anti-Marxists, and the appearance of new men—Kuroshima Denji, Senda Koreya, Akaki Kensuke—around whom *Bungei sensen* was reorganized. The theory they worked under was termed "Fukumoto-ism." In this theory it was maintained that in order to begin a strong fight across the whole social scene against the challenge of Japanese capitalism, which was seen as entering a period of decline, it was necessary to foster a strong revolutionary consciousness by means of a total theoretical confrontation. To this end the Japanese Communist Party was reorganized in December of 1926 under the leadership of Watanabe Masanosuke (1899–1928) and Ichikawa Shōichi.

The unifying idea of the Nippon Puroretaria Geijutsu Remmei, Japan Proletarian Arts League, was Marxism, but within the group there were two factions. In June, 1927, the two sides split, with part of the membership remaining with the League and publishing a journal called *Puroretaria Geijutsu* (*Proletarian Art*). The other faction reorganized into the Rōnō Geijutsuka Remmei, Worker and Farmer Artists League, and published in *Bungei sensen*. The split was over adherence to the ideas of "Fukumoto-ism," with the League members pro-Fukumoto and the *Bungei sensen* group opposed. But this was not the end of factionalizing. Within the Rōnō Geijutsu Dōmei were two groups which can be called the "legalists" and the "illegalists." When these factions separated the legalists remained with *Bungei sensen,* while the illegalists, those opposed to working within the legal system, formed the Zen'ei Geijutsuka Dōmei, the Vanguard Artists League, and began publishing a magazine called *Zen'ei* (*Vanguard*).

The affiliations of the various writers may be seen in the following list.

1. Nihon Puroretaria Geijutsuka Renmei: Nakano Shigeharu, Kaji Wataru, Tani Hajime, Hisaita Eijirō, Kibe Masayuki
2. Zen'ei Geijutsu Dōmei: Fujimori Seikichi, Kurahara Korehito, Hayashi Fusao, Yamada Seisaburō, Taguchi Ken'ichi, Sasaki Takamaru, Murayama Tomoyoshi, Kawaguchi Kō
3. Rōnō Geijutsuka Remmei: Aono Suekichi, Maedakō Hiroichirō, Kaneko Yōbun, Imano Kenzō, Satomura Kinzō, Hayama Yoshiki, Kuroshima Denji, Hirabayashi Taiko, Komaki Ōmi, Tsuruta Tomoya

In this period writers associated with *Bungei sensen,* such men as Hayama Yoshiki (1894–1945), Kuroshima Denji (1889–1943), and Hirabayashi Taiko (b. 1905), were highly active. Hayama alternated between writing and working as an ordinary seaman and his writings were tense with a fierce spirit growing out of his experiences at sea. He was widely acclaimed in literary circles for his sketches *Inbaifu* (*A Woman of the Streets*), 1925, and *Semento-daru no naka no tegami* (*Letter in a Barrel of Cement*), 1926. In these works there is a mixture of reality and reverie particularly successful in expressing a raw will for life. In what is perhaps his best-known work, *Umi ni ikuru hitobito* (*Men Who Live on the Sea*), published in 1926, he demonstrated the literary potentials of the proletarian novel in a story that tells of the requests made by the crew to their captain who ignores their distress—and the ultimate step to forceful resistance by the men.

Kuroshima Denji's life was much less spectacular than Hayama's, but he revealed in detail the mean and austere lives of the farming people on his native island of Shōdo-jima through such novels as *Dempō* (*The Telegram*) in 1925, and *Nisen dōka* (*Two Copper Pennies*) in 1926. His best work, as seen in *Hansen bungakuron* (*On Anti-War Literature*), appears in his writings about Siberia and in his anti-war novels, such works as *Yuki no shiberia* (*Siberia of Snow*), 1926, *Sori* (*The Sleigh*), 1927, and *Uzumakeru tori no mure* (*A Swirl of Birds*), 1928. In them he describes the fearsome plight of soldiers trapped and dying in the great snowy wastes of Siberia.

Hirabayashi Taiko, a woman writer in the movement, wrote with a great power of anarchistic resistance in her *Seryōshitsu nite* (*In the Charity Ward*) of 1927. Her style stands in contrast to another woman writer in proletarian literature, Sata Ineko (b. 1904), author of *Kyarameru kōba kara* (*From a Caramel Factory*), published in 1928. Satomura Kinzō brought a peculiar wildness to his writing in such work as *Kūrīgashira no hyōjō* (*The Face of a Coolie*), published in 1926. Not all proletarian writers were new writers and among the established ones who shifted to this genre was Fujimori Seikichi, whose work includes *Haritsuke mozaemon* (*Crucified Mozaemon*), 1926, and *Naniga kanojo o sō saseta ka* (*What Made Her That Way?*), 1927.

In July, 1927, the Comintern opened its meeting in Moscow and adopted a "Program Regarding Japan." The program severely criticized "Yamakawa-ism" (after Yamakawa Hitoshi, a non-Communist socialist) and "Fukumoto-ism." The Program prescribed for Japan a bourgeois-democratic revolution which would change into a socialist revolution. The Communist Party was to lead the struggle of the workers and the farmers by providing organization under the slogan "dictatorship of the proletariat," with the Party directed to "draw near to the people."

While the proletarian literary movement generally continued its internal dissension, there came an opportunity for partial unity with the formation of Nihon Sayoku Bungeika Sōrengō, Japan Federation of Left-Wing Writers, combining members of Nihon Puroretaria Geijutsu Remmei and the Zen'ei Geijutsuka Dōmei. The initial publication of the new group, known as Sōrengō, was a collection titled *Sensō ni taisuru sensō* (*The War Against War*), which appeared in 1928. The problem of unity became acute at that time with the arrest of well over one thousand persons, members of the Communist Party and other left-wing groups, on March 15, 1928, just two days after the formation of Sōrengō. The two groups mentioned above then combined to form Zen-Nihon Musansha Geijutsu Remmei, the All-Japan Proletarian Art League, known as "Nappu" after its Esperanto name, "Nippon Artista Proleta Federatio," NAPF. In May, 1928, Nappu began publication of its journal *Senki* (*Battle Flag*), out of which grew an extended rivalry with *Bungei sensen*. The formation of Nappu by radical intellectuals, such as Nakano and Kurahara, gradually brought the organization, as the literary effort of the Communist Party, to a leading position in the whole left-wing movement. Their rivals were such "legalists" as Hayama, Satomura, and Kuroshima; these men all had backgrounds as laborers, but they gradually fell into a secondary role in left-wing art.

In these years Kurahara Korehito (b. 1902) supplanted Aono as leader and theoretician in the Communist left, his most influential work being *Puroretaria rearizumu e no michi* (*The Road to Proletarian Realism*), published in 1928. The theory expounded in it went a step beyond "consciousness of the objective" to the following affirmation: "The only way to proletarian realism is this: First, look at the world through the eyes of the proletarian vanguard. Second, describe the world with an attitude of strict realism." Kurahara's ideas influenced Nappu to proclaim the primacy of political considerations and the proletariat in literature, thus aiming for an intensification of Marxism in literature.

In the same year that Nappu was formed an argument broke out between Kurahara of the old Zen'ei Geijutsuka Dōmei and Nakano Shigeharu (b. 1902) of the Nihon Puroretaria Geijutsu Remmei on the matter of popularization of art. In November of 1928 a reorganization of Nappu was approved by its members and in February of the next year the Nihon Puroretaria Sakka Dōmei, Japan League of Proletarian Writers, was established as an affiliate organization. The basic tenets of the new group were thus stated: "We resolve on the establishment of a class literature which will serve in the liberation of the proletariat" and "We will struggle for removal of all political repression inflicted on our movement." The central committee of the organization was founded on the thesis that "dialectical materialism was the main principle of labor and the masses." They resolved that popularization of the arts was most necessary.

In April, 1930, Kurahara (under the pen-name of Satō Kōichi) published in *Senki* a thesis titled *Nappu geijutsuka no atarashii nimmu* ("The New Duty of Nappu Artists") in which he called for "the establishment of a Communist art" which would be an encouragement to all members of Nappu. He also asked for the participation of all

Nappu artists in the "illegal" movement: "The theme of artistic activity will be the problem which confronts us at the present time—to be taken up by our country's proletarian art and its political party."

Another argument arose at that time around the dualistic thesis published in 1929 by Hirabayashi Hatsunosuke under the title *Seijiteki kachi to geijutsuteki kachi* ("Political Values and Artistic Values"). The question raised by Hirabayashi was that of how to judge work which had excellent artistic values and yet was negative in its political value. This was, of course, a direct challenge to Kurahara's thesis of the supremacy of politics in art, and in the same year Nakano Shigeharu published an article called *Geijutsu ni seijiteki kachi nante mono wa nai* ("There is No Such Thing As Political Values in Art"). The debate on this point grew furious and eventually involved many writers: Kawaguchi Kō, Katsumoto Seiichirō, Miyamoto Kenji, Ōya Sōichi, Komiyama Akitoshi, Kubokawa Tsurujirō, Miki Kiyoshi, and Tanigawa Tetsuzō. An illuminating article by Miyamoto Kenji, under the title *Seiji to geijutsu—seiji no yūisei ni kansuru mondai* ("Politics and Art—The Question Regarding the Dominance of Politics"), clearly revealed that the whole argument involved a shift of emphasis from social class to political party.

Kobayashi Takiji (1903–33) was one of the writers who, through his creative work, gave artistic life to the great tide of theoretical activity. He was born in a poor farming household in Akita Prefecture. After graduation from Otaru Commercial High School in Hokkaidō he wrote a story about a merciless interrogation by the secret police titled "1918–3–15" ("March 15, 1918"). His place as a proletarian writer was secure with the publication of his *Kani kōsen (The Crab-Canning Ship)* in 1929. In this novel the workers on a crabbing ship revolt against the brutal treatment by the bosses—a revolt which is suppressed by elements of the Imperial Navy. Kobayashi went to Tōkyō in March, 1930, and joined the Communist Party in January, 1931. In a novel called *Tōseikatsusha (The Life of a Party Member)*, published in 1933, he portrayed the inner workings of the Party from the viewpoint of Kurahara, revealing also the Party members' rather conventional attitude toward the role of women. Following what was called the "standard of selection of material" set down by Nappu, he produced such novels as *Fuzai jinushi (Absentee Landlord)* in 1929, *Kōjō saibō (Party Cells in a Factory)* in 1930, and *Tenkeiki no hitobito (Men of Epoch-Making Ages)*—all of which were seen through "the eyes of the vanguard." He was arrested and died in prison in 1933.

Tokunaga Sunao (1899–1958) ranks with Kobayashi as a proletarian realist. His *Taiyō no nai machi (Sunless Street)* of 1929 was solidly constructed, taking as its subject the workers' strike at the

Kyōdō Printing Works in 1926 where the author himself was a participant. The novel deals with the capitalists' side of the conflict as well and gives a well-rounded account of the inevitable defeat of the strikers. In 1930 he produced a sequel, *Shitsugyō toshi tōkyō* (*Tokyo, City of the Unemployed*), and later such stories as *Fassho* (*Fascism*), 1932, but gradually he slipped into banal and stereotyped writing. Among Nakano Shigeharu's writings is *Nakano shigeharu shishu* (*Collected Poetry of Nakano Shigeharu*), 1935, a finely wrought group of poems in modern form. His work in fiction includes a number of excellent stories, such as *Harusaki no kaze* (*Early Spring Wind*), 1928, and *Tetsu no hanashi* (*The Story of Iron*), published in *Senki* in 1929.

There were, of course, many other writers with leftist sympathies. Among the more prominent were Kataoka Teppei (1894–1944), author of *Ayasatomura kaikyoroku* (*The Heroism of Ayasato Village*), in 1929, and *Aijō no mondai* (*A Problem of Love*), in 1931; Takeda Rintarō (1904–46), author of *Bōryoku* (*Violence*), published in *Bungei shunjū* in 1929; Fujimori Seikichi (b. 1892), author of *Hikari to yami* (*Light and Darkness*) in 1929, and other works mentioned above; Kishi Yamaji (b. 1899) also wrote in the genre of popular proletarian novels. In *Senki* a succession of writers appeared, among which the following are representative: Tateno Nobuyuki (b. 1903) and Sui Hajime, writers of agricultural stories; Sata Ineko (b. 1904; married name Kubokawa) who wrote stories of girls who worked in the cloth mills; and Hashimoto Eikichi (b. 1898) who wrote novels of the lives of miners.

At the International Conference on Revolutionary Literature held in Kharkov in November, 1930, a statement was introduced, labeled "On Proletarian Literature of Japan," in which it was made clear that the Nappu position was regarded as correct, as opposed to the views of Rōnō Geijutsuka Dōmei. Rōgei, as the group was called, gradually had been shifting toward social-democracy in its political stance and, while left-wing, it was plainly anti-Communist, embracing authors of talent comparable to those in Nappu, but as the leading force in proletarian literature shifted to Nappu, Rōgei succumbed to internal dissent. These internal blowups followed one after another. Those who left the group moved to Nappu while the few remaining members dissolved Rōgei and organized under the name Rōnō Bungaku Dōmei, Workers and Farmers Literary League.

Before its dissolution, Rōgei counted some excellent writers in its ranks. Iwafuji Yukio (b. 1903) produced the best fiction published in *Bungei sensen*. In his novel *Tetsu* (*Iron*), 1929, he skillfully drew the terrible labor conditions in an iron foundry and the strains within the life of the hero's family. Hirabayashi Taiko, a woman writer, showed considerable skill in such works as *Naguru* (*I Hit Him*), 1928, and *Fusetsu ressha* (*Construction Train*), 1929, but she left the Rōgei group rather soon and was sharply critical of its harsh qualities. Maedakō Hiroichirō wrote a number of plays and in 1929 published *Shina* (*China*), a novel based on the Chinese revolution. The same year saw publication of his *Semuga* (*Semuga*), a story of the Kamchatka fishing grounds told with great irony. Hayama Yoshiki, in such stories as *Idōsuru sonraku* (*Migratory Village*) of 1930, showed a fine grasp of the character of the common man. Kuroshima Denji drew the Chin-nan (or Tsinan) incident of May, 1928 (in which Japan temporarily seized the railways in Shantung, China), in his *Busōseru shigai* (*Armed City*). This work was a strong indictment of the use of Japan's military forces. For the most part other writers lacked what Nappu termed "positiveness of theme" and offered nothing to alter the static quality of *Bungei sensen*. Another of the critically acclaimed pieces of fiction of 1930 was Hosoda Tamiki's *Shinri no haru* (*Springtime of Truth*), which appeared serially in the Asahi Newspaper and revealed the inner workings of the world of finance.

Modernism and Tradition

The currents of change which began in the late Taishō period brought a break with the past and set the stage for the new literature of the Shōwa period. The transition is marked by the deaths of two writers: Akutagawa Ryūnosuke who, in a fit of "vague malaise," committed suicide in 1927, and Kasai Zenzō who died the following year. The group called Shinkankakuha, the Neo-Impressionists, is identified with the magazine *Bungei jidai* (*Literary Age*) which began in 1924 and terminated in 1927. Another coterie called the Shinjinseiha, New Life School, began *Fudōchō* (*Non-Cooperation*, published 1925–29), standing in opposition to both the proletarian writers and the Shinkankakuha. Nakamura Murao (1886–1949), then editor of *Shinchō* (*New Currents*), a monthly dating back to 1904, was the chief figure in this group, which included the following writers: Okada Saburō (1890–1954); Asahara Rokurō (b. 1895), Togawa Shūkotsu (1870–1939), and Ozaki Shirō (1896–1964). Among the writers of the Shinkankakuha were: Ishihama Kansaku, Kawabata Yasunari, Yokomitsu Riichi (1898–1947), Nakagawa Yoichi, Jūichiya Gisaburō, Kishida Kunio, and Inagaki Taruho (b. 1900).

Nakamura Murao challenged the proletarian movement, advocating "a literature of the individual rather than a literature of 'ism' " in a *Shinchō* article of 1928 titled *Dare da? Hanazono o arasu mono wa!* ("Who is This Invading the Flower Garden?"). In the same year Yokomitsu, writing in the magazine *Bungei shunjū*, attacked

Kurahara's *Senki* article *Geijutsu undō tōmen no kinkyū mondai* ("Urgent Problems Facing the Art Movement") and gave strong support to a formalistic approach (*keishikishugi*). The formalistic view was supported by Nakagawa, Kawabata, Inukai Takeshi and others who joined in the debate which resulted in a movement aimed at unifying the anti-Marxist writers. Late in 1929 this activity brought about the formation of the elegantly-named "Barairo no Shokkō o Abite Jōtō ni Tatsu Jūsannin no Kishi," meaning: "Thirteen Knights Who Stand at the Top of the Castle, Bathed in the Rosy Light of Dawn," a group which included Asahara, Iijima Tadashi, Kawabata, Kamura Isota, Hisano Toyohiko, Nakamura, Okada, Ozaki Shirō, and Ryūtanji Yū, all from either the Shinkankakuha or the Shinjinseiha. This was a wide representation, including writers from the Waseda group and men who published in *Kindai seikatsu* (Modern Living), *Bungei toshi* (*Literary Capital*), *Bungaku* (*Literature*), *Mita bungaku* (*Mita Literature*) which were among the *"dōnin zasshi"* or coterie magazines of early Shōwa. Promoted by Ryūtanji, the Shinkō Geijutsuha, New School of Aesthetics, was organized in April, 1930, providing an association homogeneous only in its opposition to Marxism. Besides the writers already mentioned, the membership included: Abe Tomoji, Ibuse Masuji, Fukada Kyūya, Funabashi Seiichi, Hori Tatsuo, Kobayashi Hideo, Nagai Tatsuo, Narasaki Tsutomu, and Tsunekawa Hiroshi. The general principles of the group were stated by Tsunekawa in a *Shinchō* article titled *Geijutsuha sengen* ("Proclamation of the Artistic School"), but the Artistic School lacked a unifying principle except that provided by the group's common background in journalism.

In 1930 the Shinkō Geijutsuha published a collection of thirty-one stories under the title *Geijutsuha varaetei* (*Aesthetic's Variety*), and a twelve-author anthology *Modan tokio enbukyoku* (*Modern Tōkyō Waltz*). The writers of this group were published by various houses, but their presentation before the general public was fostered particularly by the Shinchōsha publishing company in which Nakamura Murao was a central figure. The group was accused by the Marxist writers of extreme frivolity, of describing the empty pleasures of modern life in Tōkyō, of *"ero-guro-nansensu,"* meaning "eroticism, grotesqueness, and nonsense." Ryūtanji Yū (b. 1901) was a principal author in this area. His *Hōrō jidai* (*Wandering Years*) of 1928 was followed in 1929 by his critically acclaimed *Apāto no onnatachi to boku to* (*Women of the Apartment and I*), a hedonistic work in a fast tempo and brilliant style which was a great popular success. Nakamura Masatsune (b. 1901) was also an active journalist; his story *"Makaroni"* (*Macaroni*) of 1929 was excellent, and in 1930 a collection of his pieces appeared under the title of *Inseki no nedoko* (*The Meteorite*

Bed). Among the men who were regarded somewhat as oddities, a few, such as Kamura Isota, author of *Gōku* (*Retribution*), 1928, Kajii Motojirō (1901–32), Ibuse Masuji (b. 1898), and Hori Tatsuo (1904–53), cultivated truly new fields in writing. As a group, the Shinkō Geijutsuha offered no unifying principle and within a short while it was ignored by the public and individual authors were left to their particular talents. Two men, Kuno Toyohiko and Asahara Rokurō, during 1931–32, attempted to broaden the concern of the group and formed the Shinshakaiha, New Society School, together with a few men from the roster of the declining Shinkō Geijutsuha.

A second offshoot of the Shinkō Geijutsuha, and one considerably more effective, was Shinshinrishugi, New Psychology School, which was inspired by Freudian psychology and European writers like Joyce, Virginia Woolf, and Marcel Proust. The search for a new aesthetic among the modern writers of Japan took several directions. One of them was *Shi to shiron* (*Poetry and Poetic Theory*), a quarterly magazine begun in 1928 by a group which included Haruyama Yukio and Kitagawa Fuyuhiko as editors, Takiguchi Takeo, Ueda Toshio, Kambara Yasushi, Takenaka Iku, Miyoshi Tatsuji, and later Sasazawa Yoshiaki, Nishiwaki Junzaburō, Hori Tatsuo, Yokomitsu Riichi, and Watanabe Kazuo. In addition to publishing the work of Japanese poets, the magazine introduced the poetry and aesthetic ideas of twentieth-century Europe, presenting on its pages pure poetry, surrealism, and the writings of Max Jacob, Jean Cocteau, André Breton, T. S. Eliot, Herbert Read, André Gide, D. H. Lawrence and others. Haruyama also edited the series *Gendai no geijutsu to hihyō sōsho* (*Contemporary Art and Criticism*) which included articles on Cocteau's poetry, surrealistic poetry, literature of intellectualism, literature and the new psychology, and so forth. The spirit and the techniques were fresh, and a new direction in writing resulted. New writers joined the movement. Joyce's *Ulysses* first found its way into Japanese through a translation by Tsujino Hisanori and Nagamatsu Sadamu. The magazine *Bungaku* (*Literature*), which was begun in October, 1930, by Hori Tatsuo, and which received support from Inukai Takeshi, Kawabata Yasunari, Yokomitsu, Nagai Kafū and Yoshimura Tetsutarō, offered translations of Proust's *Du côté de chez Swann,* Gide's *Les Faux-monnayeurs,* plus writing by Paul Valéry and others. *Bungaku* and publications like it were not notable for displaying the new work of Japanese writers, but they were quite successful in presenting new ideas, particularly those concerning the new view of man growing in the West, which became the seeds for the flowering of a generation later.

The leftist magazine *Kaizō* (*Reconstruction*), begun in 1919, published Yokomitsu's story *Kikai* (*The Machine*) in its September,

1930, issue, and this piece of fiction had a considerable effect on literary circles. Earlier, Yokomitsu's *Nichirin* had presented a beautifully turned historical romance, and in *Shanhai* (*Shanghai*), published in 1929, he brought a strong challenge to proletarian literature's social awareness through his own manipulation of emotion and a brilliant technique. In *Shanhai* he worked with the internal monologue learned from Proust, making the technique his own and offering an extraordinarily penetrating psychological study of a group of factory workers. Yokomitsu's story *Shin'en* (*Imperial Tomb*), 1932, pursued the technique and refined his idea of human life being judged and guided by a "machine" of fate.

Kawabata Yasunari in *Suishō gensō* (*The Crystal Illusion*), published in *Kaizō,* 1931, worked with a Joycean stream of consciousness and the experiments in the new psychology begun by Yokomitsu. In *Izu no odoriko,* 1926, poetic sentiment was the vehicle for a love story. In *Asakusa kurenaidan* he portrayed nihilism and evil through the denigrating world of a gang drifting through life in the Asakusa entertainment district. There is a kind of lonely, orphaned feeling in Kawabata's writing. Through his eyes we gaze on something inanimate and unfeeling—as in *Jojōka* (*Lyrical Song*), 1932, or *Kinjū* (*Birds and Beasts*)—and presently find ourselves transported to a realm of delicate and unearthly beauty.

Hori Tatsuo brought a finely honed style to his *Seikazoku* (*A Holy Family*), which appeared in *Kaizō* in 1930. In *Rūbensu no giga* (*An Imitation Rubens*), 1929, he attempted a more relaxed style closer to European writing and succeeded in producing a work of great delicacy which gave body to abstractions and portrayed internal movement. Kajii Motojirō, who died quite young, also benefitted from the new influences and kept a remarkable artistic integrity in his work. His *Remon* (*Lemon*) is a vivid and well drawn story, and his *Aru gakeue no kanjō* (*Feelings at a Certain Precipice*), 1928, and *Nonki na kanja* (*An Easy Patient*) are excellent psychological studies which closely examine the mood of restless ennui. Ibuse Masuji, one of the Shinkō Geijutsuha writers, came to write good-humored stories, sometimes pathetic, after such early works as *Sanshōuo* (*The Salamander*), 1924, and *Koi* (*Carp*), 1928, in which he was highly sentimental in the treatment of his subject.

Kobayashi Hideo (b. 1902) was awarded a prize in criticism for his *Samazama naru ishō* (*Various Ideas*) which appeared in *Kaizō* in 1929. His entrance on the literary scene had a specific purpose: to support the traditional main current in Japanese literature. Kobayashi wrote in a strong and persuasive style. Using the "Current Criticism" (*Bungei jihyō*) pages of *Bungei shunjū* as his vehicle, he wrote clear analyses of the work of Shiga Naoya and Yokomitsu

Riichi, standing opposed to the deceptions of aesthetic ideologies and their consequent utilitarianism. His position was clearly anti-Marxist and Charles Saint-Beuve (1804–69), the French master of the biographical method of criticism, was his guiding light. Kobayashi was a student also of the thought of Paul Valéry and André Gide. He adopted as his own the art of Europe and was unhesitant in calling for a total reconstruction of the Japanese literary world. The strength of his self-confidence all but overwhelmed his generation.

Itō Sei (b. 1905), inspired by Joyce and Proust, became an advocate of psychological literature, although somewhat academic in his approach. In his *Bungaku ryōiki no idō* ("The Shifting Realm of Literature") published in 1930, and in *Jeimusu Joisu no metoodo "ishiki no nagare" ni tsuite* (" 'Stream of Consciousness,' the Method of James Joyce") of the same year he began his advocacy of the psychological method. He pursued this idea, searching for deeper views into the human mind, and published a major study titled *Shinshinri-shugi bungaku* (*The New Psychological Literature*) in 1932. He applied his views to various works of fiction, among them *Kanjō saibō no dammen* (*A Specimen of Feeling*), 1930, *M hyakkaten* (*The M Department Store*), 1931, and *Seibutsusai* (*Festival for Living Creatures*), 1932.

In another direction, Abe Tomoji (b. 1903), following the literary ideas of Eliot, Huxley, and Read, found emotional and psychological depth through critical observation and intellectual approaches to description, publishing in 1930 a study called *Shuchiteki bungakuron* (*An Intellectualistic Theory of Literature*). His ideas had areas of agreement with the new psychology writers and were much indebted to the introduction of European speculative thinking. In *Nichi-doku taikō kyōgi* (*Rivalry Between Japan and Germany*) and *Shiroi shikan* (*A White Officer*), 1930, and in *Afurika no doiru* (*Doyle of Africa*), 1931, he experimented with the new psychology ideas in actual works of fiction.

Attacked by both the proletarian writers and the modernists, the established authors soon lost the base in journalism they had when newspapers published their work. Naturalistic writers and the writers of first-person novels, the Shirakabaha writers, and the writers who published in the magazine *Shinshichō* (*New Currents of Thought*), all could either keep silent or pander to popular taste. Rather orphaned and apart in all this were writers of the Aesthetic School, although they managed to continue active, creative lives. Outstanding among the neo-romantics or individualists was Tanizaki Jun'ichirō (1886–1965) who produced one fine work after another.

After the great earthquake of 1923, Tanizaki established his home in western Japan. It was a physical and intellectual move away from the bustling life of Tōkyō and with it Tanizaki directed his attention to the traditional arts of Japan and attempted to capture the rich flavor of the region through use of the Kansai dialect in his writings. Beginning with *Manji* (*Swastika*), 1928–30, a monologue spoken by a woman of Ōsaka, he continued working with the materials of traditional Japanese culture. This is evident in *Tadekuumushi* (*Some Prefer Nettles*), 1929, and in *Mōmoku monogatari* (*Tale of a Blind Man*), 1931, in which a fine sense of beauty infuses a story about the upheavals during the wars from 1467 to 1568. His *Shunkinshō* (*The Story of Shunkin*), published in 1933, showed a well-wrought classical style and was received as a masterpiece by the literary world. His essays, such as *In'ei raisan* (*In Praise of Shadows*) of 1933, were outstanding, as was his examination of the Japanese language as an aesthetic medium in *Bunshō dokuhon* (*Remarks on Writing*), 1934. He produced a translation into modern Japanese of the Heian period novel *Genji monogatari* (*The Tale of Genji*).

The height of the proletarian literary movement came in the years 1928 to 1932, during which period modernism, the opposing aesthetic, remained in the doldrums until it was succeeded by a traditionalist literature in which Nagai Kafū was one of the outstanding writers. In *Tsuyu no atosaki* (*Before and After the Rainy Season*) of 1931 he dealt with the strange life of a café waitress, and in *Hikage no hana* (*Flower of the Shade*) of 1934 he made a sensitive exposition of the inner life of a streetwalker. *Bokutō kidan* (*A Strange Story from East of the Sumida River*) is perhaps Kafū at his best. The story is highly lyrical, acutely sensitive to the mood of Tōkyō seasons, and filled with voluptuous sensuality as it tells of the hero's infatuation with a prostitute who lives in miserable circumstances in the Tamanoi district of the capital.

Satō Haruo (1892–1964) was a prolific writer, publishing serially such works as *Kamigami no tawamure* (*Gods at Play*) in 1928, and *Kokoro ogoreru onna* (*Haughty Woman*) in 1930. These works were carefully plotted and well received by the public. In 1929 he made use of Freudian analysis in the serialized *Kōseiki* (*A Rehabilitation*), which also earned him a reputation as a modernist. Then in 1932 he experimented in the area of crime and the detective story with *Uiin no satsujin yōgisha* (*The Viennese Murder Suspect*). His *Musashino shōjo* (*Girl of Musashi Plain*), written in 1931, attracted many readers for its sense of beauty and delicate style.

Murō Saisei (1889–1962) experimented widely, attempting a major change of style in two works of 1930, *Ashi, depāto, onna* (*A Foot, a Store, a Woman*) and *Uwakina bummei* (*A Fickle Culture*), both of which are uncertain in handling their materials. The real development of his writing came with *Fukushū* (*Revenge*) pub lished in 1935, while his *Ani imōto* (*Brother and Sister*), 1934, a study of feminine vindictiveness, anticipated his *Onna no zu* (*Portrait of a Woman*) the next year.

Masamune Hakuchō (1879–1962) wrote many short works in the first-person style which are of slight literary consequence, but in such critical studies as *Bundan jimbutsu hyōron* (*A Critique of Literary Personalities*), 1926, his seriousness and enthusiasm are evident through a particularly enlightened discrimination in art and a fine perception of human nature. Naturalism itself seemed almost irrelevant, and Tayama Katai, its early exponent, after setting down thoughts from his later years in *Momoya* (*A Hundred Nights*), 1927, fell silent and died a forgotten writer in 1930. Tokuda Shūsei (1871–1943) as well, after completing *Tsuchi ni iyuru* (*Healed by the Earth*) in 1928, gradually fell silent, writing of the loss of creative power in such stories as *Rōku* (*Age and Suffering*) in 1930. In 1933, however, he made a comeback on the literary scene, with much of his earlier spirit, through a story titled *Machi no odoriba* (*A Dance Hall in Town*). It was followed by *Shi ni shitashimu* (*Intimate with Death*), and, in 1934, by *Hito-kuki no hana* (*A Single Flower*) which examined the mental state equated with elegant simplicity. With *Kunshō* (*The Award*), in 1935, he produced a masterful examination of the sad, dreary lives of the common people. Then in 1935–38 he wrote a much acclaimed and autobiographical love story called *Kasō jinbutsu* (*A Man Disguised*).

Kasai Zensō completed his last work, *Suikyōsha no dokuhaku* (*Monologue of a Whimsical Man*), in 1927 and died the next year. From that time on, the first-person novel genre fell into sharp decline. Kamura Isota (1874–1933), a man close to Kasai, turned to aestheticism in a deliberately simplistic style with such works as *Gake no shita* (*Under a Precipice*) in 1928, *Ashi zumō* (*Foot Wrestling*) in 1929, and *Tojō* (*On the Road*) in 1932. Makino Shin'ichi (1896–1936) also had been influenced by Kasai and from the first years of Shōwa, about 1927, wrote in a way that brought together fantasy, nihilism and reality in such stories as *Mura no sutoaha* (*Village Stoics*), 1928, and *Tsurikago to gekkō to* (*A Hanging Basket and Moonlight*), 1930. He was regarded as having switched to a new approach then, but in 1931 with *Zēron* (*My Horse Zeron*) and other works he sounded removed and impersonal, self-intoxicated with his own aesthetics. After writing *Kiruimura* (*Hard-hearted Village*) in 1934 he took his own life in 1936. In 1928 Uno Kōji fell ill and suspended work on *Yoki oni, waruki oni* (*Good Devil, Bad Devil*)—a novel eventually published in 1939—and for several years worked only on children's stories to support himself. After his recovery he worked on his coterie magazine *Kiseki* (*Miracle*) and completed *Kareki no aru fūkei* (*Landscape with*

Dead Trees) which appeared in *Chūō kōron* (*Central Review*) in 1933. This story, conversational in style, was a psychological study of its hero, Saeki Yūzō, an approach Uno Kōji repeated and refined in two succeeding works, *Kareno no yume* (*Dream of Desolation*) and *Ko no raireki* (*A Child's Life*).

The first-person novel found a few more exponents in such writers as Toyoshima Yoshio (1890–1955), Takii Kōsaku (b. 1894), and Uno Chiyo (b. 1897) whose autobiographical *Iro zange* (*Amorous Confession*) published in 1933 was considered her masterpiece. Hayashi Fumiko (1904–51) entered the genre in 1930 with the novel *Hōrōki* (*Wanderings*) in which she lyrically but nihilistically wrote of her poverty and wandering. She continued the motif in *Seihin no sho* (*A Book on Honest Poverty*) and *Nakimushi Kozō* (*Weeping Little Monk*) and became a best-selling writer in 1931.

Literary Revival

The phrase "period of literary revival" (*bungei fukkōki*) is the usual label for the transition in Japanese letters which took place about the year 1935. Change indeed was the major key of the time, and we might briefly consider the reasons why the literary pioneers of the day so readily attracted followers. There was, of course, an abundance of intellectuals, men interested in the humanities, and these people provided the audience and the participants necessary for development. The proletarian literature movement found many sympathizers on the left, but there was no great rush to the movement by intellectuals in general—men who would not assent to the destruction of humanism, who took a moderate and tolerant position between proletarian literature and traditional literature, who seemed to be balanced intellects. Such people were often critical of the left-wing movement in literature, and sometimes grew very heated in the debate.

Hirotsu Kazuo was particularly sensitive to the problems of those years and, having given up the traditional and romantic aesthetic, brought to a first-person style his interest in the intellectuals who were attracted to the commotion of Marxism. His writings mirror this interest, from *Shōwa shonen no interi sakka* (*Intellectual Writers of Early Shōwa*), published in 1930, to *Fūu tsuyokarubeshi* (*A Rainstorm Must Be Strong*), serialized in 1933–34. Miyamoto Kenji—who coined the phrase *dōhansha sakka* or "fellow traveler writer"—termed Hirotsu "a negative element" among the "proletarian authors who came from the intelligentsia."

Yamamoto Yūzō might be characterized with Hirotsu. In the format of the serialized newspaper novel he dealt with topics of social consequence from the point of view of a humanist sympathetic to the revolutionary movement, and he appealed to a wide range of readers. In *Iki to shi ikeru mono* (*All Living Things*), 1926, his first long novel, he drew the tragedy of the salaried man's life; and after the publication of the love stories *Nami* (*Waves*) in 1928, and *Kaze* (*Wind*) in 1930, he described in *Onna no isshō* (*A Woman's Life*), 1932, the steps by which a youth grew socially conscious and entered the left-wing movement. *Onna no isshō* focuses on the conditions of human happiness rather than on the revolution, Yamamoto not being a writer to avoid the broad complexity of human life.

Nogami Yaeko (b. 1885) may be termed a literary fellow traveler also, but one sharply critical of the general proletarian literary movement. She was emphatic in stressing the primary importance of the individual and deals with the lives of her female protagonists in such terms rather than in terms of the revolutionary movement. She was opposed to fascism and showed herself a progressive humanist in such works as *Machiko* (*Machiko,* a woman's name), published 1928–30; *Wakai musuko* (*Young Son*), 1932; and *Kuroi gyōretsu* (*Black Parade*), 1936. The emerging opposition to fascism and militarism in the years between the Manchurian Incident of 1931 and the outbreak of the war with China in 1937 was shared by Hirotsu and Yamamoto, both of whom took a position similar to that of Nogami. This point of view was the same as that of various writers who might be characterized as fellow travelers, such as Serizawa Kōjirō (b. 1897), author of *Burujoa* (*The Bourgeoisie*) in 1930, and Shimomura Chiaki (1893–1955), author of *Tengoku no kiroku* (*An Account of Heaven*), published in 1930.

The so-called "period of emergency" which began with the arrests of March 15, 1928, brought a quickening of historical events in Japan. The revolutionary movement on the left adopted a radical, combative posture which only served to invite repression. The "Program Regarding Japan" of 1927 was succeeded by the "Thesis of 1932" which aimed for a bourgeois-democratic revolution that would provide the basis for the step into socialism; it gave special importance to the anti-military and anti-war movements. From the point of view of the Comintern, there was a threat from the Japanese army. But through lack of any clear program the left wing movements in Japan failed as a political force, and the government irremediably moved toward fascism and war.

In November of 1931 the Nihon Puroretaria Bunka Remmei, Japan Proletarian Culture League, known as KOPF or "Koppu" from its Esperanto name, was put together out of left-wing cultural organizations which included Nappu and various farm and factory groups. This reorganization was recommended by Kurahara, who wanted the separate parts brought together into a pyramid-type organization. However, beginning in March, 1932, Koppu came under new pressure from the government with the jailing of a number of its leaders. Those who escaped capture were forced into hiding. Almost as soon as it was formed, Koppu was put into the position of an outlaw group, and the proletarian literary movement itself began to decline. The reasons for this decline, however, were not exclusively external. In 1931 Kurahara published *Geijutsuteki hōhō ni tsuite no kansō* ("Thoughts on Artistic Methodology") which revised and extended the ideas of the previous year published as *Nappu geijutsuka no atarashii ninmu* ("The New Duty of Nappu Artists"). The new dictum demanded even more conformity by authors in selection of topic and in the shock value of their treatment. Such strong ideological demands could not help but bring on near abandonment of literature by real writers in the movement.

Hayashi Fusao was released from prison in April, 1932, and immediately published two articles, *Bungaku no tame ni* ("For the Sake of Literature") and *Sakka toshite* ("As a Writer") stating why one should write for the glory of Marxism, a proposition in which Kamei Katsuichirō (b. 1907) concurred. Nonetheless, Hayashi was attacked for his lack of orthodoxy and for reactionary tendencies—possibly in response to his novel *Seinen* (*Youth*) of 1932—by Miyamoto Kenji and Kobayashi Takiji. The situation describes the widening rift between the avant-garde of the left and the public in general. Kobayashi was killed in 1933 and Miyamoto was thrown into jail, but by this time the left-wing literary movement was collapsing. The activities of Koppu became impossible while the Nihon Puroretaria Sakka Dōmei dissolved itself in 1934. A period in Japanese literary history had ended.

Government pressures and internal dissatisfaction led to the "conversion" of many writers who abandoned the far left. This movement was led by Sano Manabu (1892–1953) and Nabeyama Sadachika who published jointly a "statement of conversion" as an essay in *Kaizō* of July, 1932. Many writers followed suit, with opinions ranging from continued resistance to the authoritarian state to more cautious attitudes in support of the country at war, or the impossibility of following Communism at that time. About 1934 a succession of works began to appear by authors who had taken either a pro-government or an apolitical position. Representative of such writing from 1934 are: *Seikibyō* (*The Century's Illness*), by Fujisawa Tsuneo; *Rai* (*Leprosy*), by Shimaki Kensaku (1903–45); *Yūjō* (*Friendship*), by Tateno Nobuyuki (b. 1903); *Fūun* (*Wind and Clouds*), by Kubokawa Tsurujirō (b. 1903); and *Fuyugare* (*Winter Withering*), by Tokunaga Sunao. These men were "converted," it seems, through necessity rather than conviction and they regarded those who resisted as being more heroic than themselves. But a number of men showed enthusiasm and made this change of attitude a theme in their work, for example: *Byakuya* (*White Night*), 1934, by Murayama Tomoyoshi (b. 1901); and *Dai-isshō* (*Chapter the First*), 1935, by Nakano Shigeharu. Nakano created a great furor by making a sudden turnabout the same year with the story *Mura no ie* (*Houses in a Village*) in which he rejected his "conversion."

There was at that time considerable interest in the Russian philosopher Leon Chestov (1866–1938), generated by *Higeki no tetsugaku* (*Philosophy of Tragedy*) of 1934, a work translated with an introduction by Kawakami Tetsutarō, Abe Rokurō, and Tanigawa Tetsuzō. Chestov's "philosophy of malaise" was discussed by such men as Kobayashi Hideo, Masamune Hakuchō, and Miki Kiyoshi and as a result the ideas became popular among the intellectuals. The viewpoint was adopted by Kamei Katsuichirō in his story *Ikeru yuda* (*Living Judas*), 1935, which related Chestov's ideas to problems facing the "converted" writers. In 1936 he dealt with the theme again in *Ningen kyōiku* (*Education of Man*). Considered long after the fact, the "conversions" of these various writers reflect adversely on the Communist movement in Japan. The programs of both 1927 and 1932 were handed down directly from the Comintern as though to a colonial people, and the Party leaders in Japan, eager for power themselves, treated the situation with bureaucratic rigidity. But the "literature of conversion" of that time had not yet come to grips with such problems.

Established writers, as we mentioned, gradually reappeared on the creative scene and two substantial novels are of particular interest: *Yoakemae* (*Before the Dawn*) by Shimazaki Tōson (published in *Chūō kōron* between 1929 and 1935); and *An'ya kōro* (*Road Through the Dark Night*) by Shiga Naoya (published serially in *Kaizō* beginning in 1921 and completed in 1937).

Yoakemae opens with a famous description which begins: "The whole length of the Kiso Highway lies within the mountains." It is a long novel, centering on the post station of Magome on the Kiso road. Aoyama Hanzō, the man of dreams and ideals and Tōson's hero in this work, was modeled on his father, Shimazaki Masaki. The novel describes the revolutionary changes in Japan which came with the Meiji restoration. Tōson clearly explores his own past through this examination of the long and complex Meiji period and brings a skillful realism to his description of the life of Hanzō and the role of Hirata Atsutane's national studies (*kokugaku*) philosophy. In this aspect the novel survives critical evaluation even today. However, in the matter of capturing the broad theme of Meiji period history, the novel seems less successful: out of touch with the broad themes of the people and infatuated with obscure detail. If the overall plan of the author was not completely successful, the story has been inspiration for a considerable number of historical novels.

An'ya kōro, while sometimes failing in structure, is unsurpassed in the beauty of its parts. Its hero, Tokitō Kensaku, is imaginary, but he shares with the author a disposition to turn personal tastes into ethical judgments. The story takes the individualism of the hero as the basis for his struggle to overcome his illegitimate birth and, as a husband, his trials with his unfaithful wife and his efforts to fulfill his duties as head of the family. Perhaps Tokitō is representative of the intellectuals of his time. The story is uncompromisingly realistic. The basic struggle drawn by the story was that of man with himself, a struggle for self-affirmation. For writers such as Oda Sakunosuke (1913–47) and Dazai Osamu (1909–48) it was an inspiration, but others saw it as an undesirable trait.

The military coup d'état of February 26, 1936, was the final step into fascism and ultimate catastrophe. The event was also a clear dividing line for the literary world of Japan. Before that, however, there was a period of creative literary activity, known as the "literary revival" (*bungei fukkō*). In his article *Sakka toshite* ("As a Writer"), Hayashi Fusao spoke of it as a "proletarian renaissance," while Takeuchi Yoshimi maintained that "proletarian literature was a step toward ultranationalism." Whatever the case, there was a sense of creativity in the air which showed itself in new publications, one of which was the coterie magazine *Bungakkai* (*Literary World*—different from the Meiji journal of the same title) begun in 1933 by Uno Kōji, Fukada Kyūya, Kawabata Yasunari, Hirotsu Kazuo, Kobayashi Hideo, Takeda Rintarō, and Hayashi Fusao. In describing the philosophy of the publication, Takeda said: "The magazine is a challenge to suppression of freedom of literature and expression; from a literary standpoint it is also a challenge to the popular, low-class literature which goes by the name of *taishū shōsetsu* (fiction for the masses) . . . it will try to protect the claims of real literature and help the younger writers. It is a writers' self-defense movement. Whatever it may seem to be, this is a positive undertaking by writers who have a strong spirit of resistance." The new publication provided a meeting ground for the Shinkō Geijutsuha, the authors of "conversion literature" (*tenkō bungaku*), and those associated primarily with the publication. The authors were united by their liberal political views in opposition to the growing authoritarianism in Japan and they were encouraged by the addition of Kikuchi Kan to their group in 1937.

The magazines *Bungei* (*Literary Art*) and *Kōdō* (*Action*) were also started in 1933. *Kōdō,* begun by Abe Tomoji and Funabashi Seiichi, sought to enlist writers who were not associated with *Bungakkai.* Its philosophical standard was liberal humanism and activism (*kōdōshugi*), the latter derived from Malraux and his novels of men of action in the twentieth century. The theme was introduced in a *Kōdō* article of 1934: *Futsubungaku no ittenki* ("A Turning Point in French Literature") by Komatsu Kiyoshi (b. 1901). Komatsu also edited *Bunka no yōgo* (*In Defense of Culture*) which taught the need for a popular front in opposition to fascism.

The maturing of militarism and fascism in Japan quickened the dissolution of any remaining moderate middle ground of ideas. Kobayashi Hideo was aware of the changes and in *Kokyō o ushinatta bungaku* (*A Literature that Has Lost Its Home*) in 1933 he traced the process which he called "the socialization of self." He developed the thesis further in *Shishōsetsuron* (*On the First-Person Novel*) of 1935, showing that he had long been aware of the impending crisis. This "socialization of self" was a call for humanistic and liberal writers to reconstruct the individuality which they had lost sight of through the theory of the primacy of politics. But while showing the way by which a unity of artistic method could be created, he also conveys a presentiment that tradition would soon override the whole discussion. The argument he had with Masamune Hakuchō on "thought and real life" was simply an extension of his ideas on individuality.

Yokomitsu Riichi, from the time of *Kikai* in 1930, had provided subtle studies of the intellectuals' excessive self-consciousness. In *Monshō* (*Family Crest*), 1934, he took up questions of self and freedom for the intelligentsia following the high-tide of Marxism. In 1935 he published *Junsui shōsetsuron* ("On Pure Fiction") in the magazine *Kaizō* in which he stated: "If there is such a thing as a literary renaissance, then it is the popular novel which fills the role of pure literature; there is simply no literary renaissance besides this." Indeed, for the purpose of drawing the image of the self-conscious intellectual, Yokomitsu advocated the definition of a grammatical category of a "fourth person"—a proposition which greatly agitated literary circles. In *Kazoku kaigi* (*Family Council*), 1935, he attempted to put his idea into practice, but the result was nothing more than an ordinary genre novel, like some illustrated story for adults.

The literary renaissance encouraged the emergence of another genre, the *fūzoku shōsetsu* (genre novel or novel of manners). This was at a time when Japan's efforts in foreign affairs as well as within the nation were designed to enhance Japan's position in Asia and to promote the development of Southeast Asia and the Pacific Ocean— Japan was to be the leading country in the Greater East Asia Co-Prosperity Sphere. Japan's economy was stimulated by the war-time prosperity, and the country seemed to regard its own development as secure. Doubtless, the boom in publishing owed much to the prevailing war-time conditions. The literary ideas of Abe Tomoji followed on the heels of Yokomitsu's essay on pure fiction. There was considerable debate having to do with the content of fiction under the banner of *sambun seishin* (the spirit of prose), involving Hirotsu Kazuo, Kikuchi Kan, Satomi Ton (b. 1888), Satō Haruo and others. Those who favored the *fūzoku shōsetsu* abandoned the search for the hidden interior of man and focused on externals, generally through flashy subject matter and style. The writers turned their eyes to the manners and customs of the world of activity. "Pure literature" in these heady times began to find a place in the realm of the serialized newspaper novel and seemed to acquire many readers. The genre novel, however, leaned in the direction of national policy. The principle of expediency was soon evident in this kind of writing sometimes cooperating, but always avoiding confrontation with the military government.

Yokomitsu's novel *Kazoku kaigi* showed that he was working toward the genre novel, but the conception of his work as a novel with a theme, the argument of dual cultures, East and West, places it as a preparatory work for his long novel *Ryoshū (Lonely Journey)*, which began to appear in 1937. The story actually went unfinished until 1943. It successfully developed a panoramic view of the whole world, but with the intellectuals who appear in the story there is a painful revelation of the author's exclusiveness, his clinging to Japan.

Takeda Rintarō, only gradually getting over the feeling of despair aroused by political "conversions," attempted portraits of the misery of the common man in the urban world of Japan. Here he found a viable mode for himself and his work became reminiscent of Saikaku in such pieces as *Shiseiji (An Incident in the Vulgar World)* in 1933, and *Ginza hatchō (Eight Blocks of the Ginza)* in 1934. By the time of *Gekai no nagame (Look Down on the Earth)*, 1935–36, and *Fūsoku gojū mētoru (Wind Velocity Fifty Meters)*, 1937, his writing is well into the *fūzoku shōsetsu* style. Takami Jun (b. 1907) also moved into the *fūzoku shōsetsu*, avoiding description in favor of dialogue with such works as *Kishō tenten (Various Poetic Sentiments)*, published in *Bungei shunjū* in 1935, and *Ika naru hoshi no moto ni? (Under Which Star?)*, published in *Bungei* during 1939.

The *fūzoku shōsetsu*, the genre novel, was welcomed by the stagnant times and new authors appeared who handled the style masterfully: such writers as Ishikawa Tatsuzō (b. 1905) and Niwa Fumio (b. 1904). Ishikawa's *Sōbō (The People)*, 1935, a story of immigrants to Brazil, was the first work to be awarded the Akutagawa Prize in literature and this provided further encouragement. *Sōbō* was followed by Ishikawa's *Hikage no mura (Village in Shadow)* in 1937, and *Kekkon no seitai (The True Nature of Marriage)* in 1938, among other works which made his position as a novelist of manners unshakable. Niwa Fumio published a series of love stories called *madamu mono* ("madame" stories) and *haha mono* ("mother" stories), which had great vigor and skill. One of these works is *Zeiniku* (*Plump Flesh*) of 1934.

Two important coterie magazines of the thirties were *Nihon rōmanha* (*Japanese Romanticism*), begun in 1935, and *Jimmin bunko* (*Literature of the People*), begun in 1936. *Nihon rōmanha* brought together some thirty writers, including Yasuda Yojūrō (b. 1910), Kamei Katsuichirō, and Dazai Osamu. Yasuda was the chief organizer of *Nihon rōmanha*, but the movement was led by Hayashi Fusao. The magazine and the movement were politically right wing and Yasuda rode the tide of Japanism with such articles as: *Taikan shijin no goichininsha* ("The Greatest of the Poets Laureate"), published in the magazine *Kogito* (*Cogito,* circulated 1932–44 and concerned primarily with the classics); *Gotoba-in* ("Retired Emperor Gotoba"), 1942; and *Man'yōshū no seishin* ("The Spirit of the Man'yōshū"), 1942. His sparkling style somewhat reflected the poetic spirit of medieval Japan and a nostalgia for tradition and elegance—only slightly veiling pro-fascist sentiments. Kamei Katsuichirō turned to religion as solace for the sufferings of war, producing such works as *Shashin shiko* (*Giving Oneself to the Starving Tiger*) in 1943, and *Shinran* (*Shinran,* the Japanese Buddhist saint) of 1946. In such stories as *Bannen* (*The Later Years*), published in 1936, and *Tsugaru* (a place in Northern Japan), 1944, Dazai Osamu examined the suffering which was part of decadence and, while still in the dark valley of those years, achieved some success in maintaining a standard for Japanese intellectuals.

Jimmin bunko was started by Takeda Rintarō as a medium for writers who had not joined the nationalistic movement. However, like *Nihon rōmanha,* its pages were not so exclusive as political ideology might suggest. Both magazines provided a platform for new writers, and both seemed weighed down by gloomy self-reflection and abundant irony in their pages. As the war atmosphere deepened, *Jimmin bunko* turned more to the *fūzoku shōsetsu* style.

War Years

The long conflict with China began with the clash between Japanese and Chinese soldiers outside Peking on July 7, 1937. From that time on in Japan, control of public discussion of the war and other forms of government interference in the cultural life of the country became more and more overt. The pressure of government censorship was felt not only by the political left but also as a general restriction on the freedom of the intellectuals. In 1937 also political expediency led to the organization of Kokumin Seishin Sōdōin, The National Spiritual Mobilization, a movement designed to promote a spirit of sacrifice

among the people for the war effort. Arrests of members of Jimmin
Sensen, The People's Front, an anti-fascist league representing a broad
spectrum of Japanese society, began that year. The following year
Ishikawa Tatsuzō's story *Ikite iru heitai* (*Living Soldiers*), published in
Chūō kōron, was banned because of its realistic treatment of the
army.

In journalism there was a great rush to conformity by way of
literature which supported government policy and patriotic articles on
the war. The success of *Mugi to heitai* (*Wheat and Soldiers*) in 1938
by Hino Ashihei (1907–60) stimulated a rash of diaries and eye-
witness accounts by writers traveling with Japan's armies. Hino later
received the Akutagawa Prize in literature for his *Fun'nyōtan* (*Excre-
ment: A Story*), written in 1937. After *Mugi to heitai* he completed
a trilogy with *Tsuchi to heitai* (*Earth and Soldiers*) in 1938 and
Hana to heitai (*Flowers and Soldiers*) in 1939. While circumscribed by
wartime conditions, these works tried to maintain a perspective on
human relations and the individual psyche. *Kōjin* (*Yellow Dust*),
1938, and *Kensetsu senki* (*Building and War*), 1939, by Ueda Hiroshi
(b. 1875), as well as Hibino Shirō's *Usun kurīku* (*Wusung Creek*),
published by *Chūō kōron* in 1939, were works of considerable objectivity and literary quality, but the movement was clearly toward the
subjective war account and a diaristic style. Most of the popular war
literature aimed at encouraging a fighting spirit; it was propaganda and
quite deficient in literary value.

Japanese literature in this period underwent various changes.
Shimaki Kensaku with his *Seikatsu no tankyū* (*Life's Search*) of 1937
advocated an absurdly serious mode of existence through his hero
Sugino Shunsuke who had returned to the farmer's life. Shimaki was
one of the more confused intellectuals of that time, but he gained many
young readers. He was also an early "convert" to cooperation with the
government, as we see in his *Rai* (*Leprosy*) of 1934, but his conversion
lapsed as the proscription of his *Saiken* (*Reconstruction*) of 1937
indicates. A more orthodox work of the period was Shimaki's *Ummei
no hito* (*Man of Destiny*), published in 1940. The matter of conversion
or writing what suited the government was again part of literary debate
in Japan with the appearance of Hayashi Fusao's *Gokuchūki* (*Notes
in Jail*) in 1940 and *Tenkō nitsuite* (*On Conversion*) in 1941. Nakano
Shigeharu, as we have mentioned, recovered from the humiliation of
submitting to political expediency, and with *Kisha no kamataki* (*Train
Fireman*), 1937, and *Uta no wakare* (*Parting with a Song*), 1939, he
moved cautiously to an independent voice, which he more or less
achieved with *Saitō mokichi nōto* (*Notes on Saitō Mokichi*), published in 1942. Two other works of note were Miyamoto Yuriko's

(1889–1951) *Fuyu o kosu tsubomi* (*Buds Which Pass Through the Winter*) in 1934 and *Fujin to bungaku* (*Women and Literature*) in 1939.

Literature of farming life appeared, such as *Yokudo* (*Fertile Soil*), 1937, by Wada Tsutō (b. 1900) and *Uguisu* (*Nightingale*), 1938, by Itō Einosuke (b. 1903). While these were of high quality and encouraged imitators, the literature produced by the Nōmin Bungaku Konwakai, Association for Agricultural Literature, a group sponsored by the Ministry of Agriculture and Forestry, merely curried favor in the face of government power. Such was the case in other areas too. The so-called *katagaki bungaku* or "subtitle literature" which was literature about production, literature about the sea, literature about the continent, and so forth, moved right along with the political tide and was awarded the nickname *sozaiha* or the "subject matter school." Most of this writing was done by authors of the literary conversion and their work simply dealt with a topic, without regard to literary form. The product was extremely limp and, with the exception of *Aragane* (*Raw Metal*), 1937, by Mamiya Mosuke (b. 1899), not memorable.

The grip of totalitarianism completely seized the field of journalism. The intelligentsia dared criticize only the past, not the present. In 1936 in the novel *Fuyu no yado* (*Winter Inn*) Abe Tomoji wrote of the darkness enveloping intellectual life, but by the time of his *Fūsetsu* (*Wind and Snow*) of 1938, his own capitulation became quite evident. Paradoxically, the drift downward in literature was actually turned into art by Itō Sei in his *Machi to mura* (*Town and Village*) of 1939, while in *Tokunō gorō no seikatsu to iken* (*The Life and Opinions of Tokunō Gorō*) of 1940–41, using what at first glance seems to be merely the approach of another first-person novel, he offers a very critical look at the times. On the other end of the scale (for example, Asano Akira's thesis of a national literature) poets and critics who wished to show their patriotism became useful to the fascist government, although their writings are of no literary value.

Writers of the Geijutsuha, Artistic School, quietly opposed the direction of the *sozaiha* and sought to preserve the principles of humanism in their work. One of those writers was Honjō Rikuo (1905–39), whose *Ishikarigawa* (*The Ishikari River*) of 1938–39 was a work of some dimension, in which, with parallels to the contemporary world, he described Japanese pioneering efforts on the island of Hokkaidō during the early Meiji period. The work was a statement of protest and also a novel very sensitive to the nuances of human nature. Historical novels increased in popularity, some with disguised but visible comments on the times; for example: *Kentōbune* (*Ship to China*), 1936; *Uta to mon no tate* (*The Shield of a Song and a Gate*), 1940, by Takagi Taku (b. 1907); *Rekishi (History)*, 1939, by Sakakiyama Jun (b. 1900); *Watanabe Kazan (Watanabe Kazan,* a Japanese painter in European realistic mode, 1793–1841), 1935, and *Ōhara yūgaku (Ōhara Yūgaku,* an intellectual of the Tokugawa period, 1797–1858), 1940, by Fujimori Seikichi.

A similar body of writing exists in what might be called the genealogies; such stories as *Kiyō bimbō (Clever Poverty)*, 1938, by Uno Kōji. These were lengthy examinations of extraordinary characters and may be considered a variation on the genre novel. Novels like Hirotsu Kazuo's *Chimata no rekishi (History of a Place)*, 1940, and Niwa Fumio's *Aru onna no hansei (Half of a Woman's Life)*, published in 1940, mirror the shifting manners of society and achieve a fine intuitive realism. The first-person novel is represented by several new works: *Chichi haha no ki (My Father and Mother)*, 1939, by Kambayashi Akatsuki (b. 1902); and *Nonki megane (Carefree Eyeglasses)*, 1937, by Ozaki Kazuo (b. 1899). Novels in the first-person style by Dazai Osamu, Takami Jun and other writers tended to concentrate on literary devices and turned into little more than parodies of their predecessors.

There were many writers, of course, who, in one way or another, maintained their artistic integrity during those years, despite the omnipresence of khaki uniforms. In *Yukiguni* Kawabata Yasunari evoked a peculiarly Japanese sense of beauty with his story of a geisha's life in a remote mountain hot-spring resort. *Hana no warutsu (A Flower Waltz)*, 1936, and *Kōgen (High Plateau)*, 1938, are both admirable, the latter unfolding a delicate spiritual world with consummate skill. Hori Tatsuo in his 1936 story *Kaze tachinu (The Wind Rises)* gave a tender and lucid account of the love of a man and a woman facing the separation of death. In *Kagerō no nikki (A Gossamer Diary)*, 1937, Hori worked with materials from the court diaries of the Heian period, and in *Naoko* (a woman's name), 1941 he entered a strangely serene world, far distant from the clatter of guns that year.

Ibuse Masuji wrote the good-humored *Shūkin ryokō (Bill Collecting Trip)* in 1937, and then in 1937 and 1938 produced two works which handle a wide cross section of humanity in unusual circumstances: *Jon manjirō hyōryūki (The Sea Wanderings of John Manjirō)* and *Sazanami gunki (Just a Little War Tale)*. In two more stories, from 1939 and 1941, respectively, he quietly observes the sad details of the lives of common people: *Tajinkomura (Tajinko Village)* and *Okomasan (Miss Koma)*. Ishikawa Jun made his first appearance on the literary scene with *Fugen (The Bodhisattva Fugen)* in 1936. The next year his *Marusu no uta (Song of Mars)* was censored for being critical of the war. Later, in such pieces as *Sorori banashi* (*Stories by Sorori*), he made a turnabout with ironical and capricious tales that could be published. Nakayama Yoshihide (b. 1900) gained immediate acclaim with his story *Atsumonozaki* (*Pompon Chrysanthemums*), published in *Bungakkai* in 1938. It is a skillful psychological study, carefully constructed, and a prelude to the story called *Hi* (*Tombstone*) published the following year. In *Hi* Nakayama moved into historical fiction and a long exploration of the intricacies of human nature. Okamoto Kanoko (1889–1939) gained literary recognition for her *Tsuru wa yamiki* (*The Crane Fell Ill*) of 1936 in which she took historical persons as her subject. She had been given a traditional Buddhist education and wrote in a somewhat ornate style. With *Boshi jojō* (*The Love of Mother and Child*), in 1937, *Rōgishō* (*The Old Geisha*), in 1938, and *Seisei ruten* (*The Round of Life*), she demonstrated both her faith in Buddhism and her insights into the many conditions of human life. If we find in these writers a resistance to the movement of the times in Japan, we must keep in mind that some of this resistance may not have been really conscious or aware of itself, and that there was no organization to speak of among the writers opposed to fascism.

On December 8, 1941 (December 7 in the United States), the Japanese Navy in the Pacific entered into war against Britain and the United States. For the next four years in Japan the eighth day of each month was commemorated, in part by the dawn arrest and imprisonment of intellectuals, writers, and any other persons suspected of holding anti-war sentiments. The intellectuals of Japan were submerged in the clamor which accompanied the beginning of this new war, and those writers who completely subordinated themselves to the government formed an organization. With the expansion of the war in China in 1940, the right wing Taisei Yokusankai, The Policy Assistance Association, was set up and the writer Kishida Kunio (1890–1954), was made head of the Department of Culture. However, repression of culture seemed to be the organization's intent. In December of 1941 the Bungakusha Aikoku Taikai, Association of Patriotic Men of Letters, was proclaimed, and in June of 1942 a larger organization of writers called Nihon bungaku Hōkokukai, Patriotic Association for Japanese Literature, was organized and made the first steps as a positive cultural movement. At the opening ceremonies of the organization more than 2,000 writers participated, and this number increased with the formation of friendship organizations whose members were also members of the association. The association had eight committees (for novels, *tanka,* criticism, *haiku,* foreign literature, Japanese literature, long poems, and dramatic literature), each pledged to support the aims of the association. In 1942 and again in 1943 meetings were called of the Daitōa Bungakusha Kaigi,

Association of Literary Men of Greater East Asia, for the purpose of furthering Japan's war effort through literature.

Already by 1938 the government was sending writers to accompany the army in various actions. In 1941 journalistic publications were placed under government control and many writers—including Nakajima Kenzō (b. 1903), Miki Kiyoshi (1898–1945), and Shimizu Ikutarō—were sent to occupied areas as members of the Bunka Kōsakutai, Culture Building Corps. From such sources, and in various styles, a great quantity of writing and war literature was produced, including travel accounts and local-color articles. Iwata Toyoo (b. 1893), known by the pen name of Shishi Bunroku, published *Kaigun* (*The Navy*) in 1943 about nine heroes of the attack on Pearl Harbor. A similar novel was published in 1944 by Hino Ashihei, entitled *Rikugun* (*The Army*). Both works were fanatical in attitude and worthless as literature. Ibuse Masuji moved with the Japanese army from Thailand to Malaya and down to Singapore, out of which experience he wrote an excellent description of Southeast Asia titled *Hana no machi* (*Town of Flowers*), which was published in 1943. Niwa Fumio also saw and recorded the realities of combat while aboard the flagship during the Battle of the Solomon Sea, publishing *Kaisen* (*Battle at Sea*) in *Chūō Kōron* in November of 1942. As the war continued and widened in scope, attitudes toward the Chinese, the British, and the Americans changed for the worse, and except for a few outstanding works, writers either temporarily took leave of their humanity, or could write of nothing but the mechanics of war.

From about 1940 Japanese journalism was proclaiming a "crisis of the people" and welcoming totalitarianism as the intellectual current of the times, but by 1941 the demand was for a "literature of the people" and thereafter the political involvement of literature grew conspicuous. *Jimmin bunko,* the magazine led by Takeda Rintarō, stopped publication under charges of carrying on the work of the Jimmin Sensen. Under the tutelage of the *Nihon rōmanha* with Yasuda Yojūrō, and Shinkokugaku, New National Studies, with Fujita Tokutarō, there was some promotion of the idea of "The Immortal Land of the Gods" (*shinshū no fumetsu:* meaning "immortal Japan") encouraged by racial theories then current in Germany. Writers formerly associated with *Bungakkai,* the leading writers at the outbreak of the war, including Kawakami Tetsutarō, brought together representative intellectuals in Japan from philosophy, literature, history, religion, and science, and in 1942 discussed the question of the modern crisis and the preservation of culture.

As a sequel to *Yoakemae,* Shimazaki Tōson attempted a novel tracing the intellectual history of the Meiji period, giving careful attention to such people as Okakura Kakuzō (Tenshin, 1862–1913), a leader in the art world. This work, called *Tōhō no mon* (*Eastern Gate*), began to appear in *Chūō kōron* in 1943 but was incomplete at the time of the author's death the same year. Niwa Fumio turned to stories of Japanese settlers in Hokkaidō in which he achieved a Balzac-like realism. In *Gyōan* (*Darkness at Dawn*), 1941, he began this theme and continued it through *Jitsurekishi* (*True History*), 1941, *Kinnō todokeide* (*A Report on Loyalty to the Emperor*), 1942, and *Gendaishi* (*Modern History*), also 1942. The last work took as its theme the politics of a time of rapid change. Hashimoto Eikichi (b. 1898) turned from historical novels, such as *Tempyō* (*The Tempyō Era: 729–49*), 1941, and *Keizu* (*Genealogy*), 1942, to deal with the discipline of the scientific mind in *Fuji to suigin* (*Mercury and Mount Fuji*) in 1943. Tokunaga Sunao, noting pointedly that his *Taiyō no nai machi* was out of print, published *Hataraku ikka* (*A Working Family*), a story from 1938, and *Nihon no katsuji* (*Japanese Printing Type*) in 1942.

Generally speaking, next to historical novels, the first-person novels were most popular, much to the advantage of the Artistic School over the *sozaiha,* or topical school. As something of a last refuge for creative writers, such as Takami Jun, Kitahara Takeo, and Itō Sei, the first-person genre still did not live up to the expectations of its advocates. Among the successful first-person novels of the time were *Meigetsu* (*Record of a Bright Moon*), 1942, by Kambayashi Akatsuki; *Matsukaze* (*Pine Winds*), 1942, by Ishizuka Tomoji (b. 1913); and *Karidachi* (*Geese Fly Up*), by Shimizu Motokichi (b. 1918). The "literature of the people" continued throughout the war, devoid of creative energy yet producing a succession of exemplary propagandistic stories and articles.

Tokuda Shūsei (1871–1943), after completing *Kasō jinbutsu* in 1935, found his serialized story *Shukuzu* (*Miniature*) censored with the eightieth installment in the *Miyako shimbun* (*Miyako News*) of 1941. It was one of the last works of Japanese Naturalism. At that time Tanizaki Junichirō began writing *Sasameyuki* (*The Makioka Sisters*), a novel about four sisters in a wealthy Ōsaka family; with only the second installment published, the work was banned and not until the end of the war was this dazzling and panoramic novel available to the public. Government prohibition on grounds that a work was not useful to the war effort, that it was an impediment, or to generally discourage literary activity, prevented publication of a number of other excellent works by writers who were attempting to maintain their personal and artistic integrity. Among the casualties were *Nenashigusa* (*Rootless Grass*), 1942, by Masamune Hakuchō; *Sabishiki shōgai* (*A Lonely Life*), 1942, by Shiga Naoya and *Fūen* (*Fiery Wind*), 1942, by Satomi Ton.

Indeed, there were almost no writers publicly able to stand in opposition to the war. Most kept an acceptable mask over their private feelings. In *Koen* (*Ruined Garden*) of 1943–45 (a work not completed) Kawabata Yasunari traces the pains of maintaining the aesthetic approach to writing. Funabashi Seiichi (b. 1904) also worked in the serialized novel during those years, producing *Shikkaiya yasukichi* (*Yasukichi of the General Store*). His philosophy was that "during the war even sleeping with a woman was resistance." The war brought a calamity to Japanese letters. Writers lacked faith in themselves, in society; men's characters disintegrated. As a kind of artistic resistance, men adopted a pose of ignoring reality, and by this means a few writers were prepared for the return of peace. Some small light was brought to the darkness of the period by the work of Sakaguchi Ango (1906–55), as in *Shinju* (*Pearls*), published in *Bungei* in 1942, and *Nihon bunka shikan* (*A Personal View of Japanese Culture*), published in 1942. Nakajima Atsushi (1909–42), although he died very young, brought an exceptional literary talent to a study of the life of Robert Louis Stevenson on the island of Samoa. This was *Hikari to kaze to yume* (*Light, Wind, and Dreams*), published in 1942. His portraits of Ssu-ma Chien (Chinese historian of *Ch'ien* the Han dynasty), Li Ling (Chinese general of the Han dynasty), and other notable men were published in 1943 as *Riryō* (*Li Ling*).

An undercurrent existed in the form of several coterie magazines which sought quality in their pages, but even those came to a halt with the final stages of the war as Japan's armies crumbled and the home islands suffered devastating air raids. The new era in Japanese letters began with the end of the war in August of 1945.

A Selected Reading List

Translations and Studies of Japanese Literature

This list includes major works of Japanese literature available in English translation. Numerous translations and studies also have been published in French and German. An excellent bibliography is published annually by *The Journal of Asian Studies*. Readers wishing to study Japanese literature in Western languages should consult that publication as well as the other journals listed below.

Early Japanese Literature

Kojiki, Donald Philippi, Princeton University, 1969.
Taketori monogatari (Tale of the Bamboo Cutter), Donald Keene, *Monumenta Nipponica,* Volume 11, 1955.
The Man'yōshū, Introduction by Donald Keene, Columbia University, 1965.
Tales of Ise, Helen McCullough, Stanford University, 1968.
The Tale of Genji, Arthur Waley, London, 1935.
The Pillow Book of Sei Shonagon, Ivan Morris, Columbia University, 1967.
The Izumi Shikibu Diary, Edwin Cranston, Harvard University, 1969.
Japanese Poetic Diaries, Earl Miner, University of California, 1969. (Translations of *Tosa nikki, Izumi shikibu nikki, Oku no hosomichi,* and *Botan kuroku.*)
An Introduction to Japanese Court Poetry, Earl Miner, Stanford University, 1968. (A condensation of the next item.)
Japanese Court Poetry, Robert Brower and Earl Miner, Stanford University, 1961.
The World of the Shining Prince: Court Life in Ancient Japan, Ivan Morris, New York, 1964.

Medieval Japanese Literature

Translations from Early Japanese Literature, Robert Reischauer and Joseph Yamagiwa, Harvard University, 1951. (translations from *Izayoi nikki, Tsutsumi chunagon monogatari, Okagami,* and *Heiji monogatari*)
A Collection of Tales from Uji; A Study and Translation of Uji shui monogatari, D. E. Mills, Cambridge University, 1970.
Fujiwara Teika's Superior Poems of Our Times, Robert Brower and Earl Miner, Stanford University, 1967.
The Okagami, Joseph Yamagiwa, London, 1967.
The Heike Monogatari, Arthur Sadler, *Transactions of the Asiatic Society of Japan,* Volume 46, 1918, Volume 49, 1921, Tokyo.
The Taiheiki, Helen McCullough, Columbia University, 1959.
Early No Drama, P. G. O'Neill, London, 1958.
Japanese Noh Drama, Nippon Gakujutsu Shinkokai, three volumes, Tokyo, 1955–60.

Nō; the Classical Theatre of Japan, Donald Keene and Kaneko Hiroshi, Tokyo, 1966.
Twenty Plays of the Nō Theatre, Donald Keene, Columbia University, 1970.
The Ink Smeared Lady and Other Kyogen, Sakanishi Shio, Tokyo, 1960.
Essays in Idleness, Donald Keene, Columbia University, 1967.
The Ballad-Drama of Medieval Japan, James Araki, University of California, 1964.
Gikeiki, Helen McCullough, Stanford University, 1966.

Japanese Literature of the Tokugawa Period

The Narrow Road to the Deep North and Other Travel Sketches, Yuasa Nobuyuki, Penguin Books, 1966.
The Life of an Amorous Man, Hamada, Tuttle & Co., 1964.
The Life of an Amorous Woman and Other Writings, Ivan Morris, New York, 1963.
Five Women Who Loved Love, Wm. Theodore deBary, Tuttle & Co., 1956.
The Japanese Family Storehouse, G. W. Sargent, Cambridge University, 1959.
The Floating World in Japanese Fiction, Howard Hibbett, Oxford University, 1959.
Kabuki, Gunji Masakatsu and Yoshida Chiaki, introduction by Donald Keene, Tokyo, 1969.
Kabuki, The Popular Theater, Yasuji Toita, New York, 1970.
The Kabuki Theatre, Earle Ernst, New York, 1956.
The Love Suicide at Amijima, Donald Shively, Harvard University, 1953.
The Battles of Coxinga, Donald Keene, London, 1951.
Bunraku, The Art of the Japanese Puppet Theatre, Donald Keene and Kaneko Hiroshi, Tokyo, 1965.
The Twilight of Edo, Akimoto Shunkichi, Tokyo, 1952.
The Year of My Life, Yuasa Nobuyuki, University of California, 1960.
Takizawa Bakin, Leon Zolbrod, New York, 1967.
Matsuo Basho, Makoto Ueda, New York, 1970.
Shanks' Mare (Tōkaidōchū hizakurige), Jippensha Ikku, Tokyo, 1960.

Modern Japanese Literature, Since 1868

Japanese Literature in the Meiji Era, Okazaki Yoshie and V. H. Viglielmo, Tokyo, 1955.
Modern Japanese Fiction, 1868–1916, Nakamura Mitsuo, Kokusai Bunka Shinkokai (Japan Cultural Society), Tokyo, 1968.
Introduction to Contemporary Japanese Literature, Part 1, Tokyo, 1939, Part 2, Tokyo, 1959. Kokusai Bunka Shinkokai.
Synopses of Contemporary Japanese Literature II 1936–1955, compiled by Kokusai Bunka Shinkokai, Tokyo, 1970.
Modern Japanese Fiction, John Morrison, University of Utah, 1955.
Kafu the Scribbler, Edward Seidensticker, Stanford University, 1965.
Japan's First Modern Novel: Ukigumo of Futabatei Shimei, Marleigh Ryan, Columbia University, 1967.
Leftwing Literature in Japan, G. T. Shea, Tokyo, 1964.

MODERN FICTION IN TRANSLATION, INCLUDING WORKS SINCE 1945

An Adopted Husband (Sono omokage), Futabatei Shimei
Floating Cloud (Ukigumo), Futabatei Shimei

Little Master (Botchan), Natsume Sōseki
I Am a Cat (*Wagahai wa neko de aru*), Natsume Sōseki
The Mind (*Kokoro*), Natsume Sōseki
The Wayfarer (*Kōjin*), Natsume Sōseki
The Three Cornered World (*Kusa makura*), Natsume Sōseki
The Wild Geese (*Gan*), Mori Ōgai
Exotic Japanese Stories, Akutagawa Ryūnosuke
Rashōmon and Other Stories, Akutagawa Ryūnosuke
Kappa (*Kappa*, a river elf), Akutagawa Ryūnosuke
Hell Screen and Other Stories, Akutagawa Ryūnosuke
The Makioka Sisters (*Sasame yuki*), Tanizaki Ju'nichirō
Some Prefer Nettles (*Tade kuu mushi*), Tanizaki Ju'nichirō
The Key (*Kagi*), Tanizaki Ju'nichirō
Seven Japanese Tales, Tanizaki Ju'nichirō
Diary of a Mad Old Man (*Fūten rōjin nikki*), Tanizaki Ju'nichirō
Snow Country (*Yukiguni*), Kawabata Yasunari
The House of Sleeping Beauties (*Nemureru bijo*), Kawabata Yasunari
The Sound of the Mountain (*Yama no oto*), Kawabata Yasunari
Thousand Cranes (*Senbazuru*), Kawabata Yasunari
Barley and Soldiers (*Mugi to heitai*), Hino Ashihei
The Setting Sun (*Shayō*), Dazai Osamu
No Longer Human (*Ningen shikkaku*), Dazai Osamu
Homecoming (*Kikyō*), Osaragi Jirō
The Counterfeiter and Other Stories, Inoue Yasushi
Zone of Emptiness (*Shinkū chitai*), Noma Hiroshi
Japanese Tales of Mystery and Imagination, Edogawa Ranpo
Fires on the Plain (*Nobi*), Ōoka Shōhei
Harp of Burma (*Biruma no tategoto*), Takeyama Michio
The Heike Story (*Shin heike monogatari*), Yoshikawa Eiji
Woman in the Dunes (*Suna no onna*), Abe Kōbō
The Face of Another (*Ta'nin no kao*), Abe Kōbō
The Hunting Gun (*Ryojū*), Inoue Yasushi
The Buddha Tree (*Bodaiju*), Niwa Fumio
A Personal Matter (*Kojinteki no taiken*), Ōe Kenzaburō
The Sound of Waves (*Shiosai*), Mishima Yukio
Temple of the Golden Pavilion (*Kinkakuji*), Mishima Yukio
Confessions of a Mask (*Kamen no kokuhaku*), Mishima Yukio
Death in Midsummer and Other Stories, Mishima Yukio
Forbidden Colors, Mishima Yukio.
Ukiyo—Stories of Postwar Japan, Gluck, ed.

Poetry

Masterpieces of Japanese Poetry, Ancient and Modern, Miyamori Asatarō, Tokyo, 1956.
Anthology of Haiku Ancient and Modern, Asataro Miyamori, Greenwood Press, 1970.
The Japanese Haiku, Kenneth Yasuda, Tokyo, 1956.
Haikai and Haiku, Ichikawa Sanki, ed., Gakujutsu Shinkōkai, Tokyo, 1958.
An Introduction to Haiku—An Anthology of Poems and Poets From Bashō to Shiki, H. Henderson, New York, 1958.

The Poetry of Living Japan, Ninomiya Takamichi and D. J. Enright, New
    York, 1957.
The Penguin Book of Japanese Verse, G. Bownas and A. Thwaite, 1964.

Theatre

The Japanese Theatre, Faubion Bowers, New York, 1952.
Five Modern No Plays, Mishima Yukio, New York, 1957.

Other Books of Interest

Anthology of Japanese Literature, compiled and edited by Donald Keene,
    New York, 1955.
Modern Japanese Literature, compiled and edited by Donald Keene, New
    York, 1956.
Literary and Art Theories in Japan, Ueda Makoto, Western Reserve Uni-
    versity, 1967.
The Japanese Language, Roy Miller, University of Chicago, 1967.
Sources of Japanese Tradition, Ryusku Tsunoda *et al,* Columbia University,
    1958.
A History of Japan to 1334, George Sansom, London, 1958.
A History of Japan 1334–1615, George Sansom, Stanford University, 1961.
A History of Japan 1615–1867, George Sansom, Stanford University, 1963.
Japan, A Short Cultural History, George Sansom, London, 1952.

Journals

Articles on Japanese literature regularly appear in the following scholarly
journals:
Monumenta Nipponica; Published by Sophia University, Tokyo, Japan.
Harvard Journal of Asiatic Studies; Published under the auspices of the
    Harvard-Yenching Institute, Cambridge, Mass., U.S.A.
The Journal of Asian Studies; Published by The Association for Asian
    Studies, Inc. (the *Journal* was formerly *The Far Eastern Quarterly*)
    Ann Arbor, Mich., U.S.A.
    The annual bibliography published by the *Journal* is a valuable guide
    to translations and studies of Japanese literature.
Literature East & West; journal of the Oriental-Western Literary Relations
    Group of the Modern Language Association. University of Texas,
    Austin, Tex., U.S.A.

Index